# THE MID-TUDOR CRISIS, 1545–1565

# British History in Perspective
## General Editor: Jeremy Black

# THE MID-TUDOR CRISIS, 1545–1565

## DAVID LOADES

MACMILLAN
LONDON

First published 1992 by
The MACMILLAN PRESS LTD
Houndmills, Basingstoke, Hampshire RG21 2XS
and London
Companies and representatives
throughout the world

ISBN 0–333–52337–7 hardcover
ISBN 0–333–52338–5 paperback

A catalogue record for this book is available
from the British Library

Phototypeset by Intype, London
Printed in Hong Kong

# CONTENTS

# INTRODUCTION: THE CONCEPT OF 'CRISIS'

Writing less than a generation ago, in 1973, Whitney Jones declared, in the introduction to his own book *The Mid-Tudor Crisis, 1539–1563*

'. . . there is no novelty in recognition of the fact that, in retrospect, the trouble shadowed reigns of Edward VI and Mary stand in apparently sharp contrast with the Tudor 'high noons' of Henry VIII and Elizabeth I'.

Further on in the same essay he described the 'uneasy and uncharacteristic' nature of these reigns as 'readily accepted'.[1] Such views are overdue for revision in general, as they have already been revised in particular, and the whole proposition of a 'crisis period' in the middle of the sixteenth century should be called in question. The greatest constitutional and legal crisis of the century belonged to the years 1532 to 1536, and resulted in the establishment of the Royal Supremacy. The most revolutionary upheaval in property rights came with the dissolution of the monasteries between 1536 and 1540, and the greatest rebellion was the Pilgrimage of Grace of 1536. In terms of national security there was a bad scare in 1539, but nothing to compare with the threatened Spanish invasion of 1588. Only in economic affairs was the mid-century particularly difficult, with the sharpest rise in inflation coming during the 1550s, and the worst epidemic being the influenza of 1557–8. The harvests of 1554–6 were also bad, but no worse than those of 1594–7. The turbulent reputation of these decades therefore calls for some

1

explanation, as well as some consideration of what constitutes a 'crisis' in the history of a state or society. Part of the reasoning has been *a priori*. A royal minority was always a difficult time for a personal monarchy, and therefore the regency governments of Edward VI must have been less effective than that of an adult king such as Henry VIII. Similarly, a female ruler was an unprecedented experience, and therefore Mary must have had particular difficulty in imposing her authority. Such presuppositions can be readily confirmed by the upheavals which undoubtedly took place in 1549, and by the well-known complaints of the Spanish and Imperial envoys between 1554 and 1558. However, closer examination reveals that such explanations are far too simple. If Edward's councils were ineffective, how did they manage to enforce the most revolutionary changes which had ever taken place in the worship and doctrine of the English Church? And if Mary was weak willed, why was she so successful in insisting both upon the Spanish marriage and the papal reconciliation, in the teeth of considerable oppposition?[2] In fact Edward's government was not ineffective, and the problems of 1549 were caused rather by over ambitious policies and confused ideology than by any inherent weakness in the council. Contrary to what is sometimes supposed, the insurgents were not taking advantage of a regime which lacked adequate leadership so much as exploiting ambiguities in the Protector's thinking. When those ambiguities were removed by his overthrow, his successor had no difficulty in containing a situation which could easily have got worse because no remedies were provided for the ostensible grievances. Similarly Mary was not the somewhat bemused innocent of popular legend. She lacked both political experience and the ability to assess a problem objectively, but when her mind was made up she could be as resolute and uncompromising as her father, and she was quite capable of taking good advice if it did not conflict with the dictates of her conscience. Her council was sometimes weakened by her lack of experienced leadership, but it remained a powerful executive instrument, and enforced its will just as effectively as that of Henry VIII or Elizabeth.

There was consequently no general 'crisis of authority' during these two short reigns. Nor was there any economic or social crisis which was peculiar to these years. Serious inflation dates from about 1545, and was largely the result of Henry's policy of debasement, but the disruption to trade was short-lived, and no worse than that caused at other times by war or political embargo. The social and agrarian problems which certainly existed had nothing to do with the particular circumstances of the mid-century; they had been building up for half a century, and continued for another two generations. Inflation continued to rise, and real wages to fall, until at least the end of the century.[3] The Church, on the other hand, seems to present a more convincing argument. Exposed to dramatic change by the creation of the Royal Supremacy, it was forced through a protestant revolution between 1547 and 1549, only to be forcibly re-catholicized by Mary, and then returned to the Edwardian settlement by Elizabeth. This was undoubtedly a crisis of a sort, but it was the intervention of Mary which caused the main confusion. Had she lived, England might simply have remained catholic, and the whole period from 1535 to 1553 would have been seen as a failed revolution. Had she never come to the throne, the changes of 1547–9 would probably never have been challenged. It has been rightly pointed out in recent years that England did not become a protestant country in 1549, or in 1559, but gradually over the first twenty years of Elizabeth's reign.[4] It could also be said that, with the exception of the period from January 1555 to November 1558, it was not a catholic country at any time after 1535. In other words, although the most dramatic events occurred between 1547 and 1559, the religious 'crisis' was very much more protracted, lasting for at least half a century, from 1530 to 1580. Only by a certain semantic flexibility can so long and fundamental a period of change and adjustment be described as a crisis.

Nevertheless, there were crises within the mid-Tudor period. The sharpest, and potentially the most far reaching, was that caused by the Duke of Northumberland's attempt to divert the succession in July 1553. Had that succeeded (and it had a very good chance), not only would the Tudor dynasty have come to an end, but the whole newly-established competence of statute would have been discredited, and the way would have been opened to the practice of an advanced form of absolutism. By comparison the rebellions of 1549 and 1554 were pyrotechnic but relatively harmless. Edward's government would not have been destroyed had the battles of Sampford Courtenay or Dussindale gone the other way. The rebels had no alternative claimant to the throne, no leaders of substance and no policy beyond the immediate redress of their grievances. Similarly if Sir Thomas Wyatt had taken London and deposed Mary, Elizabeth would have come to the throne five years earlier and in much less auspicious circumstances; what effect that might have had on the remainder of her reign can only be guessed. In retrospect it can be seen that the Antwerp trade crisis of 1550, which was very sharp for a year or two, was a turning point in the whole development of England's overseas trade. But that was hardly apparent at the time, except, perhaps, to those who deliberately began to seek longer range outlets for investment. Both Edward's premature death and the failure of Mary's pregnancy in 1555 were dynastic crises which altered subsequent history, but they were no more serious in their implications than the death of Arthur in 1502, the death of the young Prince Henry in 1511, or Elizabeth's attack of smallpox in 1562.

Historians, in short, have become rather too fond of inventing crises, and are in danger of devaluing the word. The reason for this is simple and pragmatic. A crisis is something easy to identify, and to catch the readers' attention. It can be studied, analysed and discussed when neither time nor energy permit a more comprehensive approach. 'Crisis spotting' is not only a good way to focus a study, it is also a good way of bringing the historian's name to the attention of his interested audience. A crisis is something interesting and exciting, when mere change and development (or worse still, continuity) are not. Important changes, readjustments and new departures took place in every decade of the sixteenth century. At the same time much remained the same, or changed only slowly and imperceptibly. The true significance of the reigns of Edward VI and Mary lies less in what happened than in what did not happen. A minority could easily have seen many of Henry VIII's achievements undone; a major aristocratic reaction could have returned parliament to its late medieval status. What were the chances of the royal supremacy surviving in the hands of a child? Similarly the unprecedented insecurity first of an unmarried queen, and then of a foreign king, contingencies which Henry VIII had struggled desperately to avoid, could have converted England into a Habsburg province. None of this came about, because the English polity was too deeply rooted, and its sense of identity too highly developed. Elizabeth inherited a stable and well-governed kingdom, which was united in recognizing her claim. This was not because Mary willed it so, but because she could not avoid it. She also inherited serious problems, but they were not beyond her wit or skill to resolve. In fact the years from 1545 to 1565 should be seen in a very positive light, not as years of crisis, but as years of achievement. The sovereignty of parliament was consolidated, the Anglican Church created, and the foundations laid of the great national myth which was to sustain the most unlikely and successful empire of modern times.

In the pages which follow, I shall endeavour to examine the events and circumstances of the period under three main headings; the state, society and the Church. It will immediately be apparent that the study of two decades taken somewhat arbitrarily out of the middle of a turbulent and eventful century presents major problems of context and of synthesis. Consequently, no reader should be recommended to use this study in isolation, and a range of relevant further reading is suggested. It is a period which has no inherent unity, spanning as it does two whole reigns and parts of two others. The apparent unity provided by the concept of the Mid-Tudor crisis is artificial and in many ways unhelpful, but it is necessary to unravel the misunderstandings created by the 'ready acceptance' of Whitney Jones and others. Consequently it may be helpful to study the Mid-Tudor period in order to return it to an undifferentiated sixteenth century, in which it belongs without any distinguishing tag, pejorative or otherwise.

# I

## THE STATE

# 1

## CROWN AND COUNCIL

In 1460, when it had been suggested that the Duke of York's claim to the English throne should be referred to the High Court of Parliament, the House of Lords had disclaimed any competence in so high a mystery of state.[1] Two generations later, in 1525, when Henry VIII was struggling with the problem of the succession, and weighing the various possible options, such an adjudication did not even occur to him. But in 1534 there was passed 'An Act for the establishment of the king's succession', to be followed by further similar Acts in 1537 and 1544, and in 1571 the second Treason Act of Elizabeth 'virtually established parliamentary statute as the constitutional way to settle questions of succession'.[2] Between 1525 and 1571 the English Crown had undergone a profound change, not only in its constitutional relationship with parliament, but also in the scope of its jurisdiction, both theoretical and practical. The Ecclesiastical Supremacy, which was established by statute between 1533 and 1536 gave the King of England a type of authority which neither the Holy Roman Emperor nor the king of France could claim. The rulers of Denmark, of Sweden and of the Lutheran principalities of Germany exercised a similar control over the Church within their dominions, but without the same basis of legal principle. England had for many centuries enjoyed a degree of jurisdictional unity which had been the envy of more feudal and de-centralized realms, and that unity had been completed in 1536 not only by the reduction of the major franchise of the Church, but also by the removal of the last temporal liberties, the bishopric of Durham and the Welsh Marcher lordships. In 1536 and 1539 two further statutes had dissolved the lesser religious houses and confirmed the surrenders of the greater, bringing into the hands of the king lands with a capital value of some two and a half million pounds. It was not for nothing that Henry VIII declared in 1545 that he never stood higher in his estate royal than in the time of parliament. By then the Royal Supremacy had been firmly accepted by his subjects, in Ireland no less than in England or Wales. But the constitutional and legal implications of what had happened had not been fully understood. The first systematic exposition of the new role of parliament came in Sir Thomas Smith's *De Republica Anglorum* of 1565:

> The most high and absolute power of the realm of England consisteth in the Parliament . . . (Statute) is the Prince's and the whole realm's deed; whereupon justly no man can complain but must accommodate himself to find it good and obey it. That which is done by this consent is called firm, stable and *sanctum*, and is taken for law. The Parliament abrogateth old laws, maketh new, giveth orders for things past and for things hereafter to be followed, changeth rights and possessions of private men, legitimateth bastards, establisheth forms of religion, altereth weights and measures, giveth forms of succession to the Crown, defineth of doubtful rights. . . . And the consent of the Parliament is taken to be every man's consent.[3]

No medieval king had enjoyed the services of so omnicompetent an instrument, but the change had not been all gain. There was no room for the Divine Right of Kings in a realm where the 'forms of succession to the Crown' were determined by parliament. Nor was it quite clear where the ecclesiastical supremacy lay when 'forms of religion' were decided by the same means. In 1545 it must have seemed to Henry VIII that he had found the ideal way to make his writ run uniformly and his will to be effective throughout his dominions; but by 1565 it was beginning to become clear that his daughter was circumscribed by institutional limitations far stronger than the bonds of Good Lordship, which had been a flexible leash for monarchs over the preceeding 200 years.

One of the main reasons for this was the uncertain nature of the Tudor succession itself. Parliament had ratified the claim of

Henry VII, but only in the sense of recognizing the *fait accompli*, and tidying up the legal ends. It had not been called upon to endorse the obvious hereditary right of the young Henry to succeed his father in 1509. But when Henry VIII set aside his first wife, in defiance of the pope's ban and the hostility of the emperor, and married again, he destroyed the possibility of passing on his own crown in so uncontroversial a manner. Even if Elizabeth had been a boy, the problem would have remained. Such a son would have been legitimate in English law, but not in the eyes of the rest of Europe, nor of anyone within England who maintained the catholic position. The deaths of both Catherine of Aragon and Anne Boleyn in 1536 could have restored the *status quo*, but it did not because by then Henry had become convinced by his own propaganda, and believed that the Royal Supremacy was *iure divino*. There was no reconciliation with Rome and consequently Prince Edward, born to his third wife Jane Seymour in October 1537 was also illegitimate in the eyes of the catholic Church. Henry was perfectly well aware of this, and equally aware that, in default of heirs of his own body, the succession would naturally pass to his nephew James V of Scotland. This was a prospect which neither the king nor his subjects could regard with equanimity, and partly accounts for the support which Henry managed to attract throughout his devious manipulations. In spite of the disappointment of Elizabeth's birth in September 1533, in 1534 optimism was still running high, and the first succession Act confined itself to reaffirming Mary's illegitimacy, and settling the crown on the children of Anne Boleyn; first the sons, and then the daughters. By 1537 the circumstances of Anne's departure required a similar affirmation of Elizabeth's bastardy, and the elevation of Henry's offspring by Jane Seymour. Three wives and seven years later, in 1544, because the king still had no child of undisputed legitimacy, and it was no longer reasonable to expect this situation to be remedied, a more comprehensive settlement of the succession was called for, and was laid down in a statute which was to prove normative for the next fourteen critical years.

Henry's immediate heir was declared, to no one's surprise or regret, to be Prince Edward. Within England, and for all practical purposes, he was regarded as the king's only legitimate son. After him, the heirs of his body; and in default of such heirs, first

11

the Lady Mary and then the Lady Elizabeth. This arrangement, commended by both common sense and popular sentiment, outraged every accepted legal convention. By no stretch of imagination could both ladies have been legitimate, and as we have seen, both had been solemnly bastardized by Act of Parliament. Worse was to follow. Should the whole direct line fail the Crown was to pass, not to James V's infant daughter Mary, nor to any other descendant of Henry's elder sister Margaret, but to the children of his younger sister Mary. The king was also given the power to alter this disposition by his last will and testament if he chose to do so. The existence of Edward has tended to obscure the fact that this statute was a revolutionary measure. Both the first and second Succession Acts had claimed to declare the identity of the legitimate hereditary heir. This Act declared a succession without reference to legitimacy as normally defined, and it empowered the king to depart even further from custom if he so decided. In the event, Henry's will at the end of 1546 confirmed the statutory order, and Edward's accession a month later was unchallenged. For the time being, however, the emperor withheld his recognition, merely returning the greetings which had been sent to him in the name of the young king. 'We went no further than this', he wrote to his ambassador Van der Delft, '. . . in order to avoid saying anything which might prejudice the right that our cousin the Princess might advance to the throne.'[4] In his eyes, Mary was the true heir as the only legitimate child of the late king, but the Princess did not see herself in that light, and advanced no claim. Charles V was far too pragmatic to pursue such an argument on principle, and within a few weeks he was doing business with the new English government as though no such doubt had ever entered his mind.

Unfortunately, the heir for whose sake Henry VIII had turned his kingdom inside out, and launched it upon uncharted constitutional waters, proved to be only a temporary solution to the problem. By the beginning of 1553 Edward, still only fifteen and unmarried, had become seriously ill. His death was not considered to be imminent, but the situation focused his own mind and that of his mentor, John Dudley, Duke of Northumberland, upon the question of the succession. During the six years of his reign Edward himself, and his realm, had been converted to protestantism, a process which his sister Mary had strenuously and publicly resisted. For this reason, the king was determined that Mary should not succeed him and undo what he believed to have been the work of God. Northumberland, who appears to have joined the protestant party out of political opportunism rather than conviction, was of the same mind for more mundane reasons. Between them they drew up a 'Device' which ignored both Henry VIII's will and the statute upon which it rested, fixing the succession upon any son who might be born to Frances Grey, Duchess of Suffolk, the elder daughter of the late king's younger sister. The logic of such a course is extremely hard to unravel. The Greys were protestants, but so, apparently, was Edward's younger sister Elizabeth; and the main argument adduced for excluding both Mary and Elizabeth – that they might marry foreign princes and subject the realm to alien rule – had political weight but no legal validity. As long as the 'Device' retained its original form, it did appear to be aimed at the exclusion of female rule, and to that extent was consistent with Henry's original priority. But as the king's health deteriorated it lost even that semblance of justification. By June 1553 it had become clear that Edward had only weeks to live, and that no son would be born to Frances Grey, or to her recently married elder daughter Jane, in time to be of any relevance. The 'Device' was therefore altered, excluding all reference to Frances, and settling the crown upon 'the Lady Jane and her heirs male'. On 21 June Letters Patent confirmed the bastardy of both Mary and Elizabeth, and the dying king summoned his councillors and judges to swear to the 'Device'.[5] There was a great deal of unease, but no open resistance, partly because this strange edict clearly represented Edward's own intention, and partly because it was strenuously upheld by the Duke of Northumberland, who appeared to control substantial financial and military resources.

At the end of June writs were issued for a parliament, but Edward died on 6 July, leaving an extremely precarious situation. The king had never attained his majority, and therefore could not make a legally binding will. More important, parliament had never granted him the right to bequeath the Crown in such a fashion, and Henry's third succession Act was unrepealed. Only by the most extreme form of absolutist theory – a theory never before accepted in England – could his disposition be deemed valid. If the Duke of Northumberland could command sufficient power to establish Jane Grey upon the throne, not only would the constitutional developments of the previous twenty years have been rendered meaningless, but the English crown would have been freer from legal restraint or limitation than any monarchy in Europe. But Northumberland was deeply and widely unpopular, not only among ordinary people, but also among the gentry and his fellow peers. It was generally believed (although incorrectly, it would seem) that he had married his fourth son, Guildford, to Jane Grey in May 1553 in order to make him king, and to divert the succession into his own family. His ambition was feared and resented, and religious conservatives regarded him as an enemy because of his role in the establishment of protestantism. More seriously the protestants, in whose interests Edward had ostensibly acted, were deeply divided. Most of them regarded the king's death as a judgement from God, and accepted as lawful the succession laid down in 1544. Everything therefore depended upon Mary. In 1547 she had made no attempt to advance her claim, but in 1553 belief in her own legitimacy and adherence to her father's settlement both pointed in the same direction. Northumberland delayed the announcement of the king's death for three days in the hope of arresting her, but she was warned and slipped away to Kenninghall in Norfolk. There she proclaimed herself queen, and wrote to the council in London, demanding their allegiance. It seems clear that Mary was ready for this crisis, and Northumberland was not. Her proclamations must have been prepared in advance, because they were being read in towns and villages all over England within a few days; and the gentry of her East Anglican affinity arrived with their men, armed and provisioned, equally promptly. The Duke, on the other hand, had no force mobilized, and had taken no steps to recall the mercenaries who had been stood down in the previous year.

For a few days the issue hung in the balance. The Imperial Ambassadors, although sympathetic to Mary, believed that Northumberland held all the cards, and would win. On the other hand his fellow councillors soon began to reflect that it was one thing to obey King Edward while he was alive, but another matter altogether to uphold his dubious settlement after he was dead. As Mary's army began to build up, first at Kenninghall and then at Framlingham, several of these councillors, including the Earls of Bedford, Arundel and Shrewsbury, began to withdraw from their exposed position. By 12 July it was clear that Northumberland's hope for a walk-over had been disappointed. Not only had Mary challenged him, but she had the force to back her claim and only a military defeat could deny her. On 14 July the Duke left London with a force of no more than 600 men to confront an army which rumour had inflated to 30,000,[6] and not even his formidable reputation as a soldier could redress the odds. By 19 July it was all over; Northumberland's support had disintegrated, both in the capital and in the country, and he and his family were under arrest. Pleased as they were, the Imperial Ambassadors could scarcely conceal their amazement. At first they thought that the councillors were playing a double game, waiting for Mary to dismiss her forces before renewing the attack. Then they concluded that God had wrought a notable miracle for the sake of His Church. But the true nature of English politics eluded them, accustomed as they were to magnate factions and peasant revolts. If Mary had not acted swiftly and resolutely, her cause might well have gone by default, but what gave her victory against the apparent odds was the legal and constitutional strength of her claim. Protestants who feared her religious conservatism, and Henricians who accepted the Royal Supremacy and regarded her as a bastard, nevertheless accepted that she was the lawful heir. Mary herself never seems to have understood this, believing that the sweeping endorsement of her claim implied an equally sweeping endorsement of her mother's marriage and the old faith. But it was not so, as the behaviour of her subjects over the next five years was to demonstrate. Nevertheless in July 1553 the Tudor dynasty survived the most radical challenge which it was to face between 1485 and 1603.

If Mary had preserved the lawful succession by her positive action in 1553, she did the same again by negative means in 1558. The queen hated her half sister, and made it clear in discussion with her advisers during November 1553 that Elizabeth would not be included in any succession settlement which she might make. Mary was about to marry at the age of 37, and the risk always attendant upon child-bearing was greatly heightened by her age, so the matter was not academic. However, there were few options. Jane Grey (a prisoner in the Tower) and her protestant sisters were clearly out of the reckoning; Mary Stuart, suitably catholic, was in France and betrothed to the Dauphin, equally unacceptable to the queen and to her husband-to-be, Philip of Spain. If Elizabeth was also excluded, the only remaining candidates of Tudor blood were Margaret, Countess of Lennox, the daughter of Henry VIII's elder sister through her second marriage to the Earl of Angus, and Margaret Clifford the daughter of Eleanor, Frances Brandon's younger sister. Of these two unpromising ladies the queen preferred the former. However no formal disposition was made, or even proposed, out of deference to Mary's conviction that God would give her the child for which she longed. Her marriage took place in July 1554, and by October the queen was convinced that she was pregnant. Her body developed all the outward symptoms at the appropriate time, and some of her councillors – particularly her Lord Chancellor Stephen Gardiner – wished to make some interim arrangement for the succession in case the worst occurred. Agreement proved impossible. In the spring of 1555 Elizabeth was summoned to court, and kept under virtual arrest, but no steps were taken to debar her from the throne. Gardiner had wished in the previous year, and no doubt still wished, to repeal the Act of 1544; but in the absence of any child of Mary, the other candidates were so remote and ineffectual that he could find little support for such a course. In July 1555 the crisis passed. Mary did not die, but neither did she have a child. Her pregnancy had been a humiliating delusion, which left the queen shattered and her husband disenchanted. In August Philip left to attend to other pressing business on the continent, rightly convinced that his marriage was a dynastic failure, and Elizabeth remained heir to the throne.

The king accepted this situation much more readily than Mary, whose opinions had been reinforced rather than otherwise by the princess's conduct over the preceeding two years. In his eyes the main danger lay in the possibility of her coming to the throne unmarried, and choosing an unsuitable (i.e. pro-French) partner. The solution therefore was not to debar her in favour of some feeble unknown, but to marry her acceptably without further delay. His candidate was Emmanuel Philibert, titular Duke of Savoy and a loyal Habsburg adherent.[7] This proposal Mary consistently refused to accept, to her husband's mounting annoyance and frustration. This was not out of any consideration for Elizabeth, who rejected all ideas of marriage, but rather out of a fear that her position would thereby be strengthened.

Mary either could not, or would not, grasp the nettle of a parliamentary settlement, but she seems not to have believed that the princess was really her father's daughter. So strong was her hatred for the memory of Anne Boleyn that she had apparently convinced herself that her enemy's daughter could only have been born in adultery. Neither Philip, nor anybody else, shared this view. Elizabeth was certainly illegitimate, but not for that reason, and her political position had become increasingly strong since the failure of Mary's pregnancy. The queen herself clung to her hope of a child. When Philip returned to England for political reasons from March to July 1557, she immediately began to entertain renewed hopes of pregnancy. The following January, when she announced a forthcoming happy event, the courts of Europe could barely preserve their decorum, but she persisted in her delusion. In March, when she made her will, there was no reference to any succession apart from 'the fruit of my body lawfully begotten'. Philip could have advanced a claim of his own. Although forbidden by the terms of the marriage treaty of 1554, it could have been argued that such a claim arose naturally, and could not be barred by human law. Mary would have preferred such an outcome to the succession of Elizabeth,[8] but the king had no intention of falling into the trap. He knew perfectly well that he was deeply unpopular in England, and reciprocated the feeling heartily. It would have cost him a civil war in England, which honour would have required, but for which the resources were not available. As Mary's health deteriorated during the summer of 1558, he carefully stayed away, not out of callous indifference to her wishes, but out of a fear of being trapped in England by her death.

It was not until October, when her illness was already far advanced, that Mary finally made a codicil to her will, acknowledging that there was now little hope of any child, and that Philip's interest in the kingdom would end with her life. Her crown was to pass to the next heir 'by the laws of England'. No successor was named, but when parliament reconvened on 7 November a deputation of members succeeded in persuading her to nominate Elizabeth, perhaps little realizing what a bitter defeat this represented.[9] When Mary died ten days later she had preserved the Tudor succession laid down in 1544, at the cost of all her aspirations for the future of England. The new queen understandably felt no gratitude to her predecessor for yielding to the inevitable, and set out to destroy both her achievements and her reputation. In England Elizabeth was hailed with almost unanimous delight, as Mary had been five years earlier. Once again the Tudor dynasty had survived, and the shadow of King Henry VIII still dominated the political horizon. A new phase in the succession drama was about to open; one which was to last well beyond the mid-century period. Only the king of France, with whom England was at war, at first refused to recognize her, advancing the claim of his daughter-in-law, Mary Stuart. The peace treaty which ended the war at Cateau Cambrésis the following April removed that threat from the official international agenda, but it lingered on until the death of Mary's husband, Francis II, in December 1560. Thereafter Mary's claim was to succeed Elizabeth rather than to replace her, although the distinction became blurred by many years of plotting. As long as stability depended upon the queen's life, no Englishman could sleep easy in his bed; but he got used to it over the years, and could always take comfort in the reflection that what parliament had settled once, it could always settle again.

The early Elizabethan parliaments in fact spent a great deal of time debating the relative merits of Mary, Catherine Grey (Jane's younger sister) and more remote claimants such as the Earl of Huntingdon, but the queen would never allow any conclusion to be reached.

Henry VIII had spent the last twenty years of his reign trying to ensure the preservation of his own and his father's achievements, only to be succeeded by a minor and two women. In 1544 the thought that the first three provisions of his succession Act would all become operative would have filled him with dread; and yet twenty years later the English state was, if anything, more secure than it was when he left it. One reason for this was that the lawful succession had been upheld, but another was the strength of the governmental machine itself. The personal direction of the monarch was much less important than in, for example, France, and the English crown was good at surviving minorities. It had not been the long minority of Henry VI (from 1422 to 1437) which had undermined the Lancastrian state, but his personal rule. Similarly, the fact that Edward VI succeeded at the age of nine did remarkably little to impede the effectiveness of the government which was conducted in his name. 'The king's authority to govern his realm never wanteth', asserted Stephen Gardiner, 'though he were in his cradle. His place is replenished by his council. . . .'[10] That council, led first by the Duke of Somerset as Lord Protector, and later by the Duke of Northumberland as Lord President, not only managed parliament and maintained control over the counties, but altered the whole doctrine and worship of the Church in a far more radical manner than Henry VIII had done, defeating every challenge to its authority. The Royal Supremacy was changed by the circumstances of the minority, but not in any sense weakened. Common lawyers such as Christopher St German had been worried by the supremacy which Henry had created, seeing its personal nature as a possible route whereby the monarch could outflank the traditional limitations of the law. He had consequently urged the importance of parliament as a partner in the Supreme Headship, and the minority made that partnership more real – or at least more important. Mary and Stephen Gardiner both argued that while the king was a child the supremacy could be only a holding operation, but that was not consistent with Gardiner's general view of the minority, and was swept aside by the determination of the reformers. The motivation of protestant bishops such as Cranmer and Ridley was certainly religious, but one consequence of their actions was that the Church became increasingly a department of state. Cranmer sought a fresh commission from the crown at the beginning of the reign, as though he had been simply a royal servant; bishops were appointed without even a show of canonical election; and the ecclesiastical courts were conducted in the king's name. Edward could not sustain his father's quasi-papal image, but that was an advantage because it meant that the ecclesiastical supremacy ceased to be a rogue element in the constitution and became subsumed into the normal functions of the royal office. When Elizabeth took the title of Supreme Governor in 1559, it was with this development in mind. She deliberately revived the situation of 1553 rather than that of 1547, because a woman, like a minor, could not exercise ecclesiastical jurisdiction, and gender, unlike age, was not a surmountable obstacle. She had to create a situation with which she could live for the foreseeable future, and the 'constitutional supremacy', which might have been a temporary expedient if Edward had lived, became a permanent feature of the Anglican settlement.

In spite of all pretence to the contrary, the Royal Supremacy had been invented between 1530 and 1533, and the precedents which had been concocted for its use had been shadowy. There was equally no precedent in England for a ruling queen. The Empress Matilda in the twelfth century had claimed the crown, and fought a civil war in pursuit of her claim, but had never exercised the office. Although there was no Salic Law, no one knew how the powers of the crown might be affected by passing into the hands of a woman. As long as she was unmarried, the issue could be safely ignored, because neither law nor custom inhibited an unmarried or widowed heiress from holding and managing her property in the same manner as a man. Mary had done just that as princess between 1547 and 1553. Consequently nothing was done in Mary's first parliament to clarify the situation, beyond a statutory reaffirmation of her legitimacy. However, the negotiation of a marriage settlement with Philip of Spain in January 1554 removed this temporary complacency, and revived the fears of female rule which had lurked below the surface of English political life since 1520. The treaty itself could hardly have been more explicit and reassuring. Philip was to exercise no authority in England without the queen's participation; he was not to appoint any non-Englishman to office; he was not to involve England in his current war with France; and he was not to claim the throne in the event of Mary's death without heirs. So disadvantageous did the terms appear to the future king that he secretly repudiated them, and his councillors claimed that his honour had been besmirched. Nevertheless, English opinion was not satisfied. The rebellion of January/February 1554 led by Sir Thomas Wyatt was briefly dangerous, and a far more direct challenge to Mary's government than the risings of 1549 had been to Edward's. It was also the tip of an iceberg of discontent. As one anonymous Member of Parliament had argued when the matter was debated there in November 1553, it was all very well having a treaty, but once the marriage had taken place, who would insist upon its terms being observed?[11] All these fears were based upon the subordinate legal status of married women. A wife was bound to obey her husband, and her property became his. Simon Renard, the Imperial Ambassador, reported anxiously before the Wyatt rebellion that certain English laywers were arguing that the queen had only a 'woman's estate' in the realm, and that it would pass to Philip by English law, no matter what any treaty might say to the contrary.

It was partly because of these arguments that the treaty was embodied in a statute by the parliament of April 1554, thus giving its terms the force of law, any preceding custom to the contrary notwithstanding. The same parliament also passed a curious-seeming Act declaring that the queen's power was identical to that of her male predecessors. Some contemporaries later claimed that this was intended to counter a semantic subterfuge, whereby Mary might have sought to emancipate herself from such restrictions as Magna Carta on the grounds that the monarch was always referred to as 'king'. However, it seems more likely that it arose from precisely the opinion which Renard had cited, and was intended to imply that the queen's forthcoming marriage would make no difference to her sovereign status. It would hardly have been tactful to be more explicit with Philip already in the offing, and Mary herself trying very hard to come to terms with her conflicting duties to realm and husband. Once the marriage had been consummated in July 1554, that conflict was never very far away. An heir was the first priority on both agendas, and after that the reconciliation of the Church with Rome. But the latter was Mary's personal agenda rather than the kingdom's, and Philip found himself siding with the English aristocracy rather than the queen over the question of Church lands. Tension between the roles of wife and sovereign probably explain a number of curious features in Mary's relationship with her husband. Her actions and her rhetoric were not always consistent. She declared repeatedly, especially when he was absent, that she depended totally upon his advice and support, and upon his 'strong hand' in the government of the realm. And yet she allocated no effective role to him when he was present, declined to crown him as king, and gave him no English patrimony.[12] Similarly, in spite of her professions of wifely duty, she refused to yield to his pressure over Elizabeth's marriage, and confessed that she had 'frequently felt his anger' in consequence. On the other hand, in 1557 she involved England in war with France, on Philip's insistence and in his interest, against the advice of the majority of her council. In spite of this extremely important decision, on balance Mary kept to her own priorities rather than his. This was partly because of his absence, and growing indifference to English affairs, and partly because of counter-pressures within England, particularly from the financial and commercial interests of London. There was little conflict over religion once the settlement was negotiated, although Philip would undoubtedly have preferred her to show some interest in the strenuous new orders which were doing such good evangelical work in Italy and Germany. In that respect the influence of Cardinal Pole remained predominant. By 1558 Mary was an embarrassment to Philip, and her death was timely from his point of view. Had she lived he must sooner or later have taken steps to end their union because, like Henry VIII before him, he needed more children to ensure the security of his dynasty. The failure of Mary's marriage may have been a tragedy for her, but it ensured that the English crown came through the experience of being held by a married queen virtually unscathed. A child of the union, or prolonged residence by Philip in England, would have had a much more profound effect. Like the accession of Elizabeth, the unchanged authority of the English crown in 1558 was a negative rather than a positive achievement. Mary had indeed surrendered the Royal Supremacy, but she had done nothing to damage the infrastructure which had made it possible, and that can hardly have been her deliberate intention either.

Beneath the rejoicings which greeted the unchallenged succession of another Tudor in 1558, lurked a renewed fear. Elizabeth made much of her Englishness, restored the Royal Supremacy and deliberately invoked the memory of her father. It seemed unlikely that she would follow Mary's example in her choice of a husband, and that was a matter for relief and satisfaction. However, when the new queen did begin to show a serious interest in matrimony, about eighteen months after her accession, the signals seemed to be equally alarming. Not only was her favourite, Lord Robert Dudley, a son of the deeply unpopular Duke of Northumberland, he was also married. When his wife died in mysterious circumstances in September 1560 the scandal was monumental, and when Dudley was cleared of any involvement by an investigating commission, it got worse. The courts of Europe held their breath, and waited for the Queen of England to destroy herself. However, Elizabeth was made of sterner stuff than her unfortunate cousin Mary of Scotland, who was to succumb to a similar temptation in 1567. After what must have been a severe personal struggle, she recognized the political impossibility of marriage to Lord Robert, and resumed her confidential relationship with Sir William Cecil, which had been disrupted by Cecil's unconcealed hostility to the proposed union. When the queen fell critically ill with small-pox in 1562 her affection for Dudley caused her to nominate him as Protector of the Realm in the event of her untimely death, but she recovered and that ill-considered intention was consigned to the archive. Appointed to the Privy Council in October 1562, and created Earl of Leicester in September 1564, Dudley gradually lost his maverick status and became a normal part of the political scene.[13] There was thereafter no chance that Elizabeth would marry 'within the realm', and little chance that she would marry at all. Whether or not she ever made a con-scious decision not to marry, she was well aware of the advan-tages of having 'but one mistress and no master'. At the cost of leaving the succession unsettled, she retained a sole and unambiguous sovereignty. In a sense this was to mortgage the future to the present, and it could be argued that Mary made the more responsible choice. But Elizabeth's longevity resolved the issue of the succession, and allowed her to reap the full benefit of her gamble. Instead of treating her gender as an inevitable disadvantage to be overcome, she was able to turn it into an exploitable asset; but she became an impossible act to follow. The crown which Elizabeth wore was a poor fit on her successors.

Like all the Tudors in varying degrees, Elizabeth had the kind of political charisma which retained the loyalty of her subjects, even when they did not much like what she was doing. After the demise of Perkin Warbeck, no rebellion aimed explicitly to depose the reigning monarch. It could be argued that both Wyatt in 1554 and the northern Earls in 1569 had that objective as a hidden agenda; but if so, the fact that they did not announce it openly is almost equally significant. Only the 'rebellion' of Mary in 1553 is a technical exception, but the outcome of that merely serves to emphasize the point. The Tudors commanded the allegiance of their subjects in a manner, and to a degree, which could not have been predicted from the history of the English monarchy over the previous 200 years. The reasons for this were complex, but since that allegiance played a critical part in preserving the political stability of

England from 1530 to 1570, they need to be understood. Henry VII scored the same kind of propaganda coup against Richard III that Elizabeth later scored against Mary. Moreover he and his agents succeeded eventually in convincing the political nation that only the Tudors stood between England and a renewal of the civil wars – wars whose violence and destructiveness were deliberately exaggerated by such writers as Polydore Vergil and Thomas More. Henry VIII's succession was not quite as smooth as it was made to appear. Henry VII's death was concealed for three days, just as his son's was to be in 1547, so that the necessary power structure could be secured. The younger Henry, partly by genetic accident and partly by careful education, had – or appeared to have – all the qualities of an ideal renaissance Prince. He was warlike, learned, cultured, magnificent. By the time his charisma was put to the test in the 1530s, it was deeply rooted in the public consciousness. His treatment of Catherine was almost universally deplored; Anne Boleyn was widely hated; and the break with Rome filled many of his subjects with acute alarm. But Henry himself was never seriously challenged, and the more his overthrow was demanded by Continental enemies, the more England rallied to his support. By the end of his reign he was a great king, dominating the realm as his image by Holbein dominated the presence chamber at Whitehall. In achieving this, as we have seen, he had subtley, and probably unintentionally, shifted the foundations of his monarchy. Without, in his own eyes, sacrificing anything of his special relationship with God, he had nevertheless placed himself, in respect of his ecclesiastical supremacy, in a new and unique constitutional relationship with his subjects. At the same time this was a relationship which echoed some of the traditional legal restraints upon the English crown expounded by Sir John Fortescue half a century before.

The fact that Edward's title rested upon statute and his father's will should never be lost sight of. Although he was hailed as king by hereditary right and by the will of God, such language was more convenient than accurate, as his councillors understood perfectly well. Nor could an image of power be readily created for a ten-year-old boy. The image which was created – that of Josias – had a selective and very limited appeal. Nevertheless no rival appeared, and no rebel claimed that a heretic child could be no true king. Although Henry VIII's apparent bid to rule from beyond the grave through the executors of his will was quickly and inevitably frustrated, nevertheless his achievement and personality continued to dominate the political scene. Mary recognized as much when she denounced the councillors who came in Edward's name to harrass her on the subject of religious conformity, as having been 'made of nothing' by her father. What the young king had, in addition to an undoubted paternity, was an undoubted Englishness; his very birth had been hailed as a sign of Divine approval, and he was a potent symbol of the gauntlet which his father had thrown down to catholic Europe. Mary by the same token was something very different, at least in her own eyes and those of the emperor who protected her. She could, and did, claim the throne by indefeasible hereditary right, and in doing so repudiated, at first by implication and then explicitly, those aspects of her father's rule which had set him apart, both from his predecessors and from his European contemporaries. As we have seen, her subjects accepted a different basis for her rule, but neither she nor they could find any potent image to express that relationship, and before she died there were signs of an approaching challenge on religious grounds. Unlike Mary, Elizabeth inherited her father's charisma, and by the time that she, too, invited religious challenge she had become 'England's Eliza', at once a potent symbol of autonomy and a talisman against civil strife. The English had a turbulent reputation, but the Tudors sold themselves successfully as political winners, and their subjects never lost faith in their ability to rule.

Although the English monarchy was less personal and more constitutional than that of France or Spain, it bore no resemblance to the system of government which we would now call 'constitutional monarchy'. With the exception of Edward the Tudors were all effective rulers, and their chief executive instrument was the Privy Council. In one sense the council was an immemorial institution, because no wise king had ever attempted to govern without adequate advice and assistance, but the form which it had attained by 1540 was a recent innovation. The medieval council had consisted of anyone whom the king chose to consult, and thus had tended to be both large and amorphous. Some councillors were office holders, and close to the king; others were powerful men whom it would have been foolish to leave out; others again were specialists, whose expertise was only occasionally needed. During periods of royal weakness it had been argued that the council 'represented' the nobility of the realm, and even that there were persons known as 'councillors born' whom the king was bound to consult; but little had been heard of such views since the accession of Henry VII. Henry had used his council in the traditional manner, as a judicial and executive instrument with regular meetings, an omnicompetent agenda and a very fluctuating attendance. But he also consulted regularly with a small group of trusted advisers, drawn from the ranks of his council but forming only a small proportion of it. These men tended to travel with him, and were somewhat misleadingly known as the 'council attendant'. They had no separate institutional identity and although they all took the councillors' oath to the king, that did not distinguish them from other regular but less intimate attenders, such as the Chief Justices. During the period of Wolsey's ascendency, from 1514 to 1529, the judicial functions of the council had been clearly separated from the rest, and the council sitting in that capacity became known as the Court of Star Chamber.[14] All councillors were in theory judges, but only a small number attended, and they became increasingly specialized. In 1526 a plan had been drawn up to rationalize the working of the council, and to reduce its size; but although these 'Eltham Ordinances' were drafted by Wolsey they probably did not suit his interests, and it was to be another ten years before the plan was implemented. By 1540, however, thanks partly to the pressure of circumstances, partly to the wishes of the king, and partly to the political ingenuity of Thomas Cromwell, the council had been reduced to twenty effective members, all office holders, who were known in the French fashion as the 'Privy Council'.

With this development it became possible to distinguish more clearly between the three traditional functions of councillors. The judicial was carried out in Star Chamber, a court with its own records and its own staff. The executive was carried out in the regular meetings of the Privy Council, and recorded by the clerk in his minute book. The political was carried out, as before, by individuals and small groups in personal consultation with the monarch. If political business was discussed in regular meetings, the clerk was excluded and the matter was not recorded. At first glance the Privy Council Register makes that body look remarkably like a modern cabinet, but the appearance is extremely deceptive. In the first place the council had no collective responsibility, each individual councillor being sworn to advise the monarch in accordance with his wisdom and conscience, and to carry out the monarch's wishes. It was very seldom that the Privy Council spoke with one voice on any issue, but that was relatively unimportant since it was the monarch who made the decisions. Secondly, the council had no responsibility to any other constituency. If it had ever had a representative function, that had long since been taken over by the parliament; and although councillors sat regularly, either in the House of Lords or the House of Commons, they could not be instructed by those Houses. A councillor's status could be terminated in a number of ways. Occasionally a councillor who was also an office holder might resign his office, as Sir Thomas More did in 1532, or Sir William Petre in 1557. He might lose the king's confidence, or be convicted of some serious crime, as the Duke of Norfolk was in 1546. But the commonest reason, apart from the death of the councillor, was the death of the sovereign. Since the council was the monarch's personal creation, all appointments ceased with his life. In theory every adult ruler started with a clean slate, although in practice the need for experience in government always guaranteed a degree of continuity, even between regimes as dissimilar as those of Mary and Elizabeth.

However, a minority provided exceptions to every rule. In the last months of Henry VIII's life an intense power struggle developed around the dying king. As long as he was sufficiently *compos mentis* to control the situation, Henry's intention was to set up a Regency Council in the form of a body of executors. Sixteen men were named to this body in his will, and their identity not only signalled a clear victory for the reforming faction over their conservative opponents, but also the king's full cognisance of that situation. However, when he lapsed into unconsciousness on 28 December 1547, the will was still unsigned, and the new regime in consequence was based upon a document authenticated with a dry stamp. This was perfectly proper in so far as the Earl of Hertford, Sir William Paget, Sir William Herbert and Sir Anthony Denny had been authorized to apply the stamp. However, it led to inevitable suspicions that the will had been doctored, and in two important respects those suspicions appear to have been justified. In the first place

Henry's last clear intention was that the Regency Council should rule by majority decision, without a single head, but when the will was declared it contained a clause giving the council full power and authority to take any action necessary for the government of the realm.[15] On the basis of that clause, within a few days the Earl of Hertford, the young king's uncle, was named Protector of the realm and Governor of his person. Secondly the council was also empowered to award posthumously in Henry's name whatever the late king had 'granted, made, accorded or promised' but had not legally conveyed during his lifetime. On the basis of unconfirmed testimony by Sir William Paget as to Henry's unfulfilled intentions, the Earl of Hertford became Duke of Somerset, William Parr Earl of Essex became Marquis of Northampton, John Dudley Viscount Lisle became Earl of Warwick, Sir Thomas Wriothesley became Earl of Southampton, and the Protector's brother, Sir Thomas Seymour, became Lord Seymour of Sudely. The Regency Council then took the inevitable step of petitioning for a new existence in the name of King Edward VI, since neither law nor precedent enabled government to be conducted in the name of a dead king, however powerful. On 6 March the council used this authority to purge its last important conservative, Lord Chancellor Southampton, and on 12 March Somerset was granted quasi-royal powers by Letters Patent, including the power to name all future councillors.

In the event he used this power sparingly, not out of any constitutional sensitivity, but simply because the council became progressively less significant. Somerset, in fact, acted more in the manner of a king than of a regent, taking much of his political advice outside the council, and using his own household servants, rather as Henry VIII had used his Privy Chamber. Of these men, Sir Thomas Smith, Sir Michael Stanhope, Sir John Thynne, William Cecil and William Grey, only Smith was appointed to the Privy Council when he became the king's secretary. The others were significantly referred to as the 'new council', and Stanhope became a key man in the Protector's system of control when he was appointed chief gentleman of the Privy Chamber and Groom of the Stool – the positions previously held by Sir Anthony Denny.[16] The Privy Council was frequently convened at Somerset House rather than at court, and the records of attendance seem to have been falsified in order to give its proceedings a greater appearance of weight.

Such methods were not so much illegal as unwise. Somerset obtained sole custody of the dry stamp of Edward's signature, and was thus able to warrant financial business and to issue commissions without reference to his fellow councillors. They naturally became suspicious of his intentions, and when he began to insist that the king's true signature was not valid without his counter signature, they saw this as an attempt to isolate Edward, and to alienate him from everyone who did not have the Protector's passport. He also showed what some regarded as an excessive tendency to issue proclamations in the king's name. The first challenge to these tactics, however, came not from a powerful council faction, but from Somerset's discontented brother. Thomas Seymour believed that he should have been Governor of the King's Person, and this pretension was encouraged when he married the dowager queen, Catherine, in July 1547. At first the Protector temporized, admitting him to the council and creating him Lord Admiral, but Seymour was not placated. When Catherine died in childbirth he laid siege to the Princess Elizabeth, and their intimacy bred scandal and alarm. With equal recklessness he endeavoured to circumvent his brother's control of the Privy Chamber, using one of the grooms, Thomas Fowler, to pass small sums of money to Edward, whose purse strings were somewhat tightly held by Stanhope. At the end of 1548 Seymour endeavoured to inveigle the Earl of Southampton into a plot to overthrow the Protector, and his irresponsible behaviour could no longer be ignored. On 17 January 1549 he was arrested on charges of high treason, and the subsequent investigation revealed a prolonged tale of desperate intrigue, including the systematic abuse of his office as Admiral. There was very little to be said in Seymour's defence, except that he had almost certainly been 'set up' by the Protector's political enemies, particularly Warwick and Southampton. Fearing that a long and acrimonious trial would bespatter him with the mud which Seymour had churned up, his brother had him attainted by Act of Parliament, and executed without further trial on 20 March.

Coming on top of his previous high-handed methods of government, this could easily be represented as autocratic, and Somerset got little credit from anyone for having rid the realm of an unmitigated pest, and restored the Earl of Southampton to the council. By the summer of 1549 he was in increasing difficulties. His determination to pursue three controversial policies simultaneously without troubling to mobilize the support of the council was overtaxing his credibility. He had from the beginning been determined to pursue Henry's war with Scotland to a successful conclusion. This was partly the *hubris* of a military commander who could not endure the prospect of being frustrated by an enemy whom he despised, and partly a genuine political vision of the union of the crowns. In September 1547 he had crossed the border with a large army and supporting fleet, and on the tenth of that month confronted the main Scottish host at Pinkie Cleugh, near Musselborough. A hard fought but total victory had quickly revealed the limitations of such a strategy. Although his position in England had certainly been strengthened, he had been unable to impose a satisfactory settlement upon the defeated Scots. Instead he had established a string of expensive garrisons, from Haddington to Broughty Crag on the Firth of Tay, with the intention of maintaining a long-term military stranglehold to enforce eventual submission. These garrisons had swiftly become hostages to fortune. Even without significant French assistance, the Scots proved fully capable of harassing them and enforcing expensive relief and supply operations – a retaliation which had been made inevitable by the brutal *chevauchée* with which Somerset had followed up his victory. His policy had already been in difficulties when 6,000 French troops arrived in Scotland in June 1548. Within a few weeks the English had been outmanoeuvred both militarily and politically. In a treaty signed under the noses of the hard-pressed garrison of Haddington, the Scots had placed themselves under the protection of the king of France, and agreed that their infant queen should marry his eldest son. In July Mary had sailed for France, safely eluding the English ships which had been sent out to intercept her.

Further major efforts by Somerset in August 1548 and January 1549 had proved as futile as they were expensive. But in spite of having lost his ostensible war aim with the removal of Mary to France, and in spite of the opposition being created by the ever mounting cost, the Protector had persisted with obsessive intensity. By the summer of 1549 he was hopelessly bogged down in protracted and inconclusive sieges, and seemed to have lost all sense of political reality. At the same time unfulfilled expectations of an effective anti-enclosure policy, which had been aroused by the establishment of commissions of enquiry, and by Somerset's own well-publicized views, had resulted in widespread agrarian revolts; and the new protestant liturgy was generally resented. Each of these policies had been individually justifiable, but the first had long since lost its validity, and the second was actively resisted by his fellow peers, who saw no reason why they should rally to the support of a man who had so consistently ignored them over the previous two and a half years. Sir William Paget, his loyalest supporter, bombarded him with increasingly desperate letters of good advice, urging him to repair his political fences before it was too late, but Somerset was temperamentally incapable of changing his style, and in October walked into a carefully prepared trap. The originators of this coup were a group of religious conservatives led by the Earl of Arundel, who wished to halt the progress of protestantism by getting rid of the Protector and installing the Princess Mary as Regent. Mary did not respond to their advances but Arundel found many of his fellow councillors willing to take advantage of his initiative against Somerset, including Warwick and Wriothesley. The emphasis of the plot thus shifted from the positive to the negative, and its religious aspect became significantly diluted. Victory by Warwick over the rebels in Norfolk and by Lord Russell over those in Devon and Cornwall gave the conspirators their chance. Somerset had gained neither strength nor prestige from these successes, and his enemies decided to act before their forces were disbanded. Early in October a series of clandestine meetings were held in London, and those councillors who were in the plot began cautiously to move troops into the vicinity of the capital. Sensing danger, on 6 October the Protector suddenly moved himself and the king from Westminster to Windsor Castle, and issued a proclamation calling upon all the king's subjects to muster for his defence, and that of his 'entirely beloved uncle'.

In so doing, he played into his enemies' hands, because they immediately claimed that he was endeavouring to rouse the rabble against their natural lords, as he had already done by his obstinate pursuit of enclosing landlords. After only a brief hesitation the City of London, having taken stock of the situation, came down on the side of the council, and Somerset was left at Windsor with a handful of supporters and a few unarmed peasants. On 11 October he surrendered, and was consigned to

31

the Tower. There then followed a power struggle as the coalition which had removed the Protector inevitably fell apart. Although Mary had still made no move, it seemed at first as though the religious conservatives had the upper hand, especially when they were joined by the pragmatic Wriothesley. The protestant clergy were alarmed, and wrote gloomy letters to their friends in Zurich and Geneva. At this point, however, the conservatives made an understandable but fatal mistake. They decided to take advantage of the Earl of Warwick's original support for Somerset to brand him as an accomplice in the Protector's misdeeds, and thus remove him as well. Warwick, who had not hitherto shown any very marked religious predilections, made the obvious counter move. He entered into alliance with Archbishop Cranmer, whose high ecclesiastical status and close personal relations with the young king had enabled him to survive Somerset's fall unscathed. The Earl's newly discovered enthusiasm for protestant reform also had the great advantage of commending him to Edward, who at the age of 12 was showing every sign of becoming a religious zealot. In the uncertain political climate of October and November 1549, with no identifiable head of government, control of the Privy Council became critical, and the young king was propelled into a key role. Under the influence of Cranmer, he named two strong protestants, Henry Grey, Marquis of Dorset, and Thomas Goodrich, Bishop of Ely. These two appointments, and a bargain with the elusive Paget, gave Warwick the upper hand. By the end of November the Earl of Southampton had ceased attending meetings, and before Christmas a thumping re-affirmation of the Protector's religious policy signalled the outcome of the struggle. In January 1550 the Earl of Arundel was removed from office and placed under house arrest.

There was, however, a price to be paid for this success. The attempt to brand Warwick as an accomplice of Somerset had to mean that the Protector had not been quite such a bad thing, after all. Warwick persuaded him to make a more or less graceful submission, and then persuaded parliament to embody that submission in an Act of Pardon. On 6 February 1550 he was released from the Tower, and on 10 April he was reappointed to the council, and restored to much of his property. From the beginning of 1550 until the king's death three and a half years later, the Earl of Warwick was the effective head of government, but both his style and his tactics were very different from those of his predecessor. Significantly, he made no attempt to resurrect the office of Protector, but instead chose to be called Lord President of the Council, a position which had had an intermittent existence earlier in the century. Somerset had taken great care to control the Privy Chamber, but had neglected the council. Warwick did not make the same mistake. He appointed new councillors from among his own supporters, such as the young Viscount Hereford, and involved them both individually and collectively in every aspect of his policy.[17] The reason for this was clear. He could claim no blood relationship with the king, and preferred the reality of power to its trappings. He was also planning for the future; not the future which actually materialized, but for one in which the king would attain his majority, and retain his trusted chief minister in office. Warwick was a statesman, not just a politician, and he knew that the interests of the kingdom required difficult and unpopular decisions. He ended the wars with France and Scotland which had resulted from Somerset's tenacious pugnacity, knowing that in both cases the treaties would have to be virtual surrenders. He pressed on with the policy of religious reform, knowing the young king's mind and judging that it would be more dangerous to stop or to retreat than to press on. If Edward had lived, he would undoubtedly have been right. He also knew that the social order, shaken by the upheavals of 1548 and 1549, had to be firmly reasserted. Consequently he ruled as the leader of an aristocratic team, using the council as his chief instrument, and the protestant clergy as his propagandists. It was effective rule, and it coped well with the problems, both financial and political, which he had inherited. But it was fragile, because in spite of valiant attempts to demonstrate the contrary, it was Warwick's rule, and not the king's.

Because he was basically a self-made man, and a not a prince of the blood, Warwick could not afford to take anything for granted. He secured the Dukedom of Northumberland for himself in October 1551, but neither that dignity, nor the great estates which went with it could give him the *manred*[18] of an ancient noble house. He had made his career as a soldier and a courtier, and the circumstances of his triumph in the autumn of 1549 also left him as the leader of a party, or faction, with many enemies, so his control faced a number of threats and challenges. One of these came from the Duke of Somerset, who seems to have learned little from his narrow escape, and by the summer of 1550 was intriguing to recover his former power. With him the Earl of Warwick was cunning and ruthless, trapping him with accusations of treason which were scarcely even plausible, but were sufficient to bring about his execution in January 1552. Another came from the Princess Mary, who publicly and repeatedly refused to accept the liturgy imposed by the Acts of Uniformity, and denied the validity of any statute of which her conscience did not approve. With her Warwick was pertinacious, but ultimately unavailing because of the consistent support which she received from the Emperor Charles V, and the impossibility of contemplating a complete breakdown of diplomatic relations in that quarter. A third came from an unexpected source. In order to keep his political following in good heart, Warwick had to allow them rather more access to the patronage of the crown than was good for the health of the common weal; and this included the lands and revenues of the Church. In a sense the evangelical zeal of the protestant bishops had left them exposed to this sort of attack, because the quickest way to 'unlord' a prelate was to relieve him of his estates. Nevertheless, when it started to happen on an increased scale after 1550, Cranmer was the first to take umbrage. Revenues which were very properly being diverted from the maintenance of episcopal pomp should have been devoted to pious and charitable purposes, not distributed as political sweeteners. In his zeal for the Royal Supremacy, the archbishop began to realize that lay control of the Church had been allowed to go too far, and his alliance with Warwick steadily cooled. By 1553 more radical reformers, such as John Knox, were denouncing the Lord President as a 'carnal gospeller', and were beginning to feel that they had betrayed their own trust in allowing him too free a hand.[19] For all these reasons, and in spite of his political skills, Warwick's control of the council was less than solid when the crisis provoked by Edward's declining health struck him in the early summer of 1553. Paget and Arundel, imprisoned and disgraced for their alleged implication in Somerset's notional treason in November 1551, were unconvincingly rehabilitated. Forced into a desperate gamble by the king's unthinking religious zeal and his own ambition, when Edward died the Duke of Northumberland did not command either the loyalty of the obedience of those with whom he had collaborated closely during the previous three years, let alone those whom he had excluded, humiliated and imprisoned. With the king's death the council once again ceased to exist, and this time there was no body of executors to bridge the gap. There was only a self-appointed junta trying to claim the legitimacy of a contrived succession.

Just as a council could not exist without a monarch, so anyone claiming to be a monarch needed a council, and as soon as she proclaimed herself queen on 9 July, Mary was in that position. Although there were experienced councillors in London who supported her claim, they did not at once declare themselves, and she was forced to improvise from the material immediately to hand. Hence the so-called 'Framlingham council', which consisted mainly of her existing household officers, such as Sir Robert Rochester and Edward Waldegrave, and the leaders of her East Anglian affinity – Sir Francis Englefield, Sir John Huddlestone, Sir Henry Bedingfield. Once the council in London had split, and she had been proclaimed in the capital, the situation changed dramatically. Paget and Arundel joined her almost immediately, and several others did so, or endeavoured to do so, over the next two weeks. The queen's position was a difficult one. Her victory had been swift and bloodless, and she owed it in varying degrees to a large number of people. She needed experienced servants and advisers, and had nothing in the nature of a 'shadow council' waiting to take over. Consequently she had to exercise her judgement about every individual who offered submission; should he be welcomed, pardoned and dismissed, or committed to prison? Religion and proximity to the Dudley family provided some approximate guides. The Earls of Arundel, Sussex and Shrewsbury were all conservatives who had kept their distance from Northumberland, whereas Sir William Cecil was a protestant and deeply compromised, in spite of his professions of penitence. By the end of August Mary had substantially completed her team, and force of circumstances made them a somewhat ill-assorted group. First there were the Framlingham councillors, men of impeccable loyalty but modest talent, and no experience of high office. Then there were the acceptable Edwardians, such as the Marquis of Winchester, Lord Paget and Sir William Petre, professional administrators willing to serve the new regime. And finally there were the 'martyrs', men who for a variety of reasons had been persecuted or imprisoned under Henry or Edward; the Duke of Norfolk, Stephen Gardiner, and Cuthbert Tunstall, erstwhile Bishop of Durham. The most conspicuous political talents were those of William Paget and Stephen Gardiner, who became Lord Chancellor. Unfortunately they cordially detested each other and gave the queen conflicting advice on most issues of importance. Within a few weeks the tensions began to surface. The Framlingham councillors resented the fact that the majority of important offices had gone to the men of experience – 'the heretics' as they called them with more bitterness than accuracy. Gardiner advised Mary to press on with a catholic religious settlement as quickly as possible, and to marry an Englishman; Paget advised her to be cautious over religion, and to marry abroad.[20]

Distressed by this early evidence of discord among the men to whom she looked for support, and unwilling to give her full confidence to anyone who had held office since the establishment of the Royal Supremacy, Mary quickly began to look elsewhere for advice. She had long regarded the Emperor Charles V as her true father, and his ambassador at this juncture was the shrewd and capable Simon Renard. Renard quickly became her principal confidant, a position which he was able to exploit to great effect in persuading her to marry his master's son, Philip of Spain. Renard found a natural ally within the council in the person of Lord Paget, but the remaining councillors were not consulted, either individually or collectively, until the queen had made up her mind. Given the nature of a royal council there was nothing improper in this procedure, but it was unusual, and did nothing to improve Mary's working relationship with her chosen advisers. In one sense the Marian council never recovered from this bad start. When dissatisfaction with the queen's proposed marriage provoked rebellion in Kent in January 1554, Gardiner and Paget again gave conflicting advice, and Renard disagreed with both of them. When Gardiner tried to slip a new bill for ecclesiastical jurisdiction through parliament in April 1554, Paget and certain other councillors frustrated him, not having been consulted in advance. When Gardiner and Renard entered into an alliance to persuade the queen to have her sister Elizabeth executed for involvement in the Kentish rebellion, Paget mobilized the princess's friends to abort such a move. By the summer of 1554 Mary was complaining that she spent her time shouting at her council to no effect, and when Philip arrived in July, one of his courtiers declared that neither the king nor the queen had any authority in England, but that the councillors ruled all and were 'the lords of the kingdom'. Paget's behaviour in the April parliament had deeply offended the queen, and led to his temporary exclusion from the court, but Gardiner's triumph was short lived. Philip, rightly judging Paget to be his most effective ally in England, caused him to be brought back to the council, and the Chancellor spent the last year of his life fighting to secure the king's confidence. Renard was insistent that the root of the trouble was an overlarge council, which naturally divided into factions and cabals, but in truth that was a symptom rather than a cause. The true reason for the council's ineffectiveness at the political level was Mary's inexperience, and lack of confidence in handling conflicting advice and personalities. When an issue of policy could be represented as a matter of conscience or moral principle, she was decisive and inflexible, but over other matters she easily became confused and hesitant. Her council was no more divided or obstreperous than any other Tudor council, but its relationship with its mistress was never satisfactory.

If further proof of this explanation should be needed, the arrival of Philip brought about a marked improvement. Although he found communication difficult on account of his lack of English, and his role restricted by the terms of the marriage treaty, Philip was not prepared to allow council quarrels to disrupt business in which he had a direct interest, such as the reconciliation with Rome. Renard's complaints continued unabated, but that was partly because Philip had smartly put an end to his 'special relationship' with the queen, and he was trying to suggest to Charles V that this was having a detrimental affect upon English affairs. In November 1554 he wrote that a plan had been drawn up to create an 'inner council' of about six or eight members for advisory purposes, but it had had to be shelved because the queen's 'old' councillors – Rochester, Waldegrave and Englefield particularly, were making such a fuss about being excluded. In February 1555 he declared

'The split in the council has increased rather than diminished; the two factions no longer consult together; some councillors transact no business; Paget, seeing that he is out of favour with the queen and most of the council, is often in the king's apartments.'[21]

He was right about Paget's relationship with the king, but there is little other evidence to support his picture of confusion and impotence. Philip left England in August 1555, and Gardiner died in November, so there was a shift of emphasis by the end of that year. Before leaving the king had at last created the Select Council about which there had been so much discussion, but it seems to have existed mainly for his benefit, and no records of its business survive. Meanwhile Mary had found a new confidant in the person of Cardinal Reginald Pole, who had arrived in England as Papal legate in November 1554. Pole was not a member of the Privy Council, but he was given a curious optional relationship with the Select Council, which reflected the personal and idiosyncratic nature of his position. His influence was not as anomalous as that of Renard had been, but it produced similar strains and tensions within the council between those who approved of the advice he was giving and those who did not. In January 1557 Mary took the unusual step of formally consulting her council over the issue of war with France, and the *consulta* submitted by the majority of them survives. Their advice was quite unequivocal; England could not afford to go to war, and had no interest in the ongoing Habsburg-Valois struggle. This was not a unanimous opinion, and in the event it was ignored. Pressure from Philip and Mary's own inclination prevailed, but the reluctance of the council to support the war was reflected in the lack-lustre performance which ensued.

By the spring of 1558 the Court of Feria, Philip's special representative in England, was echoing the sentiments of Renard four years earlier '. . . numbers cause great confusion'. Like Renard, his observation was faulty. It was not the size of the council which caused confusion, but the way in which it was used (and not used) as an advisory body. For the other aspects of its work, a substantial number of councillors could have many advantages. The court of Star Chamber had a larger body of judges from which to draw, which could speed up proceedings and avoid overburdening a few individuals, and the executive functions of the council could be distributed in a manner which significantly increased efficiency. Before the Privy Council had come into existence, it had not been unusual to establish special committees of the council for defined purposes. The King's Council Learned in the Law, much used by Henry VII, had been a standing committee. With the reduction of the council to about twenty office holders this procedure had been discontinued, but as Northumberland sought to increase his following by recruiting more councillors, it began to come back. At the end of his reign, Edward had had about forty privy councillors, and Mary operated with between forty five and fifty. The average attendance at council meetings, as recorded in the register, was between ten and twelve. That did not mean, however, that the majority of councillors were inactive. Some, like Dr Nicholas Wotton, were absent on duty; but many others served assiduously on the various committees, without ever coming to the main board. In February 1554 no fewer than ten such committees were established, for every purpose from calling in debts and providing for money to examining the prisoners taken in the recent Kentish uprising.[22] Some of these were standing committees, and some were *ad hoc*. As these latter completed their tasks, they were replaced by others. In addition a number of commissions were issued, for such purposes as tracking down missing church goods or pursuing heretical preachers, and such commissions commonly included one or more councillors, often men who were not active in the higher reaches of government. Sometimes also commissions with a local significance would be stiffened by the inclusion of a councillor from the area concerned. This system worked well. It distributed the work efficiently, and kept the council closely in touch with numerous specific and local aspects of its responsibilities.

The main organizers of the council's administrative functions were Lord Paget and Sir William Petre. Paget became Lord Privy Seal in 1555, thanks to Philip's patronage, and seems to have outlived the queen's suspicion, but Petre retired in somewhat mysterious circumstances in 1557, and was replaced by the innocuous Boxall. On the whole Mary did not interfere with government at this level, dutifully coping with the immense load of paperwork which it generated, but leaving Paget and his assistants to direct matters as they thought fit. This also included the bulk of the legislative programme. Both Mary and Philip played an active part in preparing that part of the parliamentary agenda which embodied matters of major public policy, but most was hammered out in council. After Gardiner's death the quality of parliamentary management declined, but that was less the fault of the council than the result of the queen's inability to find high-quality replacements for the men she lost. Just as Petre was replaced by Boxall, so Gardiner was replaced by Nicholas Heath, a worthy ecclesiastic but an unremarkable chancellor. The strictures hurled at Mary's council by Spanish and Imperial observers were not, on the whole, justified, and were often caused by their own failure to understand how the English system worked. Moreover they invariably had their own agenda, and criticized the English council for not following it. Unfortunately the queen often listened to them rather than to her own advisers, and did not always appreciate that the latter had, and were entitled to have, their own ideas about what was in the true interest of England. They were bound by their oaths to advise her in accordance with their wisdoms and consciences, but that inevitably meant telling Mary things that she did not want to hear, which exposed her limitations as a listener.

Unlike her sister, Elizabeth was given ample time to prepare for the moment of her accession, and had marked out several of her key councillors and office holders well in advance of their appointments. She had obviously decided in advance to revert to the small Privy Council of her father's latter days, and only twenty men were named, ten of whom were survivors from the previous regime. So about thirty-five councillors lost their positions in November 1558, a far more drastic turn-over than had occurred in July 1553, in spite of the unchallenged nature of her succession. The composition of the new council not only reflected the balance of the queen's mind, but also the most crucial task which confronted her. The ten whom she took over from Mary were mostly noblemen, such as the Earls of Arundel and Shrewsbury; cautious and pragmatic conservatives, but also powerful men in their own right. They could be broadly described as Henricians, whose loyalty to the crown was stronger than any specific religious commitment, and who were strongly averse to any foreign interference in English affairs. The ten whom she appointed afresh were men of the 'new learning', equally loyal to the crown but for the most part protestants whose nationalism was strongly tinged with evangelical enthusiasm. Several of them, most notably Sir William Cecil, were experienced councillors and men of affairs from Edward's reign. It could be argued that this team, although smaller, was just as

40

ill-assorted as Mary's had been, and certainly seemed to threaten a natural division into two parts. That division never happened, although feuds and disagreements between councillors were as numerous as ever. Elizabeth had many failings as a queen, but managing her council was not one of them, and she succeeded in creating a dynamic loyalty to herself which survived a potentially divisive religious settlement and an unnerving scandal over her relations with Lord Robert Dudley. It was essential for the new queen to create a political consensus between protestants and conservatives which would shut out the fully-committed Roman Catholics who had represented Queen Mary's policies. That she eventually succeeded in doing, not least through the careful composition of her initial council. It was both a body of advisers and a working management team; unoriginal but effective both in concept and function. Elizabeth, as the Count of Feria observed within the first few days of her reign, was feared as her sister had not been, and 'has her way absolutely, as her father did'. It was an exaggeration, but an understandable one, for it reflected exactly the impression which the new queen was trying to create.

# 2

# PARLIAMENT AND FINANCE

Parliament had originated in the king's need to consult his subjects more widely than the nature of his council and court permitted. It had at first been less an institution than an event, summoned by writs when the king chose, and dissolved at his pleasure. The peers could be summoned separately, but in that event the assembly was termed a Great Council and not a parliament. Because of this, parliament tended to be used either when the business in hand specifically required the participation of the Commons – for instance the voting of taxation – or when the king for some reason needed to make a demonstration of consensus. When Richard II wished to restrict papal access to his kingdom he had proceeded by means of statutes of Provisors and Praemunire. By the end of the fifteenth century custom had defined both the composition and the function of parliaments. For the raising of any kind of extraordinary revenue the consent of the Lords and Commons was essential. Unlike their counterparts in France, the kings of England had never succeeded in emancipating themselves from this constraint, nor were the Tudors to do so. Such revenues normally consisted of tenths and fifteenths, levied on real and personal property, which were granted specifically on request, and tonnage and poundage on goods passing through the ports, which was granted to each monarch at the beginning of his reign. The pretext normally required to justify a grant of tenths and fifteenths was war. Neither loans nor 'benevolences' (theoretically free gifts) were covered by these constraints. Parliaments were also used when statements of exceptional weight or authority were required, particularly when the law needed to be extended or 'interpreted'.

Thus the classic definition of High Treason was provided by a statute of 1352, and acts of parliament were used to define the law-making rights of guilds and corporations.[1] More recently Henry VII had experimented by successfully using a statute to incorporate the liberty of Tynedale into the county of Northumberland, an alteration of legal status which had extensive implications. The composition of the House of Lords had settled down by the middle of the fifteenth century, when it had finally been decided that peerage was a status created by the king, and acknowledged by an individual writ of summons. Theoretically the king could withhold such a writ, even from a man whose peerage was not in doubt, but such discrimination was contrary to custom, and was hardly ever used. For all practical purposes every adult male peer was a member of the House of Lords. So, too, were the bishops – known as the 'spiritual peers' – and a selection of the more important heads of religious houses, called the mitred abbots. The definition of a mitred abbot was still flexible, and although the heads of such major houses as Glastonbury or St Albans were invariably summoned, custom still allowed the king a certain amount of discretion in this area. At this point the House of Lords was much the more important of the two Houses; the Commons did not even have their own meeting chamber until 1547. It was also, in a sense, more amenable to royal control. Not only could the king create peers at his discretion, he also had a decisive voice in the appointment of bishops. Nevertheless, and in spite of the political upheavals of the late fifteenth century, the size of the House remained remarkably constant; about 50 secular peers, 26 bishops and a similar number of abbots. The House of Commons was quite differently provided, being representative of two specific constituencies – the knights of the shire and the burgesses of incorporated boroughs. The knights were the *nobiles minor*. In theory they were elected at the county court by the votes of those freeholders in the county with lands worth more than 40s a year. Each county had two such representatives, and in practice they were normally chosen by agreement among the more substantial gentry families, or by pressure from the nearest effective peer. The burgesses (two for every borough, except London which had four) were elected by a variety of franchises; in some cases the electorate would include every householder, in others the vote was confined to freemen or guild members. In theory borough representatives had to be resident in the towns they served, and were paid by those towns. However, by the end of the fifteenth century it was becoming increasingly common for members of gentry families to be chosen. The main reason for this seems to have been the desire of civic authorities to secure influential backing from the aristocratic network to which such men belonged, but the fact that they were often willing to serve without pay may not have been without influence. Gentlemen were willing to serve because the goodwill of a wealthy borough could be useful, and because parliament was becoming a handy, if sporadic, means of access to the court and the world of high politics. In 1500 the House of Commons consisted of 74 knights and 222 burgesses.[2]

Between 1500 and 1545 a number of important developments had taken place. Parliaments were meeting more frequently, and the functions of statute had been greatly extended. These two features were closely related. It had always been true that the purpose of a parliament was to do the king's business, and that that business consisted largely of legislation. By 1545 this was much more obviously the case, as parliament extended its control to the Church, and provided for the succession to the crown. Treason was redefined, and censorship of the press introduced. As a consequence of this extension, private legislation also increased as particular interests sought to give themselves the benefit of the enhanced prestige of statute. Between 1509 and 1523 Henry VIII called only four parliaments, each for a single session. Between 1529 and 1545 he called five, for a total of fourteen sessions.[3] Only 1530, 1535, 1537–8 and 1541 did not see a meeting, and the legislative output was unprecedented. This had many consequences, apart from the impact of the legislation itself. From being an occasional event, parliament became a regular (if not yet continuous) part of the constitution – one of the king's normal channels of business and authority. This in turn made membership of the House of Commons more sought after, and accelerated the invasion of the chamber by gentlemen and lawyers, who might have a variety of other business in the capital. For reasons for his own, the king had also encouraged the Commons to insist upon their traditional privilege of freedom from arrest during sessions. Whereas in the past such privilege had been enforced by a writ out of Chancery (on the grounds that it was the king's business which was being impeded) in Ferrer's case of 1542 his release was effected upon the authority of the House itself, 'by warrant of the mace' as it was later termed, a move which could only have been made with the king's permission. The composition of both Houses was also significantly modified. After 1540 the mitred abbots disappeared from the House of Lords, destroying the balance between temporal and spiritual peers, and leaving the latter in a permanent minority. At the same time the shiring of Wales and the enfranchisement of the Welsh counties increased the number of knights in the Commons from 74 to 90. A number of Welsh boroughs were also incorporated, although with one member rather than two, and the total number of burgesses was increased to 251. Nevertheless the House of Commons was no more representative in the modern sense in 1545 than it had been in 1500, or in 1400. The consent of parliament was the consent of the political nation, the interest groups which contributed money or manpower to the king's service, it had nothing to do with the population at large, or with numerical majorities. The only interest group which was conspicuously not represented was the lower clergy. They had sent members in the early fourteenth century, but the practice had been discontinued, and their representative institution became the lower house of Convocation. By 1547 Convocation had lost all semblance of political power, and the lower clergy petitioned to be readmitted to the parliament. They were unsuccessful, and the Church continued to be represented only by the bishops in the House of Lords.

The practice of frequent parliaments continued under the minority governments of Edward VI. Two were summoned in six years, and 1551 was the only year without a session. The encroachment of parliament upon the spiritual domain also continued apace, as the English Church was converted to protestant worship and doctrine without reference to the Convocations. Priests were permitted to marry, and the legitimacy of their children recognized; ecclesiastical courts were to be held in the king's name; and justices of the peace were given the power to investigate such purely religious matters as the eating of meat in Lent. Each of these measures, and many others, were tenaciously resisted by the conservative bishops in the House of Lords, but they could never, on a straightforward religious issue, muster sufficient voting strength to make their opposition effective. Only when issues of property were involved did Edwardian parliaments become recalcitrant, a characteristic which they shared with both earlier and later assemblies. The first version of the bill to dissolve chantries in 1547, passed by the Lords was rejected by the Commons. The reason for this seems to have been that careless drafting had included all craft guilds and lay corporations within its scope. When this had been rectified there was still opposition, mainly from the burgesses of King's Lynn and Coventry, who argued that chantry revenues were necessary to them for civic purposes. A special proviso was inserted to buy off that opposition, and the measure passed.[4] There was no sign of any principled resistance to the confiscation of property lawfully devoted to spiritual purposes, because the dissolution of the monasteries had set too massive a precedent. In 1552 the House of Commons also protested against a bill to deprive the conservative Cuthbert Tunstall of his see of Durham. The charge against him was misprision of treason, and the procedure was analogous to that of an Act of Attainder but, when some members requested to hear the bishop speak in his own defence, the measure was dropped. The reason for their doubt seems to have been unconnected with Tunstall's religious views, and probably reflected dissatisfaction with such an extra-judicial conviction. Tunstall was later deprived by commission, but the charges against him were never substantiated.

Although it was a vehicle for much important public business, and consolidated its position as an essential element in the constitution – particularly in connection with the Royal Supremacy, parliament was not much involved in the political in-fighting of the minority. Perhaps the most significant consti-tutional measure was that which repealed a Henrician statute enabling Edward, on reaching the age of twenty four, to annul by Letters Patent any Act passed during his minority. It had already been established that a statute could only be annulled by repeal, so the Henrician Act was internally inconsistent. Nevertheless by repealing it in 1547 parliament removed what could have been a fatal weakness in its own authority. No such measure was ever enacted again. While Henry VIII was alive, although there could be opposition within parliament to mea-sures which the council had prepared on the king's behalf, there was no question of either House attempting to set the political agenda. However during a minority strange things could happen, and it seems that in November 1548 Thomas Seymour planned a parliamentary coup against his brother. His exact purpose is unclear, but he apparently told Lord Clinton and the Marquis of Dorset that he intended 'to put a bill into the parliament houses', having first obtained a letter of endorsement from the young king. The purpose of this bill must have been to annul the Protectorate, possibly on the grounds that it had been established without parliamentary consent. Nobody else believed that parliamentary consent was necessary for such an arrangement, but Seymour had, or thought he had, many supporters in both Houses. The Protector was not popular with his fellow peers, and Seymour's extensive patronage through his many offices had enabled him to place a number of clients, such as William Sharrington and Sir Francis Fleming, in the lower House. News of his intention leaked out, partly because he went around those whom he thought to be his friends, trying to drum up support in the Lords, and he was arrested before he could put his scheme into effect. One of the charges against him, drawn up on 17 January 1549 was that he had 'determined to . . . come into the Common House himself and there with (his) favourers and adherents before prepared to have made a broil or tumult and uproar. . .'.[5] His purpose was certainly more constructive than the creation of a riot, but whether he could have used parliament as an instrument for the seizure of power must remain a subject for conjecture. Perhaps only such an imaginative and desperate gambler as Seymour could have conceived the idea, and it was to be many years before circumstances would favour another similar attempt.

The council took him seriously enough to prepare his attainder with great care, but did not fear his influence sufficiently to have him tried by commission of Oyer and Terminer instead. Councillors sat in both Houses while the matter was under discussion, and the bill passed the Lords without difficulty. The Commons, however, were as unhappy as they were to be later over Tunstall. They debated the matter long and hard, asked to see the evidence, and treated the whole prosecution case with grave suspicion. The issue became one of the Protector's credibility, and eventually the bill was passed, but not before its opponents had forced a division, against the wishes of the Speaker. Parliament touched the politics of faction again in January 1550, when Somerset's submission was presented as a means of getting his supplanter, the Earl of Warwick, out of an embarrassing difficulty. It is even possible that the former Protector may have borrowed an idea or two from his ill-fated brother, because in the autumn of 1550 it was rumoured that he intended to denounce the new regime in parliament as men governing without respect for the laws and customs of the realm, and oppressing the people with new and unnecessary taxes. If such was his intention he never carried it out, and parliament had to wait until the reign of Charles I to hear an opposition spokesman deliver so thoroughgoing a denunciation of the government of the day.

Constitutionally, Edward's parliaments are less memorable for what they did than for what they did not do. They had no hand in either the establishment of the Protectorate or its destruction, and they were not asked to make any provision for the succession. This does not seem to have been because Northumberland doubted his ability to carry parliament on so controversial an issue, but rather because he mistimed the whole operation. In March 1553 the king's illness was not yet diagnosed as fatal, and the Duke was understandably reluctant to raise such an issue before it was necessary. By the time that it was known that Edward's days were numbered, it was too late to get any further than issuing the writs. The parliament which should have met on 18 September convened instead on 5 October, in the name of Queen Mary. One significant development did take place, however, which affected both the status and the procedure of the House of Commons. Until Henry VIII's death the Lords had met in the White Chamber and the Commons in the Chapter House or the Refectory of the nearby Abbey of Westminster. When Edward's first parliament assembled on 4 November in that year, the Commons were granted St Stephen's Chapel to use as their permanent home, and in due course the two tiers of facing seats were to have a profound influence on English political habits. The fact that there were seats at all seems to have contributed to the length of debates, as under the previous arrangements the majority of members had to stand. The most immediate and noticeable affect was probably upon the practice of voting. Previously voting had been by acclamation, the Speaker deciding which party had the stronger 'voice'; only when the issue was close, or the Speaker for some reason was uncertain, was a count taken. This probably took place in the chamber itself by a show of hands or some similar method of indication. But soon after the acquisition of St Stephen's a procedure was adopted which became known as the 'division'. Those supporting the motion under consideration withdrew to the antechamber, and were counted upon re-entering the House. By 1553 the total membership of the Commons had increased to 375 by the incorporation of several new boroughs, and there may have been some pressure upon the seating capacity when the matter under discussion was of general interest. By the end of the century, when the membership had reached 460, it was claimed that the division system caused many motions to be lost because members were reluctant to relinquish their seats in order to be counted.

Mary's parliaments acquired in later years a reputation for cantankerousness, but as recent research has demonstrated, that was hardly justified.[6] As with other aspects of Mary's reign, subsequent developments produced a distinctly tinted hindsight. Protestants, including some close to Elizabeth, wished to make it appear that parliament, and particularly the House of Commons, had endeavoured to resist Mary's 'popish tyranny'. Consequently there grew up a kind of folklore about the rearguard action which was fought in the first parliament against the restoration of the mass, and the rejection of the 'Exiles' Bill' in 1555, which inflated those episodes out of all proportion to their true importance. In fact Mary's council passed almost every measure of importance which it brought to parliament, and when it failed the issue was invariably one of property rights rather than policy or ideology. The first bill to restore the ancient bishopric of Durham was 'dashed' in the Commons on 5 December 1553, almost certainly as a result of lobbying by the burgesses of Newcastle, which stood to lose its recently acquired control over the former episcopal town of Gateshead. In April 1554 the Lords threw out a proposal by Stephen Gardiner to restore some measure of ecclesiastical autonomy, fearing for their control over the secularized Church lands; and the main reason behind the rejection of the Exiles' Bill seems to have been the fear that it would have given the crown a right to confiscaste property without due process of law. The most significant constitutional development was quite unintentional, and resulted from the advance in the authority of statute which had taken place over the previous twenty years. Mary probably, and

Cardinal Reginald Pole certainly, believed that every piece of legislation affecting the Church which had been passed since the twentieth year of King Henry VIII was invalid because it had been enacted *ultra vires*. In his view the positive law, as represented by statute, was inferior in authority, not only to some generally conceived law of God, but also to the canon law of the Church. This was also the view which had been held, with fatal consequences, by John Fisher and Thomas More. The queen, however, was persuaded by her lay advisers that only a process of parliamentary repeal could remove the laws which she found offensive from the statute book. By the time that was completed in January 1555 it was no longer possible for either side to claim that parliament had acted consistently under the guidance of the Holy Spirit. An institution which could remove the English Church from papal to royal control and back again, and could alter the official teaching of that Church not once but three times, was clearly not answerable to any higher authority.

Mary's parliaments were also more involved in political issues than those of her brother had been. When rumours were beginning to spread about the queen's intended marriage in November 1553, the House of Commons took it upon itself to send a deputation of members, led by the Speaker, to petition the queen to marry within the realm. They were unsympathetically received and told, in effect, to mind their own business; but it was significant that such an initiative should have been taken. A few months later parliament was called upon to ratify the terms of the marriage treaty, a procedure for which there was no exact precedent. Both royal marriages and international diplomacy had hitherto been matters exclusively for the prerogative. In Mary's third parliament there was also a sharp struggle over the extension of the treason laws to cover Philip as king consort, and to grant him the regency in the event of Mary leaving an heir under age. It was the debates and disputes which inevitably accompanied these unusual discussions which helped to give the House of Commons its reputation for fractiousness. At the same time the House of Commons was drawn into the political arena by the activity of the French ambassador, Antoine de Noailles. Noailles had been a thorn in Mary's flesh since the beginning of the reign. Since the queen's marriage was a direct threat to French interests, his brief was to cause as much disruption and instability in England as was consistent with remaining at his post. He had been deeply involved in the conspiracy which led to the Kentish uprising in 1554, and had narrowly escaped expulsion. The failure of Mary's pregnancy in the summer of 1555, and the general loss of momentum which the regime suffered in consequence, gave him a fresh opportunity. At the beginning of the fourth parliament, in October 1555, he reported

'. . . it is said that the reason for the assembly of this parliament is no less than to place absolute authority in the hands of the king, to enable him to dispose of its resources at his pleasure.[7]

Who was saying this, apart from Noailles himself, is not clear, but it was exactly the kind of rumour to cause alarm and suspicion in both Houses. The Venetian Giovanni Michieli, who was much more objective, believed that there was an intention to settle the succession in the event of the queen's death without heirs, and that Elizabeth would be 'utterly excluded', which is much more plausible. Much later it was said that the council had intended in this parliament to entail the crown upon Philip in the event of Mary's death, but that was part of the Elizabethan 'Black Legend'.

Whatever intentions the queen or her advisers may have harboured, nothing was said publicly about the succession, or about Philip's position. Nor was the much canvassed question of his coronation raised. This may partly have been due to the subterranean activity of the French ambassador, who had a number of friends in the House of Commons, and cultivated them assiduously. These men were not slow to spread rumours about the nefarious intentions of the Spaniards, even after Philip had returned to the Netherlands. Circumstances also conspired to favour their agitation. The harvest had been bad, prices were rising, and Pole had had to work extremely hard to persuade Pope Paul IV to ratify the dispensation which his predecessor had granted to the holders of Church property. Moreover the council's chief parliamentary manager, Lord Chancellor Gardiner, was mortally ill and died before the end of the session. One of the principal reasons for convening the meeting had been the need for a subsidy – the first which Mary's government had sought. Noailles' friends boasted to him that they would bring about its rejection, but they were not nearly numerous enough to do anything so radical. They did succeed in stimulating a prolonged and acrimonious discussion which persuaded the queen to remit a part of the intended grant, but the main subsidy bill passed on 2 November. Two days later a much more controversial measure was introduced into the House of Lords, which ran into trouble without any help from French agents or sympathizers. This was a bill to restore to the Church all the revenues diverted into royal coffers over the previous twenty years, and such former ecclesiastical property as remained in the hands of the crown. On 19 November Mary summoned a large number of peers and a representative group from the Commons to explain that this measure was for the discharge of her conscience. A modified version of the bill then passed the Lords, but the Commons were unconvinced. It was committed, debated, altered, and finally passed after a stormy division by 193 votes to 126. Opponents of the bill immediately cried foul, claiming that several of their number had been locked out on the Speaker's orders, but it was sufficiently remarkable that in a House which by this time numbered 398, 319 should have attended a single division.[8]

The bill to recall all those who had gone into exile for religious reasons was meanwhile wending its way through the Upper House. The Commons regarded this measure with equal suspicion, not because of protestant sympathies but because the penalty for non-compliance was to be the forfeiture of property. When it came to its third reading on 6 December, an alert group of those hostile to the bill following, as they claimed, the precedent of the Church property bill, seized the keys of the chamber while they were in a temporary majority, and forced a division, which they won. The queen was furious. Three days later the parliament was dissolved and the leader of the coup, Sir Anthony Kingston, was sent to the Tower. Shortly after Noailles wrote somewhat smugly to Henry II that the Queen of England had been forced to dissolve her parliament without having gained any of her main objectives. This was true only in terms of his own perception of those objectives, because in fact every official measure had been passed except the last, and it was by no means unusual for an occasional government bill to go astray. The dramatic events of 6 December did not really signify the appearance of a powerful and organized opposition, nor a loss of control by the council, but a bold demonstration of dissent by a few men who happened briefly to have captured the sympathy of a larger number of their colleagues. The fact that Kingston and a few other members were among those arrested and interrogated for their part in Henry Dudley's conspiracy against the queen in March 1556 is significant. They were a part of Noailles' network, probably in receipt of French pensions, and their actions in parliament were partly dictated by that fact. The ambassador was heavily implicated in Dudley's plan to rob the Exchequer and import mercenary troops from France, and was finally expelled in May 1556.[9] By the time the last parliament of the reign assembled in January 1558 England and France were at war, and political interference from that quarter was out of the question. Perhaps that was why Mary found this assembly more satisfactory than its predecessors, so that it was prorogued instead of being dissolved in March 1558, and reconvened a few day before her death.

Michieli attributed the unruliness of the House of Commons in November and December 1555 to the unusually large proportion of gentlemen in the House. But we now know that his observation was inaccurate; the proportion was no larger than usual, and the real cause of the trouble lay elsewhere. Nevertheless Mary's council was unusually sensitive to the process of election, commanding sheriffs on more than one occasion to ensure that only men of the 'wise, grave and catholic sort' were returned. Philip was also careful to send similar instructions concerning the first parliament to meet after his departure – ironically the one which was to prove so troublesome. It would be a mistake to assume that any of Mary's parliaments was 'packed'. No Tudor government could command, by pressure or patronage, more than a small proportion of the seats in the Lower House. Even enlisting the co-operation of the peers who controlled county or borough seats could not guarantee a voting majority. On the other hand such a majority was hardly necessary, as the business of the House was very seldom conducted by means of divisions, and it would be totally anachronistic to think in terms of 'government' and 'opposition'. Mary's reign saw an unusually large number of elections; one in 1553, two in 1554, one in 1555 and one at the end of 1557. There was no session or election in 1556, and no session in 1557. In spite of this there was a high degree of continuity in the membership of the Commons, not only from parliament to parliament within the reign, but also from the last session of Edward's fourth parliament and into the first session of Elizabeth's first. This serves to emphasize the fact that these meetings were pimarily called for the routine business of government, and that the settlement of religion came into that category. Ideological commitment was comparatively rare, and it was essentially the same body of men who passed the second Act of Uniformity in 1552, repealed it in 1553, and re-enacted it in 1559; each time in conformity with the will of the monarch. The bulk of the legislative programme was much less dramatic, and it would be a mistake to see either House as an arena which was regularly used for the gladiatorial combats of politics. The normal issues contested were those between group and private interests. Affairs of state might be vigorously discussed if they were brought before the Houses on the initiative of the council, but very rarely were the express wishes of the queen questioned or opposed. The untoward events of 1555 were the exception to prove the rule, and at least as much the result of weak council management as of exceptionally articulate opposition. In 1553 eighteen Privy Councillors had sat in the Commons, and seventeen in each of the sessions of 1554, but in 1555 there were only ten. Apart from Sir John Baker and Sir William Petre, they also lacked political experience, and were ill-equipped to deal with the exceptional agitation which was stirred up. The political strength of Mary's council was in the House of Lords, and the only occasion on which official business ran into difficulties in that chamber was when the councillors fell out amongst themselves.

Elizabeth's first parliament met on 25 January 1559, overcast by the continuing war with France and by the need for a new religious settlement. On this occasion the management was provided by Sir William Cecil from his seat in the Commons, and the main problems arose in the House of Lords. There were nineteen returned exiles in the Lower House, but they did not form a coherent group. Not all had 'fled for religion' under the previous regime, although all had been in some degree its opponents. Those who had been religious exiles had for the most part belonged to the Prayer Book congregation at Frankfurt, and cannot therefore be classed as radicals or extreme protestants. The queen had already sent out some clear signals of her intentions, by ending the persecution, allowing protestant sermons at Paul's cross, and demonstrating enthusiasm for the

English Bible, so the attitude required of a loyal subject was clearly going to be different from that required twelve months before. The Commons did little more than respond to that expectation. A bill restoring the ecclesiastical supremacy to the crown was introduced into the Lower House on 9 February, and passed in a slightly amended form, but without great controversy, on 21 February. It was then taken to pieces in the Lords, and sent back, heavily altered in a conservative direction, after a sharp tussle with the bishops who would have no truck with the Royal Supremacy in any shape or form. Cecil reconsidered the situation, and thinking that this might be the best that he could get, persuaded the Commons to accept it on 22 March. The queen, however, was not satisfied, and on 24 March parliament was prorogued, instead of being dissolved as had been expected.

Two things happened during the recess which were to have a significant impact when business was resumed, and both seem to have owed their inspiration to Cecil and his friends. The first was a highly artificial disputation between theologians of the 'old' and 'new' faiths, held in Westminster Hall on 31 March, which resulted in the arrest and imprisonment of two of the more outspoken catholic bishops, White of Winchester and Watson of Lincoln. The second was an obscure tussle at court, involving several leading councillors, between those who wished the queen to leave well alone, accepting a highly conservative supremacy, and those who wanted to press for a full Edwardian settlement. Among the latter, it seems, were Francis Russell, second Earl of Bedford, the most outspoken protestant among the peers, and Cecil himself. Elizabeth, already inclined in that direction, may have needed little persuading, particularly as the Treaty of Cateau-Cambrésis had in the meanwhile freed her both from the burden of the French war and of the Spanish alliance. On 10 April a new Supremacy bill was read in the Lower House, designating the queen as Supreme Governor rather than Supreme Head. With this concession, which was far more than semantic in its significance, the measure passed both Houses, receiving the assent of the Lords on 26 April; once again all the surviving bishops voted against it. If this act had stood alone, a situation similar to that at the end of Henry VIII's reign would have resulted. This was probably what most people, including the majority of the lay peers, would have preferred, but in the circumstances of 1559 it would have been impossible. Not only had the existing bishops shown themselves to be consistently opposed to the Royal Supremacy, the lower houses of the Convocations, meeting at the same time as parliament, had reaffirmed their loyalty to a fully catholic Church. The queen therefore had no option but to turn to an entirely different ecclesiastical leadership; and that meant the protestants. The result was a carefully constructed compromise, in which the lead was taken by Cecil, and by those protestant leaders, such as Grindal and Aylmer, who still supported the Royal Supremacy. The reformers conceded ecclesiastical authority to the queen, and she gave them the Prayer Book of 1552, with one or two modifications to accommodate her own tastes. This compromise was embodied in the Uniformity Bill, introduced into the Commons on 18 April. It passed in that House without difficulty, and was accepted by the Lords ten days later, nine lay peers and all the bishops dissenting.

As in 1549 and 1552, the convocations had been ignored in the making of this legislated settlement, and the subsequent battles over its enforcement, and about the need for further reformation, also belonged to parliament. This was largely because of Elizabeth's political need to maintain the delicate balance between conservative and protestant groups at court, and in the country at large. When Convocation produced a new set of doctrinal articles in 1563, the queen would not allow them to be embodied in a statute, because she wished to maintain as much ambiguity and uncertainty as possible. It was only after the Bull *Regnans in Excelsis* in 1570, which was virtually a papal declaration of war, that she allowed Cecil and her other protestant advisers to carry out the kind of enforcement policy which they had been advocating. Even then such issues did not dominate the parliamentary agenda. The puritans certainly used the House of Commons as a forum for presenting their case, much to Elizabeth's annoyance, but in doing so they consumed only a small part of its time, and of parliament's legislative energy. The Reformation Parliament of 1529–36 remained unsurpassed in its output of statutes, but the five sessions of Edward's two parliaments produced 164, and the four sessions of Elizabeth's first three parliaments produced 122.[10] Only Mary, with 104 statutes from six sessions operated at a somewhat lower output, because the Acts of Repeal left parliament with no further role in ecclesiastical matters. Apart from that temporary withdrawal the twenty years following 1545 saw the steady consolidation of the striking constitutional gains which parliament had made between 1530 and 1545. The fact that a minor was followed on the throne of England by two women contributed to that outcome. A powerful king might have followed a different course, but Edward, Mary and Elizabeth all needed the co-operation of the Lords and Commons, just as Henry had done when trying conclusions with the pope, and the strong roots which were put down during this period were to survive all the storms of the next 200 years.

Other aspects of Henry's legacy had been less positive. For a few years the dissolution of the monasteries had made him wealthy, but his whole style of government was based on lavish expenditure, and in 1545, after two years of war with Scotland and France, he was in deep financial trouble. The fundamental problem was that the revenues of the English crown were not geared to war. The king's 'ordinary' expenditure, that is his household, the central offices of the administration, and the upkeep of his ships, garrisons and missions, was supposed to be covered by his ordinary income, derived from his lands, the customs and the profits of justice. This was known as the king 'living of his own'. It could be done, as Henry VII had demonstrated, by stretching some legitimate resources to the limits of credibility, and by virtually renouncing war as an instrument of policy. But it was an obsolete concept by the sixteenth century, belonging to the days when the realm had been the king's private honour, and Henry VIII never made any serious attempt to implement it. Extraordinary revenue could be obtained in a number of ways, but the most important were loans of various kinds, and parliamentary grants. The traditional tenths and fifteenths had long since become ossified, and in 1513 Wolsey had developed a new type of direct tax, confusingly known by the old name of subsidy.[11] The essence of the Tudor subsidy was individual assessment on oath by local officials under the supervision of nationally appointed commissioners. The commissioners then calculated the tax due from each person, which was collected by other commissioners on a county basis. This was heavy on time and energy, and had the additional drawback of requiring a parliamentary vote, but it was flexible and realistic. Similar taxes could be levied on the clergy through the more amenable instrument of convocation, but they were less productive and convocation only met in association with parliament. Five subsidies were granted between 1513 and 1523, providing a total of £322,099. Traditional tenths and fifteenths brought in £117,936 between 1512 and 1517, while clerical taxation yielded £240,000 over the rather longer period from 1512 to 1529. However, this was not free revenue. All parliamentary and convocation taxes were by custom linked to the waging of war, and the war of 1512–14 alone cost upwards of £900,000. Extraordinary expenditure nearly always exceeded taxation income, so that additional sources of revenue were required, In 1522–3 Wolsey succeeded in extracting a further £260,000 in the form of short-term 'loans'. Because these were in theory to be repaid they did not require parliamentary approval, but in practice the king's creditors never saw their money back, and when the Cardinal tried a similar device in 1525, the so-called 'Amicable Grant' was universally refused.[12] The English war effort ground to a halt, and Wolsey's credit with the king never entirely recovered.

When Henry VIII mortgaged his political credit to parliament between 1532 and 1536 in order to obtain the Royal Supremacy, he also forfeited any chance of being able to impose direct taxes without a formal grant. Thomas Cromwell did, however, succeed in modifying the accepted definition of 'extraordinary' to include defensive preparations as well as the actual waging of war, and on that basis extracted subsidies in both 1534 and 1540 when the country was at peace. The subsidy act of 1534 marked a significant change in the perception of how government should be financed, but the advantage was never fully exploited. Subsidies were voted in the majority of parliaments called between 1514 and 1571, and instalments were collected in almost every year. So parliamentary taxation became a normal part of the royal revenue; but it could never be taken for granted, because although a vote was never refused, the sum granted was often less than that asked for, or spread out over a longer period. So in spite of their frequency, and the less exacting circumstances in which they could be granted, subsidies could never be classed as 'ordinary' revenue. By 1545 they were, in fact, indispensable for the normal conduct of government, which left the crown increasingly vulnerable to parliamentary pressure as the century drew to a close. This also helps to explain the urgent need to find and exploit other sources of income. Loans were an obvious expedient, but after the disastrous experience of 1525 Henry was understandably reluctant to make another general approach to the taxpayers along those lines. It was not until 1542 that he tried again, when blank Privy Seal letters were issued to commissioners in every county, inviting selected individuals to contribute to the king's necessities in accordance with their assessed capacity to pay. Repayment within two years was promised. This loan raised £112,229, and was converted into a tax in the following year, when parliament remitted the king's obligation to repay. By 1545 the country was at war with both France and Scotland, and the danger of a French invasion was real, which may have made Henry's subjects more willing to dig into their purses than would otherwise have been the case. The Benevolence of that year never held out any hope of repayment, but perhaps it was recognized that honesty was the preferable policy, and £119,581 was raised.

In the last seven years of Henry's reign subsidies realized £656,245, and forced loans a further £270,000, but these sums, large as they were, came nowhere near meeting the war expenses, which totalled 2,134,784. The shortfall was made up from three sources, each in its own way damaging to the health of the crown's revenues. Between 1536 and 1540 the crown had obtained, by a mixture of statutory dissolution and forced surrender, the property of rather over 600 religious foundations of various sizes. The capital value of that property was somewhat in excess of £1.5 million, and should have yielded an annual return of about £75,000, enough to transform the ordinary income of the crown, which then stood at £150,000.[13] Whether Thomas Cromwell intended this land to form a permanent endowment or not continues to be debated. He was responsible for the first round of grants and sales, without the immediate pressure of a war, but it may have been the king who was unable to resist a quick profit. By 1547 about a half of the total acquisition had been sold for £700,000. The second source consisted of commercial loans, taken up at 12 or 14% on the Antwerp bourse. Henry employed his own financial agent, Stephen Vaughan, to negotiate these loans, which were individually modest in size and usually for a period of months. Security was provided by the City of London, and particularly by the Merchant Adventurers. Every sixteenth-century government had a cash flow problem, and a certain amount of government borrowing helped to stimulate the market, but such loans were expensive and the debt had to be serviced. When he died Henry VIII owed £100,000 in Antwerp. The third source was the debasement of the coinage. This was always a temptation to an impecunious government, because the mint was a monopoly and the crown controlled the bullion supply. Henry VII had tampered with the currency in a very small way in 1492, but on the whole the temptation had been resisted until an issue of base coin was made for Ireland in 1542–3. This was also on a modest scale, probably no more than £4,000, and may have been used as a trial run for the bigger operation which was to follow. Large-scale debasement began in all the seven English mints in 1544.[14] Both gold and silver was affected, but whereas the metallic content of the gold coins was only slightly reduced, that of the silver came down by as much as 60% on some issues, and was to go lower in the following reign. The ratio between gold and silver coins was thrown into confusion, the exchanges unsettled, and prices began to rise steeply. Between 1544 and 1546 the king took a profit of £363,000, and the total gain down to the time when a halt was called in 1551 was £1,270,684. The price was paid by the king's subjects in economic disruption, so debasement could be described as a form of indirect taxation. However, an increasingly sophisticated money market had its own way of exacting revenge for such irresponsible conduct, and credit became both more expensive and more difficult to obtain.

Financially, 1547 was not a very significant year. The French war had come to an end in 1546, removing the greatest single cause of expenditure. But Protector Somerset's determination to continue the struggle in Scotland, and to retain and fortify Boulogne meant that there was no immediate prospect of retrenchment, or of returning the finances to a normal peacetime footing. Henry VIII's death in itself altered nothing. Somerset's Scottish campaigns between 1547 and 1549 cost £580,393, and the military expenditure for the whole six years of the reign amounted to £1,386,687.[15] The French war was briefly renewed in August 1549, but after the protector's fall in October a radical reappraisal of English policy led to the Treaty of Boulogne in March 1550. The remaining English garrisons were withdrawn from Scotland, and Boulogne itself was returned to the French for £133,333. Expenditure on the navy and upon fortifications continued, but the massive costs of war ceased and a serious attempt was made to get the crown's finances back onto an even keel. Edward's debts were probably at their worst in the spring and summer of 1550, when they may have approached £300,000. William Paulet, Marquis of Winchester, was appointed Lord Treasurer in February 1550 with a reforming brief, but when the situation was assessed in May 1552, after two years of peace, the estimates still varied between £235,000 and £251,000. At least £132,000 was owed to bankers in Flanders, and £108,800 to the king's own subjects. To meet this heavy burden the sale of crown lands, monastic and otherwise, continued. At least £100,000 was raised in this way, and a further £110,486 was realized within a year from the sale of the chantry property confiscated by statute in 1547. Parliamentary taxes contributed £336,000, and the continuing debasement of the coinage a massive £537,000. In the circumstances persistence with this pernicious policy was unavoidable, although the council knew perfectly well how much harm it was causing. The Earl of Warwick, as Lord President of the Council, made a number of attempts to ease the situation by 'crying down' the currency – that is, reducing its face value – but it was not until 1551 that the mints returned to producing a sound coinage, and 1560 before the base coin could be called in and confidence restored.

In June 1551 Warwick declared a financial policy; regular income must match regular expenditure and the king's debts must be liquidated. This was much easier to say than to do, but thanks to the extraordinary ingenuity of Sir Thomas Gresham, the Antwerp debts were paid off within two years, and the overall burden reduced to something of the order of £180,000.[16] No amount of ingenuity, however, could balance the ordinary account without the continued sale of capital assets. The situation is difficult to represent accurately because every available set of figures is either incomplete or misleading, but a survey conducted at the end of 1551 represented the net ordinary revenue for the year 1550–51 to have been £168,150. Over the same period ordinary expenditure was calculated at £131,600. However, this definition of 'ordinary' did not include the admiralty, the ordnance, the privy purse, or Ireland. As the peacetime military establishment was costing at least £80,000 a year at this point, there would consequently have been a deficit of about £50,000 on the year, instead of the surplus of £36,550 which the survey hopefully declared. On 23 March 1552 a more ambitious commission of enquiry was established 'for the survey and examination of the state of all his Majesty's Courts of Revenue', which reported to the council on 10 December. This investigation produced startlingly different figures; an income of £271,912 and expenditure of £235,398 for the same financial year, but ignored taxation, land sales and the mint as well as military expenditure. Its purpose was more to put pressure upon the crown's creditors than to present an accurate picture of the situation, and the suggestions for radical reform which were also included in the report never even got as far as the council. It was thought that the crown was owed £100,000, but most of this was probably bad debt as only £16,667 is known to have been recovered. During the last year of the reign the Duke of Northumberland was in a cleft stick. The financial situation was so tight that even the £20,000 which it was expected to raise from the sale of Church goods was considered to be worth the political price, and yet he was constrained by his own insecurity to go on making grants and preferential sales of land to his friends and supporters on the council. It was in this way, rather than through any incompetence or perversity in government that the circumstances of the minority impinged upon the royal revenue. Had Edward been of full age it is hard to imagine him being so lavish, or having any occasion to be so.

In spite of all difficulties the Northumberland/Winchester programme of retrenchment enjoyed a fair amount of success. Expenditure was effectively pruned, and loans renegotiated, but little could be achieved to increase ordinary income, especially during a bad slump in the cloth trade, which occurred between 1550 and 1552. Once mint profits had been returned to their normal modest level, the crown was dependent upon land sales and taxation to balance what was supposed to be the ordinary account. This continued to be the case after Edward's death. Indeed, Mary's re-appointment of the Marquis of Winchester as Lord Treasurer ensured a fundamental continuity of policy, which was immediately disclosed in the reorganization of the revenue courts. The old and formal machinery of the Exchequer had been largely bypassed since the early part of Henry VII's reign by what is normally called the Chamber system of accounting. From about 1490 until the mid–1530s the bulk of the king's income had passed through the Treasury of the Chamber, which was an office of the Household, and the Treasurer had been immediately responsible to the king. By 1540 this system had been largely replaced with a series of autonomous revenue courts, each handling a defined sector of business; General Surveyors, First Fruits and Tenths, Wards and Liveries, and above all Augmentations. The Treasury of the Chamber continued to operate at a reduced level, just as the Exchequer had done for years. However, this system had been partly created to suit Thomas Cromwell's individual style of control, and within five years of his fall was appearing unnecessarily clumsy and byzantine. After an enquiry set up in 1545, the Courts of General Surveyors and Augmentations were merged in January 1547 to form the Second Court of Augmentations. Winchester's appointment in February 1550 led to further pressure in the same direction, and before Edward's death plans had been drawn up to abolish Augmentations altogether, and re-route the majority of the royal revenue back to the Exchequer. This was done in January 1554, and for a transitional period from December 1553 to the autumn of 1555 all revenue was placed in the hands of Sir Edward Peckham, the Treasurer of the mint.[17] The Court of First Fruits and Tenths was abolished when those revenues were returned to the Church in 1555, and from then on all income (apart from minor operations such as the Duchy of Lancaster) passed either through the Exchequer or through the Court of Wards and Liveries. The accounting procedures of the Exchequer were modified in the process, but it remained a profoundly conservative institution, and its lack of flexibility was a handicap in revenue management for the remainder of the century.

In spite of the Lord Treasurer, Mary's council initially took a propagandist view of its predecessor's financial operations, which led to some strange inconsistencies. On the one hand it was alleged that the queen's inheritance was bankrupt on account of Northumberland's self-interested mismanagement, and early memoranda referred to 'the great debts which be owing many ways'. At the same time the queen decided to remit the last instalment of the subsidy which had been voted earlier in 1553 on the grounds that the Duke had oppressed the people with unnecessary taxes. The Imperial ambassadors, who presumably drew their information from a source within the council, reported first that the queen owed £500,000, and then £700,000. The true debt seems to have been about £185,000, of which fresh operations on the Antwerp bourse accounted for £60,000. By comparison with Charles V or Henry II of France, Mary's financial situation was extremely healthy. Thomas Gresham, continuing his operations in the Low Countries, never had serious difficulties about raising loans at standard rates of interest; and as the cloth trade recovered between 1553 and 1555 his task became easier. Nevertheless, the underlying problems remained unchanged. Ordinary expenditure was rising, largely on account of inflation, while revenues remained static or declined because of customary and conservative assessments. The customs, for example, declined from £23,386 in the fifth year of King Edward to £22,407 in the first year of Mary. Household expenditure, £66,000 in 1552–3, rose to £75,000 in 1554–5. Mary's council, like Edward's, rummaged around for minor economies, while the queen's politically motivated decision to remit £50,000 in parliamentary taxation cost the crown just as much as the late Edwardian 'plunder' which was so much condemned. In April 1554, about nine months into the reign, the Lord Chancellor estimated the current level of debt at £200,000, so in spite of the brave words and the absence of extraordinary expenditure, the steady downward trend in indebtedness, visible since 1551 had been reversed.[18] The queen had not been irresponsibly generous with rewards, but she had given at least as much as she had received in the reshuffling of grants and attainders which followed her accession, and she had demonstrated again the crucial role of taxation in maintaining royal income.

By September or October of 1554 the crown's debt in Antwerp had shown a massive increase to £150,000. This was not the result of mismanagement, but of another politically motivated decision, this time to seek a large loan in Spain. The reason for this is not entirely clear, but it was connected with Mary's decision to marry Philip of Spain, and her need to demonstrate close political links with the Habsburgs. These dealings, which tied up large sums of money and made the management of the debt extremely difficult, taxed even Gresham's skill. But he was not above exaggerating the difficulties in order to increase his own reputation, and he succeeded in containing a situation which had very little to do with financial dealing in the ordinary sense. Thereafter policy changed, and the position began to improve. Between the spring of 1555 and August 1557 over £312,000 passed through Gresham's hands as he paid off old obligations and entered into new ones. By January 1556 the Antwerp debt had been reduced to £109,000, and by the time he closed his account it had disappeared. This conjuring trick was accomplished with the aid of the Merchant Adventurers and Staplers of London, who undertook to discharge the queen's debts in Antwerp and to accept repayment in sterling in London. This was not financially advantageous to them, but they were under political pressure to agree, and were able to extract their own price in a different way by forcing the council into gradually withdrawing the privileges of the Hanseatic League, which Mary had renewed at the beginning of her reign. These domestic debts were not free of interest, but they did not cost anything like the £32,000 a year which had to be expended servicing the foreign debts in the second, third and fourth years of the reign. Meanwhile, even without such an additional burden, the ordinary revenue was still in deficit. Between Easter 1554 and Easter 1555 expenditure passing through the Receipt of Exchequer, which was handling just about everything except the mint, totalled £138,326, while income for the same period was about £132,000.[19] In spite of continued efforts on the part of the council to control expenditure by means of special committees and commissions, and to call in outstanding debts, the underlying problems were unsolved.

Realization of this fact drove the council reluctantly back to parliament in October 1555. Although a valiant attempt was made to plead new circumstances, this appeal for a subsidy tacitly admitted that the queen had made a fool of herself two years earlier. It was singularly unfortunate that Mary insisted on returning First Fruits and Tenths to the Church at the same time as seeking a grant of taxation, and there were speakers in the Lower House who were bold enough to suggest that she might look for her money elsewhere, but in the end the subsidy act passed without great difficulty. This may have been partly because it was realized that the surrender of First Fruits would be accompanied by the ending of responsibility for monastic pensions. In the short term the two transactions balanced. A new and detailed subsidy assessment was ordered, and the collection was efficient. Over the two years from Michaelmas 1555 to Michaelmas 1557, £181,000 was received from taxation – over 40% of the revenue. A further £42,000 was raised from a Privy Seal loan in the autumn of 1556, but that was scrupulously repaid a year later and made no difference to the overall situation. Between Easter 1555 and Easter 1556 the crown's income was £184,279, and for the next financial year £211,515, so it might appear that, with the aid of parliament, victory had been achieved. Unfortunately that was not the case, as recorded expenditure was running at about £215,000 a year over these two years. This was partly the result of the struggle to shift the Antwerp debt, and the situation would very probably have improved by the end of 1557 as the advantage of reduced repayments began to become apparent. Unfortunately, in June 1557 Mary declared war on France, and the struggle for solvency was overtaken by a new damage limitation exercise, similar to those which had been conducted in 1544–6 and 1549–51.

When she asked their advice in January 1557, Mary's councillors told her frankly that England could not afford to wage war

'. . . all yet talking of the smarte of the last warres (and) it might be very daungerous to entangle them now with new warres, especially where necessitie of defence shall not require the same. . . '.[20]

However, war was a political decision, not a financial one, and rested with the queen. At first it was hoped that the main expenditure could be shifted onto Philip, as it was his war and he had pressed very hard for the declaration. He paid virtually the whole of the £48,000 which it cost to send an expeditionary force to the Netherlands in July 1557, but such a tactic could not be repeated and the king's financial plight was, in fact, far worse than Mary's. As the second instalment of the 1555 subsidy had only just been paid, there was an understandable reluctance, to call another parliament immediately after the outbreak of war, however great the need. Instead the council decided to repeat the successful Privy Seal loan of the previous year on a larger scale. There was a great deal of grumbling, and even some resistance, but almost £110,000 was raised, which repaid the earlier loan and put about £65,000 of free money into the Exchequer. This was useful, but nowhere near enough to support the cost of war, which according to one estimate was

£30,700 a month, and by another £350,000 a year. By the end of 1557, in spite of a fresh round of land sales, the debt was rising rapidly and inexorably. According to her own clearly expressed intention in 1555, Mary was due to return to the Church all the former ecclesiastical lands still in the hands of the crown, but in the event she confined her generosity to the £2,000 worth which was given in endowment to the restored religious houses. The rest she continued to sell, in exactly the same way as Edward had done, and it is difficult to see how she could have done otherwise. Private loans were raised in London to the tune of some £46,000 in the autumn of 1557, and on 12 March 1558 the council was forced to abandon its policy of abstinence in respect of the Antwerp money market. Gresham was sent back with instructions to raise £200,000. It is difficult to be sure exactly how bad the situation had become by the time that Calais was lost in January 1558, but the main argument used against mounting any immediate expedition for its recovery was once again cost. Philip's agents made no secret of the fact that they regarded the English council as pusillanimous, and it may well have been that the influenza epidemic had a more inhibiting effect upon military operations than the Exchequer, but the problem was real enough. The navy was costing £80,000 a year, and the garrisons and border fortresses a further £97,000 before any field operations were mounted at all.

The loss of Calais, however, had the beneficial effect of jolting the parliament which met soon afterwards, into granting another subsidy which was also matched by convocation. In due course another £230,000 would be collected, but it was spread out over three years, and the need was immediate.[21] One answer to this was loans, expensive but not prohibitive at 14%; another was to grasp the nettle of the long obsolete customs dues. These had not been revised for many years because of the need of successive governments to maintain good relations with the powerful merchant companies, and their value had been steadily eroded. In April 1558 new rates were imposed, without consultation, and new dues were introduced on certain categories of cloth. There was an immediate outcry, and the legality of the new Book was tested in the courts during the summer, but the judges ruled it to be a legitimate use of the prerogative, on the grounds that the queen had the right to control the movement of her subjects' persons in and out of the realm. By extension, therefore, she had the right to control the movement of their goods, and to charge what she chose for her licence and indulgence. This could have been an historic breakthrough in the provision of ordinary revenue, but Mary did not live to see its benefit, and Elizabeth almost immediately began to retreat. The customs of the last year of Mary realized about £29,000, those of the first year of Elizabeth about £80,000, but the new queen began to allow objections and exemptions after 1559 in order to recover the favour of the Merchant Adventurers, and a part at least of the new income was lost. When Mary died on 17 November 1558 this extra revenue had only just begun to be collected, and of the parliamentary taxes voted in the spring, only the tenth and fifteenth had come in. At the same time the Antwerp debt stood at about £92,000, with a number of transactions in mid-air. The total debt was not calculated, but probably stood at about £300,000, approximately where it had been in the summer of 1551, when the last battle for retrenchment had commenced. On the whole, Mary's financial management had been tight and effective, with one or two lapses. She had continued to mint good coins, except for Ireland, which was always the Achilles heel of the mint, and her council had laid plans for a recoinage, but had decided at the last moment that they could not afford to redeem the existing base circulation. But she could not afford, any more than Edward or her father could afford, to wage war on the basis of any level of taxation which parliament was likely to grant. And although she made one brave attempt, she was no more able than they had been to find a way round that limitation. She had not been absurdly generous, and certainly not to the Church. That was a myth created by Elizabeth's councillors when they faced the unpleasant realities of her financial legacy, and wished to create the impression that the new queen could avoid making the same mistakes.

Elizabeth did eventually bring the situation under control, but it was a long hard battle, and made her few friends. Nor could she provide a long-term solution. When she was forced to go to war in earnest in 1585, all the familiar problems reappeared, and by then she had lost the will to insist on realistic subsidy assessments, so that the yield of parliamentary taxes steadily declined. In the early years of her reign she applied conventional remedies with a certain courage and determination. The Marquis of Winchester was reappointed Lord Treasurer at the age of about 85, and was to serve his third sovereign in that capacity for some thirteen years. Although the war with France was ended at Cateau Cambrésis, it was not until 1563 that expenditure returned to a normal peace-time level. First there was intervention in Scotland in 1559–60, and then the Le Havre expedition. Neither amounted to full-scale war, but each was costly, particularly the latter. Like her sister in 1554, Elizabeth resorted to the bourse, and to the services of Thomas Gresham. By July 1559 the debt there had gone up to £133,680, and by April 1560 to £279,565. When Gresham submitted his next account in 1562, almost £700,000 had passed through his hands in a little over three years, at a cost to the Exchequer of about £105,000.[22] The domestic debt correspondingly fell, from about £200,000 in November 1558 to £100,000 in October 1559 and £69,000 by the spring of 1560. In February 1559 parliament granted a further subsidy, and two fifteenths and tenths, in spite of the fact that collection of the previous year's grant was not complete. A second grant followed in 1564. During this period also, Elizabeth's council grasped the nettle of recoinage, and found it to be a beneficial herb. The process started in the autumn of 1560, and was substantially completed within a year, although some minor parts of the operation may have gone on for almost a decade. The difficult part was to fix the redemption price for the base coin, given that it had been minted over several years at a number of different levels of fineness. Too high a rate, and the mint would make a disastrous loss; too low a rate and people would not surrender the coin they had. Preferring a loss to the failure of the operation, the council screwed up its courage, and emerged with a profit of about £50,000. The reversal of Mary's religious settlement brought both ecclesiastical revenues and the lands of the refounded religious houses back to the crown, but there was no large windfall from attainders as there had been in 1553. Without the inherited debt, Elizabeth's government would probably have been solvent by 1563, but with that legacy she was forced to resort to further land sales, continuing a process which had been going on steadily since 1540. £90,156 was received from that source in 1560, and a further £172,866 as a result of the commissions of 1561 and 1563. In spite of the consequent reductions in annual revenue, by 1565 the financial situation had markedly improved. With wars over, and the foreign debt virtually discharged, a new equilibrium had been reached, and the steady development of overseas trade during the 1560s more than offset Elizabeth's somewhat feeble handling of the customs issue. Subsidy acts in 1567, 1571, 1576 and 1581 kept the taxation income trickling in from year to year, and with that supplement a frugal manager like Elizabeth could just about balance her recurrent expenditure. It was an undignified predicament for a renaissance monarch, but she never suffered from delusions about Divine Right, and was inclined to make a virtue of depending upon her subjects' love.

# II
## SOCIETY

# 3

## Towns and Trade

Mid-sixteenth century England boasted only one city to compare with the major urban centres of Germany or the Low Countries. In 1550 London had about 120,000 inhabitants, having doubled in size over the previous half century. It did not compare in either wealth or international prestige with Antwerp or Augsburg, but was nevertheless a sophisticated and rapidly developing financial centre some years before the foundation of the Royal Exchange.[1] The Merchant Adventurers of London dominated England's overseas trade, particularly in the main export commodity, broadcloth, and led the struggle against alien control, which had excluded English merchants from many markets over the previous 150 years. Observers from Italy, and other countries accustomed to urban development, noted a handful of other towns which they were prepared to acknowledge; Norwich, with about 12,000 inhabitants; York and Bristol only a little smaller; Newcastle, Exeter, Salisbury and Coventry with between 5,000 and 10,000. Less discriminating English commentators were prepared to designate about 50 other places in the same way, although not always for the same reasons. A few places were conventionally known as towns on the basis of their population and economic activity, in spite of the fact that they lacked chartered incorporation. Lewes in Sussex was such a 'town', although its status was that of a seignorial borough. The great majority of towns, however, were distinguished more by their constitutional privileges than by wealth or population. These privileges, such as the right to hold and control markets, were intended to be economically supportive. Only the inhabitants had the right to produce and sell their goods within the

73

confines of the town, while strangers were charged substantial fees, or excluded altogether. Such control also frequently included the right to licence the goods themselves after quality inspection, a system which could similarly be used to deter competition. Such restrictions, however, did not always work as intended. In 1536 the ropeworkers of Bridport in Dorset alleged that their trade was being ruined by the unscrupulous competition of 'outdwellers' who were evading the controls and selling cheap, inferior rope. They obtained statutory support for their monopoly, but the real problem seems to have been that protection had made them complacent and incompetent, and big shipbuilders, particularly the royal dockyards, were buying Russian rope instead. A similar problem later afflicted weaving towns such as Halifax, where the hidebound controls of the civic authorities later drove enterprising craftsmen to seek greater freedom and opportunity in the surrounding villages.

Nevertheless corporate status and the degree of self-government which went with it was much sought after as the demographic recovery, which had begun around 1470, began to gather pace after 1520. Many substantial old towns, such as Lincoln, Coventry and York, had suffered serious economic decline during the fifteenth century, and Tudor governments had quickly demonstrated a supportive sympathy for their problems. Poor towns were frequently granted full or partial remission from parliamentary taxation, as much as £12,000 being deducted from the total grant to make such provision. The inexorable tendency for the yields of taxation to decrease was not unconnected with this generosity, as there was no corresponding willingness on the part of newer or more prosperous boroughs to take the place of their afflicted brethren. But as only corporate towns, which were assessed collectively, could enjoy this sort of benefit, the attractiveness of incorporation increased. In 1550 a scheme was even proposed to remit the payment of fee farms of all English towns and boroughs for three years, in order to set up a scheme for the employment of the poor on public works. The scheme actually reached the statute book, but was quickly amended by a council which could not face the additional loss of revenue. The originators of the proposal may have been social idealists, inspired by recent writings on the stewardship of wealth, but they may equally have been citizens taking advantage of another perquisite of incorporation, that is representation in parliament. The rapid growth in the number of borough members, from 251 in 1547 to 308 in 1558, represented an alliance of interests. Representation was not only prestigious, it could also bring significant and tangible benefits, as when the burgesses of Coventry and King's Lynn succeeded in securing the amendment of the 1547 Chantries Act in favour of their towns. A large proportion of the specific economic legislation which passed parliament between 1540 and 1565 was the result of lobbying by urban and commercial interest groups. Such lobbying could affect public legislation, and might even be an embarrassment to the council. In 1553 and 1554 the burgesses of Newcastle-upon-Tyne strenuously (albeit unsuccessfully) resisted the re-erection of the diocese of Durham, a measure to which Queen Mary was personally committed.[2] On the whole, however, the crown and the nobility also gained by securing greater scope for their patronage in a forum which was enjoying increasing political weight and importance. It would be an exaggeration to claim that the councils of Edward VI and Mary enfranchised boroughs in order to increase government support in the House of Commons, but Mary's creation of 23 new boroughs in 5 years must certainly rank as a deliberate policy.[3] Perhaps it was felt that returns from new boroughs could be more easily influenced, or perhaps the council was seeking to use urban corporations as an additional means of controlling religious dissent, which was primarily an urban phenomenon.

During the 1550s economic hardship was particularly severe, and the government deliberately protected the vested interests of the urban elites in order to secure their co-operation in the maintenance of social discipline. In 1543 the tapiters, or specialist worsted weavers, one of the most numerous and prosperous groups in the city of York obtained a statutory monopoly of their industry north of the Trent. More significantly, in 1546 the Londoners succeeded in persuading the council to restore the differential customs rates for aliens, and in 1552 the financially beleaguered regime of the Duke of Northumberland withdrew the traditional privileges of the Hanseatic League. The German merchants were then allowed to carry English cloth only to their own Baltic and North German ports, and not to the main English market of Antwerp. This was not only a resounding victory for the Merchant Adventurers, it also reflected the power which the City of London was beginning to derive from its ability to secure government loans in Antwerp by the use of cloth credits. The following year Mary, apparently acting on the principle that everything which Northumberland had done must be wrong, restored the Hanseatic privileges. After her marriage in 1554 King Philip strenuously defended the interests of the 'merchant strangers'. This not only earned him the lasting hostility of the London merchants, it also proved futile. Not only did Mary's financial policy urgently require the co-operation of the Adventurers and the Staplers, the events of Wyatt's rebellion and the simmering religious discontent of the country's largest protestant community necessitated amicable relations between the council and the City Fathers. As a result the restored privileges were steadily eroded, until they were again suspended amid increasing acrimony in 1557. This quarrel seriously strained relations between Philip and Mary, because the latter really had no option but to support her own subjects. However, she had no reason to complain of the attitude of the London magistrates when it came to enforcing government policy.

The government needed prosperous towns, and took seriously the complaints of urban blight and decay which had been resounding on all sides since the middle of the fifteenth century. How justified these complaints were in fact has always been a matter of some controversy. Comparing the poll tax returns of 1377 with the subsidy assessments of 1524–5, 24 towns showed a declining population. The most spectacular losses were at Bristol (12,057 to 7,597), Coventry (9,152 to 4,713) and King's Lynn (5,941 to 1,463).[4] On the other hand 22 towns showed an increase, the largest being at Exeter (3,222 to 6,825), Crediton (550 to 2,815) and Reading (1,520 to 3,452). York and Lincoln declined substantially, while London advanced by leaps and bounds, and Norwich also showed significant expansion. In terms of population the late Middle Ages seems to have been a period of urban redistribution rather than decline. The decay of wealth appears to have been greater, with five towns being assessed at over £1,000 in 1377, while the highest assessment of 1524, apart from London, was Norwich at £749. However, the comparability of the assessments is hard to establish, and it is likely that the poll tax was much more rigorous and comprehensive. In the well-documented case of Coventry there were 565 tenements unoccupied within the walls in 1523, and the decline seems to have continued throughout the mid-century period.

Tudor governments are not famous for the soundness of their economic diagnoses, and before the end of Henry VII's reign had started to resort to legislative coercion in an attempt to check this dereliction. This was part of a well-intentioned, but ultimately misguided, attempt to maintain existing patterns of settlement and land use; rural depopulation and the decay of tillage being directly linked to urban depopulation and the decay of established crafts. Starting in 1535 a series of statutes began to refer to the repair and rebuilding of dwellings within specific towns. The general idea was to compel householders to keep their properties in occupation and repair, and if they proved negligent or recalcitrant to empower the borough corporations to take over the properties and apply the remedies themselves. By 1540 these conditions had been applied to nearly 60 towns, in what was clearly a concerted campaign between the council and the borough representatives to stabilize urban population.[5]

This campaign continued through the 1540s, and was picked up by the ambitious social policies of Protector Somerset. Alongside the renewed efforts to restrict enclosure and sheep ranching he mounted a determined effort to discourage urban speculators. In June 1549 the authorities of the little town of Godmanchester in Huntingdonshire complained to the council that houses in the town were being bought up and kept vacant, or converted to other uses. In response the council ordered that all those owning more than one property should offer the additional housing for rent, and that converted dwellings should revert to their original use. At the same time all the open fields which had formerly belonged to the dissolved guilds were to be divided up for the use of cottagers. How effective this intervention was is not clear, but the purpose is obvious. The dissolution of religious houses, and later of chantries, had brought a lot of urban property onto the market. In some cases this had brought gentle, and even noble purchasers to live at least a part of each year within the town. But more often the result was speculative purchase, often followed by demolition and the sale of lead, timber and stone. A good example of this problem is provided by the borough of Boston, at about the same time, where a man named John Browne was accused of making his living by acquiring and demolishing derelict or unwanted houses, or even, apparently, houses which were still in occupation by the poorer artisans of the town. The corporation not only wished to protect its humble citizens from eviction, it also wished to prevent Browne from laying waste to important areas of the town centre. In this case they were successful through appeal to Sir William Cecil, who soon demonstrated his ability to deal with such a relatively petty nuisance. It was fortunate for those city fathers who were struggling to revitalize their communities that their efforts awoke a cultural as well as an economic response at court. A flourishing urban life had been fundamental to that classical civilization which all humanist scholars and their patrons so greatly admired. Thomas Starkey, for example, an influential writer on social and political issues in the 1530s, had spent a number of years in the highly developed urban culture of northern Italy. Just as the learning and civility of a king's court was an essential element of his honour, so too was the beauty, orderliness and wealth of his kingdom's towns. The poverty and lawlessness of contemporary English towns were not only threats to the whole social order, they were reproaches to the king and his council.

Starkey's *Dialogue between Reginald Pole and Thomas Lupset* set out both a complaint and an agenda for reform.

'Every gentleman flieth into the country; few ... inhabit towns or cities; few have any regard for them; by the reason whereof in them you shall find no policy, no civil order, almost, nor rule. . . .'[6]

This was hardly fair, and probably reflects Starkey's awareness of the contrast between England and Italy, rather than between England past and present. The English gentry never had been town dwellers, so it was not a question of tempting them back; and urban government was not conspicuously inefficient. It was Starkey's aristocratic prejudice which led him to believe that no-one could bear rule except a gentleman. Nevertheless his analysis had some validity. Rich men who aspired to be gentlemen might move out of the towns which had provided them with their economic opportunities. This was partly because their very success made them obvious candidates for expensive and time-consuming urban offices; and partly because the perception of gentle status involved an income from rented farmlands and the exercise of manorial jurisdiction. The departure of such men weakened the towns, and increased the burden on those that remained. It was also true that fewer towns were dominated or protected by noblemen. The Duke of Norfolk maintained a palace within the city of Norwich as late as 1540, and exercised a powerful voice in the city's affairs, but he was exceptional. The Tudors had deliberately eroded the power of the provincial nobility, and the granting of corporate privileges to new boroughs was one way of doing that. Starkey was quite right, therefore, in perceiving that urban government needed the support of the crown, and that it was in the crown's interest to provide it. He suggested the levying of new taxes for urban renewal, and the appointment of 'overseers' to improve such matters as public hygiene, education and civic amenities. Such highly specific remedies were not adopted, but successive governments throughout the period took steps, usually by means of legislation, to strengthen the hands of mayors and corporations, not only in economic and social regulation but also in the general enforcement of the law. Some large cities had enjoyed county status for many years, with their own sheriffs and commissions of the peace, but the appointment of mayors and other civic officers to county commissions *ex officio* represented a significant enhancement of their standing and effectiveness.

'Commonwealth' writers such as Starkey were more inclined to look to social engineering than to economic stimulus to provide a remedy for the ills which they perceived, and governments displayed a corresponding faith in legislation. To the eye of the modern analyst, and indeed of the contemporary entrepreneur, what the market needed was more freedom to develop. The fact that weavers and other craftsmen were setting up their businesses in the countryside in order to escape guild regulations is sufficient indication that they had a commercial incentive to do so. To tempt such business back into the towns the whole traditional structure of regulation and protection needed to be drastically revised. However, the best received opinion, as represented by the *Discourse on the Common Weal*, was exactly the opposite:

'. . . another thing I reckon would much help to relieve our towns decayed, if they could take order that all wares made there should have a special mark, and the mark to be set to none but to such as be truly wrought. And also that every artificer dwelling out of all towns . . . should be limited to be under the correction of one good town or another; and they to sell no wares but such as are first approved and sealed by the town that they are limited unto. . . .'[7]

In official thinking the stick triumphed over the carrot. Instead of reducing the obstacles to commercial and industrial development within the towns, in order to reduce unemployment and urban decay, the council decided to increase the obstacles to development in the countryside. This was a course which the urban authorities themselves approved and encouraged, because it enhanced their control without requiring them to abandon their deeply ingrained habits of thought and action. Beginning as a series of *ad hoc* responses to specific lobbying, this policy of increased regulation had become systematic by 1550, and the beneficiaries were the mayors, the guild wardens and their deputies. Theory and practice seem to have advanced together. The earliest statutes of this kind antedate the 'commonwealth' writers, and indeed the regime of Thomas Cromwell, and it is probable that the author of the *Discourse* was already preaching to the converted in 1549.

Once it had advanced from the specific to the general, this policy was embodied in four statutes of particular importance. The first of these was the Retail Trade Act of 1554 (1 & 2 Philip and Mary, c.7) which imposed penalties of fine and forfeit on all country dwellers seeking to retail woollen or linen cloth, haberdashery, groceries or mercers' wares except at the regular and licensed fairs. Insofar as this statute was effective, it not only caught those who were seeking to evade the market tolls, but many others endeavouring to supplement their agricultural production by developing cottage industries. The Weavers' Act of 1555 (2 & 3 Philip and Mary, c.11) was even more draconian, limiting weavers operating outside corporate towns to two looms each, and prohibiting any further clothiers from setting up businesses in such locations. Three years later the Woollen Cloth Act was equally forceful and even more explicit, blaming the 'decayed, destroyed and depopulated' condition of many towns upon the unlawful removal of cloth manufacture (4 & 5 Philip and Mary, c.5). The penalty of £5 per cloth upon those who did not comply, and the fact that this was the third similar statute in four years, convey a slight air of desperation which may have been linked to the export difficulties of these years. A question is also raised by this act because there were a considerable number of specified exemptions from its provisions. Whether these reflected doubts about the general wisdom of the policy or counter-attacks by a number of rural lobbies is not clear. The government does not seem to have changed its mind with the accession of Elizabeth, but the legislative pressure upon the clothing industry was not renewed. Probably the economic imperatives proved to be too strong, because the problem did not go away, and later governments returned to the same theme in the early seventeenth century. Urban clothworkers were not the only craftsmen to receive the protection of the law. As we have seen the ropemakers of Bridport had adopted the same tactic twenty years before, and in 1563 another important act sought to protect the livelihoods of Girdlers, Glovers, Cutlers, Saddlers and Pointmakers. It was alleged that '. . . the said artificers are not only less occupied, and thereby utterly improverished . . . but also divers cities and towns within this realm of England much . . . impaired', not by rural competition in this case, but by imported goods.[8] No-one was to import girdles, knives, rapiers, saddles, horse harness or a long list of other commodities upon pain of forfeiture. The thought that a little competition might have stimulated the craftsmen to improve their efforts or reduce their prices, would have been incomprehensible heresy, alike to the council and to the craftsmen themselves.

The search for economic salvation in the statute book did not stop with negative regulations of this kind, because the ancient canonical theory of the just price was fighting a vigorous rearguard action against inflation and market forces. The idea that it was in some sense wicked or immoral for either prices or wages to rise was deeply intrenched, and the 'commonwealth men' were moralists even before they were social engineers. The minority governments of Edward VI made several totally unsuccessful attempts to control inflation by proclamation, but the effect of reducing the face value of the coinage was merely to send prices rocketing out of control as every merchant who had the opportunity tried to minimize his losses. It was easier and more attractive, particularly for a parliament consisting largely of employers, to approach the problem from a different angle by controlling wages. This was done in a piecemeal fashion from the 1530s onwards, usually in respect of one particular craft, but at the beginning of Elizabeth's reign a more comprehensive approach was tried. In the countryside unemployment, vagabondage and depopulation were most commonly blamed upon enclosure, and that conviction inspired a whole legislative programme. But there were urban equivalents; masters who laid off their servants, journeymen or apprentices when the economic going became rough; and employers who tried to corner the market in skilled labour by paying higher wages than their competitors could afford. The remedy proposed was a complete system of labour direction, requiring every individual, unless he or she could prove independent means of at least 40 shillings a year, to serve as yearly workers in the crafts in which they had been brought up. Only married women were exempt, and any person between the ages of 12 and 60, not being otherwise employed, could be compelled to work as a 'servant in husbandry'. This Statute of Artificers (5 Elizabeth I, c.4) expressed the intention of providing 'one sole law and statute' so that 'it will come to pass that the same law, being duly executed, should banish idleness, advance husbandry, and yield unto the hired person, both in the time of scarcity and in the time of plenty, a convenient proportion of wages. . .'.

This very positive aim was, however, once again pursued by negative means. There were penalties for every infringement, but no incentives to compliance. A master who improperly dismissed a servant was to be fined 40 shillings; a servant leaving his or her master without good cause was to be imprisoned. Justices of the Peace were required to produce comprehensive schedules of maximum wages; any employer paying above the official rate was to be fined £5 and imprisoned for 10 days; any worker receiving such wages to be imprisoned for 21 days. Every Easter the justices of each county or city were to assemble together and revise or confirm their local rates and, if any justice tried to evade his responsibilities he was to be fined £10. In the countryside, where wage labour constituted only a minor sector of the economy, the impact of this statute was probably not great, even where it was rigorously applied, but in the towns it was hard to evade, and harder still to resist. The magistrates who assessed the rates were also the employers who paid the wages, so the maximum rates tended to be strictly enforced, and nothing was said about a minimum. The policy of successive governments between 1540 and 1565 was therefore to corral manufacturing industry within the confines of the corporate towns, and there to subject it to minute and rigorous regulation at the hands of its own guildmasters and officials. The ostensible reason for this was to maintain standards and revitalize the urban economy, but the real motives seem rather to have been the desire for social control, and the fear of violent protest which crowded conditions, poverty and disease could so easily produce. It is not surprising that the council and the urban elites were close allies in this programme. The gradually increasing commercial prosperity which most observers can detect in the period after 1550 owed nothing whatsoever to this well-intentioned but doctrinaire interference. When trade flourished, it was more often in spite of the government than because of it.

Poverty and violence, both of which were alleged to be increasing, have given the appearance of social crisis to this mid-century period, but in truth it was attitudes and sensitivities which were changing. Violence had been endemic in medieval towns, particularly those with sizeable alien communities. London had seen large-scale riots against the Italians in 1457 and against the Flemings in 1517. Southampton and Bristol had also been affected. In the absence of a police force, physical control was extremely difficult to achieve over the crowded streets and teeming slums. In 1517 it had been the retinue of the Duke of Norfolk which had provided the quick response force against the May Day rioters, and saved the faces of the civic authorities. In August 1553, when a protestant disturbance at Paul's Cross aroused the ire of the council, the lord mayor was threatened with the loss of the city's privileges if he did not keep better order. But the following Sunday it was the Yeomen of the Guard who policed the sermon, not the city militia. This kind of situation presented the government with an unwelcome dilemma. In general it was Tudor policy to replace quasi-feudal retinues with a better organized and equipped militia, in order to reduce dependence upon the magnates and their followers. The problem was that local levies were at their most unreliable in dealing with civil disorders. In 1536 the militia of the northern counties had provided the substance of the rebel forces; and in January 1554 the Londoners sent against Sir Thomas Wyatt changed sides.[9] When Wyatt reached the outskirts of the capital a few days later the craft guilds of London were ordered to mobilize, although 'none but householders' were entrusted with the defence of the gates. In spite of this preparation, it was touch and go whether the citizens would fight, even in defence of their homes. Some of Lord Howard's men had also joined the rebels in Southwark, and most of the militia forces mustered outside the walls simply stood aside and let the insurgents pass. In 1549 the citizens of Norwich made no serious attempt to resist Robert Kett and his followers. In return their property was respected, but they faced an unpleasant inquisition after the Earl of Warwick had defeated and captured Kett at the end of August. On the other hand the men of Exeter defended their city most resolutely in the same year, although many of them shared at least some of the rebels' grievances. This sort of uncertainty persuaded the Duke of Somerset to rely heavily upon the German and Italian mercenaries, who had originally been raised for the Scottish war, and when that war ended in 1550 led the Earl of Warwick to create the select militia which was called the 'gendarmerie'. This was virtually a return to the quasi-feudal retinue, except that it was paid for by the king, and for that reason turned out to be a short-lived experiment.

The militia unit was the county, and the responsible officer for many centuries had been the sheriff. Consequently those boroughs with county status, such as London, had always been responsible for their own forces, but the position in less autonomous towns remained unclear. Some, either by custom or agreement, conducted their own musters, others had always mustered with the shire; in others again there were disputes. Nor was government policy consistent; in June 1545 the council instructed the sheriff of Cambridgeshire to allow the town of Cambridge to muster separately, while in January 1546 the mayor of Portsmouth was instructed to muster with the county. Decisions were probably made on an *ad hoc* basis, depending upon local circumstances, and perhaps upon the attitude of the magnates and leading gentry of the county. In some instances noblemen, under pressure from the crown, were trying to assert, or reassert, a role in urban affairs, which is another reason why some of them bought vacated religious sites and built themselves town houses. After 1549 the situation began to change. Royal lieutenants had in the past been occasional appointments, made on a regional basis in times of exceptional danger, but the Earl of Warwick made a number of such appointments in Edward's name, and in 1557 Mary divided the whole country into ten lieutenancies. Two statutes of 1558 tightened up the militia organization, and the provision of armour and weapons, and in the early part of Elizabeth's reign the responsibility for mustering was moved from the sheriff to the lord lieutenant and his deputies. This did not, in itself, affect the position of the towns, but as the deputy lieutenants (who did most of the work) were also the Justices of the Peace, it was more likely that mayors and other civic officers would be given that responsibility. Indeed the Militia Act (4 & 5 Philip and Mary, c.3) was explicit on that point; if a borough charter included provision for ex officio Justices of the Peace, then that borough was accountable to no one but the crown for the mustering of its inhabitants. By 1560, therefore, the officers of a corporate town were much more likely to know exactly what resources they could call upon, not only to defend themselves against invasion or rural insurrection, but also to police their own communities. The alliance between the crown and the gentry to police the countryside was paralleled in the towns.

The urban justice, even more than his rural counterpart, was preoccupied with the problem of vagabonds. These social drifters, whatever the reason for their uprooting, tended to congregate in the towns, drawn by the opportunities for employment, support or crime, according to their tastes and inclinations. How serious the problem was at national level is a subject of much discussion and dispute,[10] but it was certainly perceived to be both pressing and dangerous. Probably a steady demographic upswing, accompanied by changes in the pattern of land use, and powerful fluctuations in the trade cycle had increased the number of social dependents. But the abrupt withdrawal of the resources of the Church between 1536 and 1540 had had a much more significant impact. This was not because monks or monastic servants were turned adrift without provision, but because those who had previously depended upon the charitable services of monasteries, nunneries and friaries could find no immediate alternative. Charity had always been the function of the Church, and although the Church had been dependent to a large extent upon lay support to sustain that function, attitudes did not change as quickly as circumstances. The problem was there before the dissolutions began, and the first acknowledgement that it was to some extent a government

responsibility came in 1536. Thomas Cromwell's statute of that
year transcended the earlier punitive approach in several ways,
acknowledging that there was a need to provide employment
and charitable relief systematically and upon a large scale. This
initiative died even before Cromwell himself, but it was not
forgotten, and in 1547 Protector Somerset returned to the
charge. Not only had the situation deteriorated since 1536, but
the new government took a protestant attitude towards charity.
No longer was almsgiving a good work in the sense that it
contributed towads the believer's salvation. Charity was a
Christian duty, but no longer motivated by teleological self-
interest. Consequently it was necessary for secular authority,
both national and local, to provide the infrastructure and the
motivating thrust. The statute of 1547 is notorious for having
prescribed slavery as the penalty for the unregenerate vagabond,
but its positive provisions were far more lasting and important.
The parish became the unit of administration, responsible both
for making collections and for preparing registers of those in
need. Because so much of it proved to be unworkable, this act
was repealed in 1550, but the parochial emphasis was retained
in the new act which replaced it two years later. In this case
the original intention seems to have been to levy a permanent
tax for the relief of the poor and impotent, to be collected and
employed at parish level. However, that turned out to be too
idealistic, and its mandatory nature disappeared in committee
and discussion. What emerged was a statute providing a structure for the administration of poor relief, but leaving the actual
contribution of cash upon a voluntary basis, reinforced by
ecclesiastical exhortation. The brief return of catholicism under
Mary was not reflected in social legislation, the act of 1555
repeating that of 1552, except that it now provided that wealthy
urban parishes could be required to assist their less fortunate
neighbours in the same town. It was not until the 1570s that
the provision of employment on a parish or town basis, which
had been a feature of the 1547 act, was restored to the statute
book, and a compulsory poor rate was finally introduced in
1572.[11]

By that time the national government was a long way behind
the best urban practice. London, which was always at the sharp
end of this sort of problem, was branding and expelling sturdy
beggars as early as 1514 and had resorted to flogging and to

begging licences for the impotent by 1524, anticipating the law by seven years. After the dissolution of the monasteries, and following appeal to the king, the hospitals of St Bartholomew and St Thomas were refounded to care for the sick and infirm, and Christ's Hospital as an orphanage. All these were civic properties, run by boards of trustees, and supported in the first instance by voluntary contributions, and by modest endowments provided by the crown. In 1547, by order of the Common Council, the weekly voluntary collections were discontinued, and replaced by an annual tax equivalent to one half of a parliamentary fifteenth, which was to be assessed and collected in the same manner as the parliamentary taxation. By the end of Edward's reign two further institutions had been added, Bethlehem Hospital for the insane, and the old royal palace of Bridewell as a house of correction for the incorrigible. Other towns also developed their own schemes, but on a much more modest scale. A cornstock under civic control to cushion the effects of harvest failure was a common expedient. Bristol had such a scheme as early as 1522, Canterbury by 1552 and Norwich by 1557. The licensing of beggars was general by about 1550, and Lincoln, Ipswich, Gloucester, Cambridge and York are all known to have practised it. Early in Elizabeth's reign Ipswich introduced a system modelled on that of London, with a school, hospital and house of correction, all supported by a compulsory levy. York was well provided with hospitals, while Lincoln had made provision for the apprenticing of poor children by 1551, and had appointed a special civic officer to deal with the affairs of the poor by 1560. By 1570 Norwich had become the model of civic initiative for those who could not aspire to London's scale of provision; but the problem remained an obstinate one, and many found themselves unable to sustain the financial effort required, even after the law had come to their assistance. The conflict of self-interest was endemic; on the one hand both civic pride and the preservation of public order required action; but on the other hand the expense steadily escalated with inflation. The more successful a scheme was, the more paupers and beggars it attracted; and the government, which was so keen to see the problem addressed, was unable to provide any of the necessary funding.

The sinew of charity, or of urban renewal, was the same as that of war – money. Without prosperity there could be no effective civic polity or culture. The crown could create chartered boroughs for its own purposes, but in spite of much optimistic idealism, it could not create prosperity by legislation. Prosperity depended upon trade, and trade depended upon the unpredictable factors of supply and demand. Politics could distort the patterns of trade, but it could only create demand in very limited and specific ways. War with France disrupted the wine trade between Bristol and Gascony; in 1494 Maximilian, King of the Romans, embargoed English cloth exports to the Netherlands; in 1563–4 a similar embargo drove English merchants to trade through Emden rather than Antwerp. The only kind of demand which could actually be created by political action was that for military supplies. Henry VIII's agents bought saltpetre, sailcloth and rope in Danzig and Hamburg. In the 1550s Sir Thomas Gresham spent large sums in Antwerp on 'almain rivets', gunpowder and pikes. Tudor governments tended to be economically aggressive, repeatedly insisting upon the use of English ships, and after 1540 systematically attacking the privileges of 'merchant strangers'. This inevitably led to reprisals and it is arguable whether the English merchants gained more than they lost, but since such policies were usually instigated by pressure from London, they could hardly complain that the government was acting contrary to their interests. Henry VII had consistently used such international muscle as he possessed to promote the interests of his merchants as they were then perceived, but his son's priorities were elsewhere. Although petitioned to do so, he showed no interest in promoting long-distance trading ventures, prefering to develop his warships for the defence of the coasts. After 1550, however, in a changing economic climate, the minority government of Edward VI began to encourage investment in exploration and the search for new markets, an initiative which was picked up and developed in new and dramatic ways in the early part of Elizabeth's reign.[12] During his years as King of England Philip did his best to inhibit English interest in southern or western trade, but Mary was as supportive as her circumstances allowed, and her council's position was consistent with that of Edward's or Elizabeth's.

Originally England's principal overseas trade had been in raw wool, and the company which handled that trade, the Merchant Staplers, had wielded great financial power. In the middle of the fourteenth century 35,000 sacks a year were being exported, but by 1420 high taxation and the beginnings of domestic cloth manufacture had reduced that figure to 10,000. In spite of this decline, by 1470 the Staplers had been constrained to accept financial responsibility for the garrison of Calais, where the Staple was situated, and this probably drove their trade deeper into recession. In 1527, with exports down to about 5,000 sacks a year, they complained bitterly to Wolsey of the hardness of their lot. The Staplers survived even the loss of Calais in 1558, but they were not a major economic force in the middle years of the sixteenth century. That role had long since devolved upon the Merchant Adventurers. Originally an offshoot of the Staplers, the Adventurers were a regulated company, membership of which was open to anyone able and willing to pay the fees. In theory the members traded as individuals, but it was the company which held the monopoly to export unfinished cloth, and by the end of the fifteenth century the London Adventurers had organized themselves into a powerful cartel. Driven from the Baltic and Scandinavia by the competition of the Hanseatic League, they concentrated increasingly upon the Netherlands. By 1530 they had a privileged base in Antwerp, and the English cloth trade was dominated by the London–Antwerp axis. In 1450 total exports had amounted to 57,000 cloths, of which London handled less than half. A century later the total was approaching 150,000, and 80% was passing through Blackwell Hall. These fundamental changes in the country's principal export commodity had many repercussions on the pattern of economic activity. Cloth-manufacturing areas in Yorkshire, Suffolk and the Cotswolds became prosperous; East coast ports such as King's Lynn withered as London expanded. However, the government resisted attempts by the Londoners to keep their provincial rivals out of the most lucrative trade. Henry VII had given the Merchant Adventurers a charter in 1505 which gave them a substantial amount of autonomy, but he had refused to allow them to make prohibitive increases in their entry fines, and in 1504 frustrated their attempt to take over the Staplers. Both Newcastle and Bristol Adventurers retained some independence, and in 1552 the latter obtained their own charter from Edward VI. Other goods were traded overseas; tin, hides, fish and manufactured goods particularly, and some small ports lived predominantly off these lesser commodities. However, by 1550 the big money was in cloth, and it was dangerously concentrated in London. The Merchant Adventurers' annual shipment was reckoned to be 'richly worth' £300,000, twice the revenue of the crown of England, and the largest single element in the complex make up of the Antwerp economy.

It was therefore extremely damaging to both cities when this lucrative trade briefly but dramatically overheated in 1551. The underlying reason appears to have been that the debasement of the English currency had unsettled the exchanges, and made English cloth relatively cheap. As a result there was a surge of demand in the late 1540s which led to some deterioration in the quality. This was followed by the Duke of Northumberland's anti-inflation measures, particularly the 'crying down' of the coinage, which sharply increased the price. Consequently in 1550–51 there was a flood of somewhat inferior English cloth at enhanced prices, and the market briefly collapsed. Figures for the next few years are uncertain. There was probably a revival in 1553–4, followed by a further sharp decline in 1558–61, and by the time that the embargoes were introduced in the mid–1560s the trade had been heavily undermined. In the long run Antwerp suffered from this more than London, because there was no alternative source of broadcloth on an adequate scale, whereas there were alternative markets if the English had the energy and enterprise to discover them. A shock of this kind, coming at the same time as their hard won and bitterly controversial victory over the Hanseatic League, proved stimulating to the Merchant Adventurers. In spite of their title, they were the most conservative of men, showing not the slightest interest in expanding their commercial horizons as long as there was a large profit to be made by the shortest and easiest route. The merchants trading to Andalusia had been granted a charter by Henry VIII in 1531, but all trade with Spain declined as political relations worsened in the 1530s,[13] and by 1547 the company was struggling for survival. At the same time Bristol merchants had begun to open up links with the Azores and with West Africa, but the Londoners were not interested, and Philip did his best to quash the initiative in 1556 and 1557. However, the collapse of 1551 began to alter attitudes in the city. Local alternatives to Antwerp could be found, such as Middleburgh and Emden; they had been used before, and would be used again, but they did not have the facilities of Antwerp, and in any case were too close to have escaped the temporary blight. Consequently, when Sebastian Cabot turned up in 1552 with a proposal to gain direct access to the potentially enormous markets of China and the Far East, he found rich men willing to listen to him.

Cabot was an old man; a Genoese whose connections with England went back to 1497, when he had sailed from Bristol with his father on one of the voyages sponsored by Henry VII. He had made at least two other voyages after his father's death, and seems to have liked working from a base in England. But after 1509 he had failed to attract the patronage of the new king, and had taken himself off to Spain. There he had made a distinguished career, rising to be Pilot Major in the service of Charles V. However in 1547 a new regime in England opened up fresh possibilities, and he returned to the north. We do not know whether the initiative came from Cabot himself, from Protector Somerset or from someone else in England. Perhaps he had done something to upset the increasingly rigorous ecclesiastical authorities in Spain or felt inclined to do something. He was given a pension, but hardly enough to tempt him away from his prestigious office. Charles V was extremely annoyed, and claimed at first that Cabot was being held in England illegally and against his will. Not only was the old man an excellent cosmographer, he also possessed an enormous amount of sensitive information about Iberian navigational technology and training methods. He was full of ideas and soon attracted the patronage of the Earl of Warwick, a former Lord Admiral who was, from the autumn of 1549, the *de facto* head of government. Between them they promoted a project 'for the discovery of the northern part of the world'; a voyage of exploration in search of what would soon be known as the North East passage. A mixed group of London merchants and courtiers was persuaded to put up over £6,000, and in 1553 Sir Hugh Willoughby and Richard Chancellor set sail upon what was to prove an epoch-making journey.

Like many such enterprises, its success was unintentional. Willoughby perished with the entire crews of two ships, having made a mistaken decision to winter on the coast of Lappland, but Chancellor succeeded in reaching the Russian port of Archangel. From there he travelled overland to Moscow and delivered to Tsar Ivan IV the effusive letters originally intended for the Emperor of China. Ivan responded favourably and, although when Chancellor returned in 1554 he found both King Edward and the Duke of Northumberland dead, the initiative was not allowed to flag. In 1555 a new company was chartered in London under the guidance of Sebastian Cabot, which soon became known as the Muscovy Company, and the tsar responded with a generous charter of privileges in the same year. The trade which then developed, based upon the exchange of cloth for furs, rope and naval stores, was modest in quantity, but showed a consistently good return on investment as long as the Russian authorities were sympathetic. Cabot died in 1557 but by that time the spirit of enterprise had taken root. In that year Stephen Borough made another unsuccessful attempt to find the North East passage, sensibly turning back in the Kara Sea, while Anthony Jenkinson struck out overland from Moscow. Reaching Bokhara by the end of the year, he reported good trading prospects further south and the Muscovy company abandoned the North East passage in favour of a new initiative in Persia. Meanwhile Stephen Borough had visited the Casa de Contratación in Seville, and Richard Eden had published his *Decades of the New World*. By the time that Elizabeth came to the throne in 1558 the narrow horizons of the Merchant Adventurers were being widened year by year. Although Philip had done his best to discourage English interest in Barbary and Guinea, trade with Spain had naturally recovered during the four-year marriage alliance, and resident English merchants could again be found in Seville, even trading lawfully to the Americans under the aegis of Spanish companies. Nevertheless, the crown had so far shown little direct interest. Edward, like his father, visited his dockyards and launched ships.[14] During his last illness he had struggled to the window at Greenwich to see Willoughby and Chancellor set off, but he had had little opportunity to show a more practical concern. Mary was dutifully concerned about the interests of her merchants, when these did not conflict with more pressing priorities, but she does not seem to have talked to the seamen and travellers who were beginning to bring England out of her relative isolation.

By 1562 Elizabeth was playing a more positive role. Many years before William Hawkins of Plymouth had made an unsuccessful attempt to break into the Portuguese trade with Brazil. In 1561 his son John decided to try again, not this time to Brazil but to the equally prohibited Spanish colonies in the Caribbean. Hawkins had connections with the court through certain West Country gentry, such as the Carews, and shared the religious sympathies of the new regime. He became *persona grata* and his illegal enterprise attracted the financial backing of both courtiers and city merchants. The queen herself invested two ships and a modest sum of money. Hawkins' plan was to sail to the Guinea coast, trade English goods for slaves and ship his purchases across to Hispaniola or New Spain, where there was a chronic labour shortage. This involved evading or defying the Portuguese authorities on one side of the Atlantic and the Spanish on the other, so well-armed ships were necessary. Hence, in part, the queen's involvement. The voyage was a success, and two years later it was repeated, again with royal involvement. Thereafter Elizabeth blew hot and cold, as her desire to support her seamen (and make a profit) struggled with her concern not to provoke Philip too far and run the risk of open war. In 1568 when Hawkins was caught and badly mauled at San Juan d'Ulloa, he was not only commanding two of the queen's ships, he also held the queen's commission. Anglo-Spanish relations barely survived the resulting fracas. By then the Merchant Adventurers' trade was worth some £800,000 a year, but less than 100,000 cloths were passing through London, and the recipients were spread from Bokhara to Vera Cruz. The bulk of the trade was still going into northern Europe, but to the Baltic and northern Germany as well as the Low Countries. During the following decade the Persian and Russian trades developed, and the Levant company reopened the routes to the Eastern Mediterranean. By 1580 English merchants had begun to venture into every part of the known world, but the critical period of diversification, when the earlier mould was broken, came between 1550 and 1570.

Overseas trade was important for a number of reasons; because of the revenue which it produced for the crown; because of the role which it played in foreign policy; and because it created the financial power of the City of London. But mid-sixteenth-century England was not the commercial power which Britain was to become 200 years later, and the bulk of commercial activity took place within the realm. Three quarters of all transactions involved internal trade, and for this the steadily increasing population was the critical factor.[15] More people

93

meant a greater demand, not only for food, but for clothing materials, fuel, housing and a wide variety of services. London created a ramifying service economy. Market gardening in Kent and Surrey supplied the city with fruit and vegetables, and the hostmen of Newcastle-upon-Tyne grew rich by supplying the capital with sea coal in ever increasing quantities. Agricultural produce was generally sold direct by the producers in a very large number of small markets up and down the country, but the demands of the royal household, and of the armed forces in time of war, superimposed a large-scale pattern upon this diffuse trade. England was at war from 1543 to 1550, from 1557 to 1559 and again briefly in 1563. Large forces were raised in 1544 and 1557, while at other times the garrisons of Calais, Berwick and the other border fortresses, together with a standing navy of 30–40 ships kept up a steady pressure of demand. After 1550 Edward Baeshe, the Surveyor General of Victuals for the navy developed a scheme of county quotas. A thousand quarters of wheat and six hundred quarters of barley from Norfolk; three hundred cheeses and two hundred oxen from Suffolk, and so on, covering about two thirds of the counties of England.[16] Some counties were exempt because they were already supplying particular garrisons; Berwick, for example, was supplied by Northumberland. These quotas were taken up at agreed prices, which were negotiated with the commissioners for each county, although Baeshe held a commission of purveyance in reserve, and could impose his own prices if the commissioners were uncooperative. Victualling was big business, involving brewers, butchers and bakers as well as the primary suppliers. Baeshe normally spent between £5,000 and £10,000 a year in peace time, and up to four times that much in war – and that was only for the navy. Purveyance for the royal household was on a much smaller scale, and a great deal more varied in its demands, but had been a standing grievance for centuries. During Elizabeth's reign it was gradually replaced by a system of commutation for cash upon a county basis, but little progress had been made in that direction before 1565.

The crown was the largest purchaser upon the domestic market, as well as the legislator who had to be appealed to to protect threatened trades or promising new industries. The unity of royal control, which had made England exceptional as early as the twelfth century and which had been completed in Henry

VIII's reign, also offered important commercial advantages. There were no internal customs barriers in England, because there were no semi-autonomous private jurisdictions. Cargoes travelling down the Rhine paid tolls to half a dozen cities and principalities because the Holy Roman Empire was more a concept than a state. A similar journey down the Seine could be almost equally expensive because although the whole river lay within the kingdom of France, the seignorial jurisdictions remained in place. A merchant shipping his goods from Oxford to London or from Hereford to Bristol, on the other hand, paid only the carriers' charges. Rivers were important highways, as they always had been, and from time to time the royal authority was also appealed to to prevent them from being obstructed by private fish weirs or water mills. The assistance of the state might also be solicited in preventing or remedying the silting up of harbours and in boosting the demand for fish by decreeing that Friday remain a fast day in spite of the move from a catholic to a protestant Church. In short, the crown and its agents were as pervasive in the world of trade and industry as they were in administration or the enforcement of the law. Nevertheless there was, and could be, no such thing as an economic policy. Apart from the overseas cloth trade and the early navigation acts, government interference in commercial activity was sporadic and had to be solicited. The crown exploited mining rights on its own estates, and Henry VIII set up his own gunfoundry at Hounsditch early in his reign, but the Tudors were usually patrons of enterprise rather than entrepreneurs in their own right. Elizabeth's council imported German miners and prospectors, giving them the right to seek for and exploit mineral resources in Cumberland and Westmorland, an activity which aroused the ire of the local inhabitants and required further intervention to protect the miners in 1566.[17] At about the same time a group of Flemish silk weavers were encouraged to settle in Norwich, and set up an industry for which there was no local skill or tradition.

The overwhelming majority of craftsmen produced their goods on a small scale for the domestic market, but the days of local self sufficiency had long since gone. Most towns specialized to some extent. In Northampton 23% of the workforce was engaged in producing leather goods, mostly shoes and boots. In Coventry 15% were making hats, caps or gloves, and many similar examples could be cited. Every town was a market centre for foodstuffs and household goods, between 20 and 40% of retail traders making their living in that manner. Most of this was locally produced, but luxury items such as spices and haberdashery were usually imported from abroad, and distributed either by specialist wholesalers or by the chapmen and peddlers who were such a feature of the roads and markets of this period. Sometimes almost indistinguishable from vagabonds, their packs would contain not only pins, buttons and ribbons, but also the latest ballads and gossipy newsheets of a kind which were becoming increasingly popular after 1547. Internal trade is almost impossible to quantify, precisely because it paid no dues in transit. We know that drovers moved cattle and sheep over long distances to satisfy the demands of large cities, but we do not know much about the size of the flocks and herds. We know that dried and salted fish was available in inland markets, but we do not usually know in what quantities. Coastwise trade, on the other hand, was recorded in the port books; so we know that between 1540 and 1560 the east coast ports shipped some 60,000 quarters of wheat to other parts of England, and that during the same period the northern ports received about half that quantity. Similarly, between 1551 and 1560 Newcastle upon Tyne exported some 29,000 tons of coal, most of it to the south and south east of England.[18] Bulk transport was both easier and cheaper by water, but such figures as we have are hopelessly incomplete because they only measure what passed through the main ports. Every stretch of coastline contained innumerable creeks and inlets; small havens which constituted a smugglers' paradise, provided endless refuges for pirates, and handled an unknown but substantial proportion of the legitimate coastal trade.

Sixteenth-century roads were a scandal. About ten main routes, listed in a guide book of 1541, had been recognized for centuries as royal highways. From time to time the king had endeavoured to protect travellers from footpads and highwaymen, but the crown had never accepted any responsibiliy for their maintenance. The upkeep of roads and bridges had always been a matter for private charity. In practice this had often meant religious houses or guilds, and with the disappearance of such foundations between 1536 and 1547, the situation deteriorated, just at the time when pressure from travellers and merchants was beginning to increase. Some charitable trusts which had no religious connotations remained, and continued to attract bequests and donations down to the end of the century, but charity was already being constrained before the religious houses went down. An act of 1530 empowered Justices of the Peace to enquire as to the state of bridges, and to compel the parishes within which faulty bridges were found to repair them, and to maintain the highway for a hundred yards at either end. In 1555 a kind of corvée was introduced, whereby every adult male was required to work on the highway for four days in every year without pay. In 1563 this duty was increased to six days, and the appointment of two surveyors in every parish was prescribed to oversee the work. Later on delinquent parishes could be presented at quarter sessions and corporately fined if they neglected their duties, so the roads in fact became compulsory parish responsibilities. Presumably some improvement resulted, but even the most important highways remained mere rutted and potholed tracks, while lesser roads could disappear completely as a result of flooding or the encroachments of farmers. By 1560 the growth of coastal piracy probably meant that it was safer to travel by land, and regular carrier services were beginning to operate between major towns, but journeys were painfully slow even in the summer, and often impossible in the winter.

Measurable economic activity in the sixteenth century took only a limited number of forms, and it is upon those that historians have naturally tended to concentrate. Clothmaking for the international market can be roughly quantified, and its crises assessed, partly because the international trade itself can be quantified, and partly because contemporary observers concentrated upon it as a barometer of economic health. Ship-building can be roughly measured because the crown took stock of available shipping from time to time, counting the ships in each port of every size from 80 tons burthen and upwards. The coal trade can be assessed because it was largely concentrated in Newcastle and the hostmen kept good records which have survived. Industrial activity is much harder to measure on a national scale, but provides good illustrative material, for example the accounts of a particular mine or forge. But the great bulk of manufacturing and internal trade is tantalizingly below the horizon. We know how many shoemakers there were in Leicester in 1552, and how many cutlers in Sheffield, and we know what regulations they worked under; but we do not know how many shoes or knives they made, how far afield they sent them or how much profit a typical craftsman might make in a year. Wage labourers are slightly more visible, thanks to the statute of artificers and its less comprehensive predecessors, which is why building workers have been used as an element of economic reconstruction. There was plenty of building activity going on, but it is difficult to say just how much, even within a single town, and impossible to say how prosperous the master craftsman himself might be. So judgements have to remain impressionistic, based upon population statistics which themselves have a very wide margin of error. However, we can be reasonably sure, for example, that far more cloth was produced for the home market than was ever sold abroad. Many of the lighter and cheaper varieties of cloth were never exported at all, and finished garments hardly ever feature as items of export. Indeed, there were vigorous complaints that some garments, particularly hats and caps, were actually being imported 'to the great impoverishment' of the English manufacturers.[19] We also have to remember that urban crafts and trade, whether internal or external, were minority activities, despite their high historical profile. England between 1540 and 1565 was predominantly an agrarian society, and far more people were affected by harvest failures, or by shifts in the relative prices of wool and corn, than were ever affected by upsets in the trade cycle or by the development of new industries. Whatever may have been the case in 1800, in 1550 England was a nation of farmers, not shopkeepers.

# 4

# AGRICULTURE AND ORDER

If there was a revolution in English agriculture, it certainly did not come in the sixteenth century. The system of crop rotation, the breeds of sheep and cattle and the familiar round of the seasons remained substantially unchanged from the fifteenth century (and earlier) until the days of Coke and Townsend. Increasing demand brought back into cultivation some marginal land which had not been tilled for 200 years, and such land was particularly vulnerable to harvest failure. But the so-called 'agrarian crisis' of the Tudor period was not a crisis of production, or of technology, so much as of law and custom. The polemical case was summed up in a tract of Edward VI's reign entitled 'Certayne causes gathered together, wherin is showed the decaye of England only by the great multitude of sheep, to the utter decay of household keeping, mayntenance of men, dearth of corne, and other notable dyscommodityes. . .'.[1] This theme was consistently pursued by moralists and preachers, going back to the days of Sir Thomas More and before, and reached a shrill crescendo between 1547 and 1553. Circumstantial details were offered:

'. . . there is not so many plows used occupied and maintained within Oxfordshire as was in King Henry the Seventh his time, and since his coming their lacketh 40 plows; every plow was able to keep 6 persons downlying and uprising in his house, the which draweth to twelve score persons in Oxfordshire'.

Nor was this the result of some natural disaster, ascribable to the wrath of God; it was the deliberate work of wicked and greedy men.

> 'Men without conscience. Men utterly void of God's fear. Yea, men that live as though there were no God at all! Men that would have all in their own hands; men that would leave nothing for others; men that would be alone on the earth; men that be never satisfied. Cormorants, greedy gulls; yea, men that would eat up men, women and children. . . .'[2]

It was in this authentic voice of paranoia that the true crisis of the period lay because these public enemies were not men in the abstract, but concrete individuals to whom names and habitations could easily be given.

> '. . . the great farmers, the graziers, the rich butchers, the men of law, the merchants, the gentlemen, the knights, the lords, and I cannot tell who . . .'

This was Thomas More's 'conspiracy of rich men', and it struck a society rooted in deference and largely unpoliced with the impact of bubonic plague.

The specific issue which aroused such fury was enclosure or, more precisely, that type of enclosure which resulted in land being converted from tillage to pasture. Two generations ago R. H. Tawney took the contemporary polemic pretty much at its face value, accepted that there was extensive conversion of land use, and blamed what he called the 'capitalist spirit'.[3] Roughly speaking, this meant the belief that a man was entitled to take as much profit out of his land as the market would yield him, without acknowledging any moral responsibility to others whose livelihood might be involved. A contemporary ascribed exactly this attitude to the objects of his hatred, accusing them of saying '. . . it is mine own; who shall warn me to do with mine own but as myself listeth'. If any sixteenth-century gentlemen or other landlord ever used such words, he did not write them down in a form which has survived, and in terms of ideological conflict the 'commonwealth men' were beating the air. If a 'capitalist spirit' existed in the sixteenth century, it found no articulate advocate. The phrase belongs to nineteenth-century economic analysis, and Tawney's propensity to see his subject in terms of early twentieth-century socialist policy invalidated much of the thesis. Ruthlessness in pursuit of gain was nothing new in the sixteenth century. Francesco Datini of Prato had carefully headed every page of his ledger 'in the name of God and of profit', and the bankers and wool merchants of the fifteenth century had been every bit as rich and unscrupulous as the landlords of whom Crowley and Latimer complained so bitterly. Recent research has suggested that enclosure was a real issue, but it was a symptom rather than a cause of economic malaise, and what the moralists were really complaining about was a very much more general change in attitudes towards social responsibility. The social theory of the medieval church was paternalistic. The king, the lord and rich men in general were responsible for the well being (and for the good behaviour) of their dependants and inferiors. It was a crude way of adjusting the facts of a hierarchical society to the theory of a people equal in the sight of God. All things came of God, and wealth was therefore a stewardship for which all men were ultimately accountable. Far from abandoning this theory when they challenged the catholic theology of justification, the early protestants reasserted it strongly. Luther and Calvin were not advocates of a new individualism, and were as hostile to usury (for example) as the medieval schoolmen.

The specific origins of 'commonwealth' theory were humanist, and although the humanists were often sharply critical of the Church, they did not in this respect depart very far from traditional Christian teaching. The first responsibility of the Christian prince, declared Erasmus in his work of that title, was to protect and preserve 'the public weal, free from all private interests'. The princely office existed, not for the glory of its holder, but to enable him to protect the welfare of his subjects, and the same responsibility lay upon those who served him in public office. What the humanists lacked in originality they more than made up for in the fashionable currency of their writings. They were the accepted educators of renaissance princes, and a scholar moralist such as Erasmus had the entrée to every court. They did not spare their reproaches. It was their own pupils who were ignoring the 'fundamental principles of equity and honesty' and allowing the self-interest of their ministers and agents to subvert the course of justice. Thomas More in *Utopia* and Thomas Starkey in the *Dialogue between Pole and*

101

*Lupset* made the same point; rulers pretend to be concerned with the common good, but all they are really interested in is their own 'profit, commodity and pleasure'. In some of these works it is difficult to tell where moral indignation ends and the intoxication of rhetoric begins, but the moral seriousness of such men as More and Sir Thomas Elyot need not be doubted. The English humanists were particularly good at showing what a modern scholar has called a 'dawning awareness of social process', and More in particular reserved many of his sharpest darts for the aristocracy. They were guilty of absurd pretentiousness '(carrying) about with them a huge crowd of idle attendants', who intimidated the innocent and became a burden on the community because they learned no useful trade. Whether he knew it or not, More was not attacking any new culture of individualism in making such remarks, but the ancient culture of magnificence. When Latimer quoted scripture to the effect that the rulers of England were the companions of thieves, he was not only speaking with the immemorial voice of Christian social conscience, but also expressing an awareness that traditional values were no longer sufficiently robust to cope with the moral imperatives of a new generation.

The roots of change were deep, and not easy to identify, but probably lay rather in the decay of lordship, and in the waning authority of the clergy than in the rise of any positive new ideology. Both these developments were connected to the rising power of the crown, and the 'increase of governance' which is generally recognized to have taken place during the Tudor period. Successive kings from Edward IV onward set out to undermine the 'natural' or autonomous power of lords, encouraging instead the idea that authority came from the crown by delegation. The increasing use of the commission of the peace is the best-known, but by no means the only, example of this. By 1547 the English gentry had, by and large, come to the conclusion that the king was a better lord than the Earl of Derby or the Duke of Norfolk, and this had a profound affect, not only upon the power of the nobility but upon the whole aristocratic culture.[4] Lordship was a seamless web, and as the gentry emancipated themselves from dependence upon the nobility, their own inferiors sought to follow the same course. At the same time the English Church ceased to be part of an independent and international institution, and also became an aspect of the royal jurisdiction. Bishops were appointed by the king, and clergy became the mouthpieces of royal propaganda. Their moral authority in consequence declined, a fact which was noticed and lamented as much by reformers as by conservatives; 'I never saw so little discipline as is nowadays . . .' declared Hugh Latimer, and he went on to observe that both the sanctity of marriage and obedience to masters appeared to have collapsed. It was therefore natural for the commonwealth men to appeal to the king as the guardian of social and moral order, not by restoring hierarchy and deference, but by transcending them. The bonds of the traditional order, they believed with some justice, had been shaken loose. Noblemen and gentlemen, no longer sure of their own positions, were compensating for their insecurity by exploiting their poorer neighbours. Rich merchants and others aspiring to be gentlemen, naturally followed the same route, wishing to conform to the new *mores*, and not averse to taking their profit. Only the king could transcend this moral confusion and insist upon the observance of traditional values. Paradoxically, of course, by responding to this appeal, and intruding the authority of the crown still further into the web of social relationships, successive governments furthered the process of change which they were ostensibly attempting to check. The main beneficiaries of the paranoid fears of the commonwealth men were the Tudors themselves.

In this process the mythology of enclosure was a catalyst. It became the symbol of that greed and irresponsibility which the moralists wished to find in contemporary English society in order to justify their own diagnosis and remedy. The facts, insofar as they can be recovered, were much less dramatic. Virtually all land was manorial, but a manor was a legal and jurisdictional entity, not a topographical one. Some manors included several settlements, a number of which might be physically detached from the *caput honoris*, or principal centre. The most extreme example of this was the royal manor of East Greenwich, which in the seventeenth century came to include estates on the other side of the Atlantic. On the other hand, some settlements were divided into a number of manors. Whatever its size or shape, a manor had two invariable characteristics – a court and a group of tenants who formed the 'homage' and were the members of the court.[5] These tenants held their land under the customary law – the law of the manor – and had originally been unfree. By the sixteenth century bondmen of condition were rare, and most bond tenures were held by men (and women) who had been personally free for generations. Nevertheless, because of their status, these tenancies could not be pleaded in the king's courts. That is to say, they were not protected by the common law. There were tenants who held manorial land as freehold, and they were protected by the common law, but they were not members of the homage of the manor. A freehold tenement was normally held for a term of years or lives at a fixed rent, and was absolutely secure for as long as the lease ran. Only when the lease expired could the terms be renegotiated. A bond tenement was held by a similar instrument, known as the copy of court roll, and was consequently called copyhold. The terms might well be identical with those of a freehold lease, but they were pleadable only in the manor court. In practice fully-registered copyholds, known as 'copyholds of inheritance', were as secure as freeholds because the customary law of the manor was protected by the crown in chancery. On the other hand, there were customary tenancies which were not protected. A 'copy' which was not registered was not pleadable, but the tenant might not discover that until it was too late; and a tenant at will neither had, nor expected, any security.

These technicalities were important, because if a landlord wished to change the use of manorial land, he had to do so within the limits prescribed by the law. By the middle of the sixteenth century England was far too well governed for a lord simply to dispossess a tenant by force and hope to get away with it. If he wished to enclose his own demesne land[6], of course he was answerable to no one, but if he wished to enclose tenurial land it had to be either by agreement or by the termination of the tenancy. Enclosure by agreement was fairly common, and in open-field areas offered advantages to all parties. Instead of a variety of strips scattered through the various fields, each tenant and the lord emerged with an enclosed farm which could be cultivated 'in severalty', without recourse to complicated agreements about crop management. In such cases the land usually remained under cultivation, and there was little controversy. The homage and the manor court remained *in situ*, although there would have been much less for the court to do. A lord who wished to convert his land to pasture, however, would have been unlikely to proceed by agreement. His aim would be unity of possession, and that meant getting rid of his tenants. A very patient man, or a very lucky one, might manage to achieve that by lawful means as the tenancies fell in; but even if he did he would have been unlikely to escape controversy. An arbitrary refusal to renew, although perfectly legal, could be guaranteed to produce a major sense of grievance. The great advantage of unity of possession was that it destroyed the manor itself. Where there was no homage, there was no court, and where there was no court, there was no manor but only a seigneury. A would-be encloser might be frustrated by secure tenancies, even under the customary law, but equally he might resort to harassment or inducement to clear his path. Alternatively, he might cease to convene the manor court in the hope that its functions would disappear, and the tenants thus become vulnerable to extra-legal action. Another possible tactic, and one which was frequently alleged, was the removal or destruction of the court records in order to make tenancy agreements unverifiable. This was not likely to succeed because the sworn testimony of the homage would normally be accepted in lieu if the case was appealed to the equity jurisdiction of the crown. False judgements might also be made in manor courts under pressure from the lord, and many such allegations were brought to Chancery, but they were not very often substantiated.

The actual incidence of conversion from arable to pasture by means of enclosure was much less than many contemporaries believed; nor was it a new development in the sixteenth century. When Cardinal Wolsey set up his commission of enquiry in 1517, the commissioners were told that the greatest number of enclosures had been carried out 'before the king's majesty's father began to reign', that is before 1485. In Warwickshire many of the enclosures went back before 1470, and at that time there had been little complaint, for the simple reason that tenements were plentiful and tenants scarce. That situation was changed by the rising level of population rather than by the growth of enclosure. Across the whole of England and Wales the total, which may have been as high as 6,000,000 in the middle of the thirteenth century, had been reduced 200 years later to something in the region of 2,500,000. Plague had been the most potent, but by no means the only reason for that collapse. After 1450, although the plague remained, the population began to recover, and by 1550 had probably reached

3,000,000, or a little more. A rise of 15–20%, most of which had occurred after 1500, had been sufficient to put pressure upon the resources of available land, although even in the open field areas of the East Midlands only a small proportion of manors had been affected by the middle of Elizabeth's reign. It was in the eighteenth century, not in the sixteenth that the great open fields were swept away and the modern chessboard pattern of fields and hedgerows produced. In others part of England, where the patterns of settlement and land use were different, there was little or no controversy. Many parts of the West and North, particularly areas of mixed husbandry, had been enclosed from very ancient times, and Wales was largely unaffected. Any quantification of enclosure for pasture, however approximate, suggests that the protests were out of all proportion to the problem. Tenants with freeholds or secure copyholds were very seldom disturbed. The tactics whereby Sir Giles Overreach plotted to undo Master Frugal belong to the early seventeenth century, and although in a sense they are timeless in their plausibility, few such cases can actually be traced in the mid-Tudor period.

> 'When I have harried him thus two or three years,
> Though he sue in forma pauperis, in spite
> Of all his thrift and care, he'll grow behindhand . . .
> Then, with the favour of my man of law,
> I will pretend some title: want will force him
> To put it to arbitrament; then if he sell
> For Half the value, he shall have ready money,
> And I possess his land.'[7]

Sueing *in forma pauperis* (an early version of legal aid) was more effective than Massinger suggested, although it only applied to the common law. The principal sufferers were those who had no security of tenure, and were consequently unprotected by any law. The eviction of such tenants raised a moral rather than a legal question, and each case was individual. Some tenants believed themselves to have a security which neither law nor custom recognized, others were indignant at the shortness of the notice or the triviality of the pretext. Henry Brinkelow leaped to the defence of such victims, complaining 'It is now a common use of the landlords, for every trifle, even for his friend's pleasure, in case his tenant have not a lease, he shall put him out of his farm . . .'.

It is not a complete defence of the landlords to say that, willingly or not, they were constrained to operate within the law; but it does invalidate the suggestion that any significant proportion of them were criminals, having their wicked way by force or fraud. Nor does a conclusion that complaints of depopulation were vastly exaggerated, necessarily mean that rural tensions were artificially whipped up by agitators. The real problem was not the landlord who wanted to convert his arable fields to pasture – the profits of wool were declining after 1550 anyway – but the landlord who wanted to charge an economic rent. Tenements or copyholds for 70 or even 90 years, whose rents had been fixed quarter of a century before, were economic liabilities in a period of inflation. Almost alone among the controversial literature of the period *The Discourse of the Common Weal of England* recognized this fact, and put into the mouth of the knight (one of the characters in the dialogue) a rational defence of such action. Increasing rents, he complained, were commonly blamed for the dearth, but the truth was the other way round.[8] A merchant or craftsman could protect himself by putting up the price of his goods; even a wage labourer could strike a hard bargain, but a landlord living on fixed rents had no remedy. His income stayed the same, while he had to pay more for everything he bought. When leases did fall in, or could be legitimately terminated, rents inevitably rose steeply, a process known as rack-renting. Some landlords undoubtedly exploited the shortage of tenements to extract all, and sometimes more than all, that a farm was worth. But the screams of indignation were not confined to such cases. Many tenants chose to believe that they were entitled to renew their leases at the same rent, because it was 'customary', or with a modest increase on a sum which probably represented no more than a quarter of the return on the land. As with depopulation, so with dearth; the landlords – aristocratic and otherwise – became popular scapegoats for a malaise which was actually rooted in the rising population and debasement of the coinage. It was not moral depravity, nor some aggressive 'spirit of capitalism', but harsh economic reality which drove them to seek an enhanced income from their estates. Customary rents, like the 'just price', belonged to a world of economic stability.

It was the same pressure which led to the erosion of common land. Some part of each manor was waste or common, that is not tilled or lived upon but available to all the homage of the manor for their lawful purposes. Usually this meant the pasturing of beasts or the gathering of fuel. Commons also offered a precarious living to the fringe members of the community, who 'squatted' or built cottages there, and caught rabbits or wildfowl according to the nature of the ground. Although unlawful, if undisturbed for a number of years such cottagers acquired the protection of custom. But common land was vulnerable. If a manor was enclosed by agreement, the common was often included in the division; and although in such cases an 'ancient' cottager would be allowed to retain his cottage, the remainder of his living would disappear. Sometimes also a landlord, enclosing his own demesne, would include a part of the common in lieu of his right on the remainder. This might, or might not, be a fair claim. And of course, any lord enclosing by unity of possession would normally take the common as well, squatters or no squatters. There was probably more justice in complaints of landlords overgrazing commons, abusing their rights and moving boundary fences than there was in any other form of grievance, but it was often the lack of any other opportunity to improve their circumstances which led to such marginal aggression.

Contemporary diagnosis of England's economic woes may have been wildly astray, but the ills themselves were real enough. The food price index, from a base of 100 in 1500, had reached 217 by 1550 and 315 by 1560 before falling back to 298 in the following decade.[9] By the same token the purchasing power of an agricultural worker's wages had sunk by 1559 to 59% of what it had been half a century before. Such figures do not mean quite what they would mean today, because most poor people, particularly in the countryside, grew the bulk of their own food. At the same time only a minority were primarily dependent upon wages, and cheap labour reduced the cost of living of their employers, but the dearth affected everyone from the monarch downward. One of the reasons why the analysts were so confused in the early part of Edward's reign was that there were no visible shortages. Whatever the evils of enclosure, corn was '. . . in a good plenty, the Lord be praised!'. It was this fact as much as anything which fuelled the search for scapegoats, because although dearth itself was depressingly familiar, it was normally associated with harvest failure. With the solitary exception of 1545, every harvest from 1536 to 1548 had been good or very good, and therefore by the best conventional wisdom, food prices should have been low. Instead they were high, and rising. And then England's luck deserted her, or God turned his face away, as some contemporaries alleged. Between 1549 and 1558 six harvests out of nine were bad, and those of 1555 and 1556 were the worst of the century, apart from the disastrous year of 1596. Perhaps it is no coincidence that after 1550 the voices of protest and complaint became increasingly muted. There was no point in railing against the will of God, and even enclosure began to slide down the agenda of *maleficium*. By 1573 Thomas Tusser could find a number of good words to say about it, on the reasonable grounds that it motivated farmers to improve their land, and increase productivity.

'Example by Leicestershire take,
What soil can be better than that
For anything heart can desire?
And yet it doth want ye see what:
Mast, covert, close pasture and wood,
And other things needful as good.

All these do enclosure bring,
Experience teacheth no less,
I speak not to boast of the thing,
But only a truth to express.
Example (if doubt ye do make)
By Suffolk and Essex go take.'[10]

Before the end of the century other voices were advocating farming in severalty as a remedy for dearth, and events were to show that they were nearer to the truth than those who sought to blame the price surge of the mid-century, and its consequent disruption, upon the greed of enclosing landlords.

There was, however, another form of enclosure which had nothing to do with economic pressures, and could not be justified along any of the lines so far explored. Noblemen and gentlemen enclosed land to create deer parks and other pleasure grounds.

Quantitatively such enclosure was insignificant, but it was given a very high profile. In one sense emparkment was a gift to the moralist who wished to create an image of the 'step-lord, the unnatural lord' who abused his rank and social authority; but it was not easy to represent such action as the result of greed, since very little income was to be derived from a park. Nor does it fit very easily into Tawney's 'capitalist' thesis. Parks were a form of conspicuous consumption, very much in the aristocratic tradition of magnificence. Among the most notable emparkers were Henry VIII at Windsor and Nonsuch, Wolsey at Hampton Court and the Duke of Somerset at Savernake Park; all champions of the tenantry and opponents of depopulating enclosure. Such paradoxes were not simply the result of hypocrisy, but of deep-rooted convictions of the privileges of rank. From the point of view of the perpetrators, such actions were not estate management, aggressive or otherwise, but expressions of a life style which they took for granted. Reactions to emparkment varied with the methods adopted. When Sir John Thynne created Longleat, or the Earl of Arundel Fersfield, the dispossessed tenants were offered other lands in exchange, and even if they were not pleased, they had little ground for complaint. At Savernake, the Duke of Somerset's agent observed

> 'The tenants of Wilton should have no manner of common for their rudder beasts in that side, which would have been to their utter undoing. . . . I praye God we may find out land, meadow, and something to satisfy them for that which they shall now forgo . . .'.[11]

Emparkment by compensation was not popular with those affected, but it created no sharp edge of grievance. Other lords were less scrupulous, or more easily misrepresented. Sir John Rodney was alleged to have pulled down several tenements, and seized 200 acres of common land in the creation of Stoke Moor Park; while John Palmer of West Angmering apparently threatened those who sought to oppose him, declaring '. . . now is the time come that we gentlemen will pull down the houses of such poor knaves as ye be'. Such stories need to be treated with scepticism, but parks were generally disliked by the farming community, which is not surprising at a time of land hunger, and tales of oppression were readily invented and believed. After

1550, perhaps under the pressure of rural opinion, but more likely out of increasing economic necessity, more parks were dismantled than were created. Hunting continued to be popular, but it became less fashionable to consume good farmland for such pleasures.

However it had come about – and the massive redistribution of monastic land must have played a part – the English country-side was simmering with discontent by the end of Henry VIII's reign. Violence was never far below the surface of any medieval or early modern society, and by the standards of sixteenth-century Germany or France England was peaceful, but the potentiality for large-scale demonstrations was there, and had probably been there since the 1520s. Nobody liked being taxed, and everybody thought that they were paying more than their fair share. Even at the end of the prosperous fifteenth century the men of Cornwall had been provoked into open revolt by the thought of paying taxes for the defence of the Scottish border. Less violent, but much more widespread and potentially danger-ous was the tax-payers' strike against the Amicable Grant of 1525, an embarrassment brought on by war and Wolsey's clumsiness. The great Northern demonstration of 1536, known as the 'Pilgrimage of Grace', had many causes, but agrarian grievances and resentment against taxation certainly played a large part.[12] Paradoxically, Henry VIII managed to extract much greater sums during the last decade of his reign, in the form of parliamentary subsidies, without arousing the same opposition. This was partly because the country was genuinely convinced of the need for a defensive war, and partly because the aristocracy was busily occupied in promoting it. In fact Henrician tax assessments were reasonably fair and equitable. The poor paid nothing; but revolts and protests are not led by the very poor; they are led by those who are a little poorer than they think they ought to be, and who think that they know the reason why. The removal of Henry's awesome personality, and the continuation of the war with Scotland for reasons which many could not comprehend, began to draw existing grievances to a head in the summer of 1548. There had been no significant deterioration in the economic or social climate since 1545, but changing political and religious circumstances drew them to the surface.

The most important person involved in bringing this about

was Protector Somerset. Somerset took his quasi-regal responsibilities with great seriousness, and accepted the arguments that his clerical and intellectual friends were propounding. In May 1548 he picked up the campaign against enclosures where Wolsey had laid it down twenty years earlier. The royal deer park at Hampton Court was disparked, and a series of Star Chamber judgements enforced the restoration of common rights in a number of test cases. In June a carefully worded proclamation repeated the standard lamentations about men being 'driven to extreme poverty and compelled to leave the places where they were born', and ordered the strict enforcement of all statutes against enclosure for grazing.[13] At the same time a commission was appointed to investigate the situation in the Midlands, and the Protector let it be understood that this was intended to be the first of many. However, he was not carrying his colleagues with him. The council was less than convinced by 'commonwealth' rhetoric, and sensitive to its socially subversive implications. Warwick, Herbert and Paget were all moderate enclosers themselves, trying, as far as we can tell, to make just settlements with their tenants. They and their colleagues were not in the mood for breast beating, and Somerset's commission was not announced. Nevertheless it began work, taking evidence upon oath, and summoning identified offenders before it. Not being a judicial commission, it had no power to do more than insist upon the observance of the existing laws, but it could intimidate and humiliate; and John Hales as its chairman was determined to do just that. After a pause during the winter, Hales recommenced his labours in the summer of 1549, by which time they had begun to assume a somewhat sinister significance which was not lost upon the chairman himself. Feeling assured of the protector's sympathy, some of the aggrieved parties had started taking the law into their own hands. For all their vehemence, this was not at all what the reformers had in mind, and Hales felt constrained to remind his colleagues that they should not 'take upon you to be executors of the statutes; to cut up mens hedges, and to put down their enclosures. . . . Be ye not breakers of the law, while ye go about to have vices reformed by the law'. Meanwhile Somerset had taken the issue to parliament, probably in the hope of getting that solid backing which he could not find in the council. His first measure was a mere gesture; an act to secure in perpetuity the protection of copyholders on his own estates. He may have seen this as a means of establishing his own *bona fides*, but as it affected nobody else, it was quite uncontroversial. The second, passed after a great struggle in March 1549, was an altogether different matter. In view of the financial situation, a demand for a subsidy would have been expected; but what Somerset actually did was to ask for a relief – a 5% tax on personal property – and a special tax on sheep.

Sheep on enclosed land were rated more highly than those on pasture or common, and large flocks more highly than small. The intention was both didactic and disciplinary, and given the composition of the two Houses, it is surprising that it passed at all. But Somerset was determined, and wielded the full authority of his office. 'Maugre the Devil, private profit, self-love, money and such like the Devil's instruments, it shall go forward . . .' he declared. But his success with parliament seems to have blinded him to the reality of the situation. Warning signs were not lacking. There had been an unusually large number of rural riots in the summer of 1548, and in August there was an outbreak in Buckinghamshire, within the orbit of Hales' commission. The Earl of Warwick blamed Hales and his colleagues for stirring up trouble, and other members of the council concurred. Hales responded with precisely the kind of self-righteous reproach most calculated to annoy a nobleman of Warwick's stamp. He was grieved, he said, '. . . that those that seemed to favour God's word should go about to hinder or speak evil of this thing; whereby the end and fruit of God's word, that is love and charity to our poor neighbours, should be so set forth and published to the world'. Whether or not there was any substance in this particular charge, broadly speaking Warwick and his colleagues were right. Somerset's declared policy, and the words and actions of Hales and his 'commonwealth' friends, were raising expectations which could not be fulfilled, given the state of the law and the economic pressures which affected landlords no less than others. At the same time they were encouraging an anti-aristocratic animus which could only undermine the structure of rural government. Whether he liked it or not, Somerset could only rule England with the support of the nobility and gentry. If he continued to use the power of his office to undermine their authority in defence of some intellectual ideal of social justice, there was a real danger that the countryside would

113

become ungovernable. Neither Hales nor Somerset had any such intention, but zeal (which in Somerset's case also seems to have included a generous measure of self-deception) blinded them to the effects of their own words. In 1548 the situation had been contained without too much difficulty, which may have induced a sense of false security, but as the summer of 1549 advanced, it looked as though the whole of southern England was on the point of social and economic disintegration. By July the foreign mercenaries, recruited for the war in Scotland, were being deployed against English rebels; and London was garrisoned and protected with artillery.

Although the troubles were very widespread, only in two areas did they transcend the power of the local authorities to deal with them. Significantly, both those areas had recently lost a dominant noble family. The Marquis of Exeter had been framed on highly dubious charges of treason in 1538, and the fall of the Courtenays had opened the politics of the South-west to a variety of conflicting gentry interests. The destruction of the Howards in 1546 on somewhat more substantial grounds had similarly destabilized East Anglia, and particularly the county of Norfolk. In spite of the crucial role which the Stanleys, the Talbots and the Howards had played in stemming disaffection in the north in 1536, it was generally Tudor policy to rely on gentry networks rather than on noblemen, and the Courtenays (at least) had been partly removed for that purpose. But for such a policy to succeed, it was crucial that crown and gentry interests should continue to coincide, and it was precisely that alliance which Somerset's ostensible idealism had undermined. As a result the gentry temporarily lost control of Devon and Cornwall, and regained it at considerable cost in bloodshed. In East Anglia the position was slightly more complicated, because there was an heir to the Howard ascendancy in the person of the Princess Mary.[14] By 1549 Mary was at loggerheads with the council over religion, and although there is no reason to suppose that she sympathized with the rebels, much less aided them, her extensive affinity was less than eager to leap to the assistance of a beleaguered Protector. Consequently, there is no reason to seek for explanations as to why discontent should have been so much more powerful in the South-west and East Anglia than in the rest of the country. The grievances were much the same everywhere, but there was an element of weakness in the government of those two regions which made them particularly vulnerable.

It is now generally accepted that the main driving force of both rebellions was social and economic discontent, and that it was directed against the local representatives of law and order rather than against the government in London. From the point of view of the council that was an academic distinction, but it mattered a great deal to the rebels themselves. They did not see their action as treasonable, any more than the Pilgrims of 1536 had done. They were full of professions of loyalty to the king, and had no desire to overthrow the Protector. What they were trying to do, in their own eyes at any rate, was to compel their local magistrates to enforce, and to obey themselves, laws which were already on the statute book. Unfortunately they could only do that by assembling together 'riotously and unlawfully', which made it impossible for the Protector do other than move against them with whatever resolution and force he could muster. Some confusion has been caused by the fact that the incidents which initially provoked these risings were very different in nature, and create the appearance of quite different motivation. Norfolk saw a straightforward anti-enclosure riot, directed against a lawyer by the name of Flowerdew, grow within a few days to a mass movement sweeping the countryside around Wymondham and Attleborough. In Devon, on the other hand, the original demonstration had, apparently, nothing to do with enclosure or with any other agrarian grievance. When the new Prayer Book was introduced on Whitsunday, in the village of Sampford Courtenay, near Okehampton, the congregation refused to accept it, and compelled their vicar to say mass in the traditional manner. This strongly religious atmosphere was reinforced shortly afterwards when the protesters drew up their demands, most of which involved the retention of traditional devotional practices. However, recent research has indicated that this appearance of religious fervour was largely created by the fact that the leadership, which in Norfolk was provided by yeomen farmers, in Devon was mainly provided by clergy.[15] The reason for this contrast lay rather in the different structure of rural society in two widely separated parts of England, than in any difference of religious beliefs. Norfolk was one of the richest counties in England, and its grievances were relative, while inland Devon was much poorer, and a good deal of it was remote. Enclosure of commons, which in Norfolk aroused the ire of the moderately well to do, like Robert Kett, in Devon was more likely to drive the poor to desperation. There was considerable hostility between the gentlemen and the commons in both counties, but the commons of Devon probably missed the Courtenay lordship more than those of Norfolk did the Howards. In both areas, too, there were some conservative gentry who sympathized with the demonstrators, but only in remote Cornwall did any of them become actively embroiled.

The only reason why the forces of discontent should have been stronger and more pervasive in 1549 than in 1548 was the increasing conviction that the Protector's good intentions were being frustrated by the agents through whom he was compelled to work. 'It boots not how many laws be made', as one commentator remarked, 'for we see few or none put in execution.' As early as mid-April reports of disorders were reaching the Privy Council, and a month later the troubles had reached a level at which national action was considered to be necessary. The proclamation issued on 23 May was eloquent of the Protector's dilemma.[16] Action was promised against unlawful and depopulating enclosure, but in the meantime 'disobedient and seditious persons, assembling themselves together in some parts of the realm, have most arrogantly and disloyally . . .' presumed to take action themselves, overthrowing pales, hedges and ditches without any commission or authority to do so. Such seditious tumults would be punished in accordance with the law, and justices were instructed to use force to break up unlawful assemblies. In June the Lord Chancellor, Richard Rich, harangued an assembly of justices in London, urging them to do their duty with diligence in order to prevent a dangerous situation from becoming worse. Rich himself then set an excellent example in his home county of Essex, which saw no serious outbreaks thanks to his energetic and effective leadership. Somerset, however, hesitated to move with equal resolution on a wider scale. A further proclamation on 14 June offered pardon to those already in arms, if they would desist and return to their homes; preachers were also sent out to persuade the rioters of the evil of their ways. There were a number of reasons for Somerset's apparent lack of resolution in what was rapidly becoming a very dangerous situation. One was that he accepted the justice of some, at least, of the rebels' complaints. Another was an unjustified faith in his own charisma and powers

of persuasion. It took him some time to accept that the malcontents were not going to be satisfied with his promises of redress,
even if they believed in his honesty in making them. In a sense he
had pledged his credit over the previous twelve months, and he
was understandably reluctant to admit that he could not redeem
the pledge. Being forced into military action on a large scale
would involve a loss of face, and Somerset was very persistent in
his self delusion. Moreover, he did not have much military force
at his command. The Scottish war was going badly, and he was
determined to make another big effort in that direction. The
French were threatening Boulogne, and in August seized the
opportunity presented by the turmoil in England to declare war.
To divert military resources for domestic purposes meant giving
up his ambition for another major campaign in Scotland, and
possibly exposing both Boulogne and Calais to capture by the
French. It was one thing to put on a show of strength to defend
London, but quite another to undertake extensive campaigns in
the Midlands, East Anglia and the South-west.

By July the Protector was being bombarded with good advice,
not only from his fellow councillors, but also from Charles V's
chief minister, Granvelle, via the Imperial ambassador, and the
theme was consistent. A few swift hangings were of more use
than 'ten thousand proclamations and pardons for the quieting
of the people'. If Somerset was unwilling to follow such advice,
others were not. Sir Thomas Wyatt and his fellow justices in
Kent carried out two executions at Ashford as early as 13 May.
Lord Rich did the same in Essex in early July, and one man from
Suffolk was hanged at Tyburn. In Surrey, Buckinghamshire,
Berkshire and Northamptonshire the gentry moved their own
retainers swiftly to counter any riots; there were no executions,
and the levies were not called upon because they were obviously
considered unreliable. The Marquis of Dorset and the Earl of
Huntingdon contained the situation in Leicestershire and Rut-
land at the cost of an unknown, but probably small, number of
lives, while Lincolnshire and Cambridgeshire sent small contin-
gents to join Kett in Norfolk. By a mixture of firmness and
conciliation, the Earl of Arundel defused a potentially explosive
atmosphere in Sussex, and the Earl of Shrewsbury prevented
the southern disorders from spreading into Derbyshire, Shrop-
shire and Nottinghamshire, where his influence was predominant. Only in two counties outside the main rebel areas was

there serious violence. Wiltshire is difficult to assess, because the evidence is scanty, but it appears that a mob attacked Sir William Herbert's park, probably in early July. They chose the wrong man because Sir William did not wait for the law to give him either protection or redress. He confronted the rioters with his own retainers and killed a number, putting the rest to flight. After this sharp lesson the men of Wiltshire showed no disposition to support the rebellion further west. Oxfordshire is better documented, and there the strife was both more general and longer lasting. It was also the only county outside the South-west where conservative clergy are known to have been active among the ringleaders. Probably enclosers had been active in Oxfordshire more recently than in most counties, because a number of more or less simultaneous attacks took place, and a large number of sheep were killed and eaten by the rioters. Somewhat ironically, religiously conservative gentry, such as Sir John Williams and the Dormers, were among the principal victims. Woodstock and Rycot were violently disparked, and many deer were also killed. The situation was virtually out of control when Lord Grey of Wilton moved into the county with 1,500 men on his way to support Lord Russell in the West. He was able to surround and defeat the rebels, who foolishly concentrated to resist him. Some were killed in the fighting, and about 200 captured, of whom at least 13 were executed at various places in the county, by way of example.[17] Grey then went about his business, but not before he had called the principle gentry together, and instilled enough confidence and determination into them, to cope with any resurgence of trouble, but none came.

In the South-west there were two trouble spots. The first was the market town of Bodmin, where a mixed bag of popular grievances was converted into rather aimless action by a group of thoroughly disaffected clergy. This became serious when the sheriff, John Milton, was unable to organize any effective response, and the rebels captured the town of Plymouth. Cornwall had a history of turbulence, based more on its remote location and sense of distinctiveness than on any substantial problems, but the gentry were somewhat divided in their attitude, and in 1549 that meant that the county was soon out of control. The second, and quite independent, focus, as we have seen, was Sampford Courtenay. For some reason which is not immediately obvious, animus against the gentry seems to have been stronger amongst the commons of Devon than almost anywhere else in England, and most unusually the riot at Sampford Courtenay was quickly stained with murder. A gentleman named Hellier, one of those who had attempted to parley with the mob, was hacked to pieces. Groups of rebels then quickly fanned out, sweeping up all sorts of restless malcontents, and soon linked up with the Cornish rebels, who were advancing from Plymouth towards Crediton with a vague intention of marching on London as their grandfathers had done in 1497. By the end of June they were sufficiently organized to send a list of fifteen demands to the council, almost all of which related to the restoration of conservative religious practices. The clerical leadership had succeeded in giving the appearance of cohesion and purpose to an essentially anarchic outburst of rage. Only one demand contained a revealing reference to restricting the number of servants employed by the gentry. There were widespread attacks on property, particularly on property owned by gentlemen who had moved into the area following purchases of former monastic lands; but enclosures were not particularly singled out, perhaps because they were few. Robert Whiting's recent study of popular religion in the area has pointed out that only a very small proportion of the adult male population was actually involved in the rising, but the use of conservative religious language and imagery created a widely sympathetic context, and made it much more difficult for the local authorities to deal with it.[18] The principal landowner was John Lord Russell, who had also been for a while after 1539 president of the somewhat shadowy council in the West, however he was both a newcomer and an absentee, and had never been able to assume the mantle of the Courtenays as Henry VIII had presumably intended. There were, however, a few reliable gentry families with court connections and enough local presence to give a lead against the rebels, if they could be suitably directed and supported. The most obvious were the Carews, but neither Sir Gawain nor his nephew Sir Peter was in Devon in June 1549. Sir Peter was summoned from his wife's estates in Lincolnshire, and in the middle of June, before the rebels' formal demands had been received, they were both sent down to Exeter.

Somerset, who may not have been very fully informed of the extent of the trouble, was still thinking of conciliation rather than confrontation. The Carews were instructed to negotiate, and to persuade the insurgents to disperse peacefully. Presumably it was hoped that scattered and demoralized gentry would also rally to them and give them enough substance to negotiate from a position of strength. The mission was a complete failure. Not only did the rebels refuse to disperse without the satisfaction of their demands, but one of Carew's servants set fire to a barn near the spot at which the parley was taking place, causing a panic which nearly set off a full-scale battle. Within a few days rebel bands controlled the whole county up to the walls of Exeter, and Sir Peter Carew returned to London to report at first hand on the rapidly deteriorating situation. The council had, in fact, already decided to send down John Lord Russell, but whether on account of Somerset's self-deceived optimism, or because no adequate force could be mustered, the instructions issued to him on 24 June did not differ greatly from those of Carew. Russell set out with a wholly inadequate force, and encountered Carew on the way. Being under no illusions about the weakness of his position, he proceeded with extreme caution, eventually setting up his headquarters at Mohun's Ottery, a house belonging to Sir Peter Carew, between 30 June and 2 July. By this time even the Protector was convinced that military action would be necessary, and reinforcements were despatched, including some German mercenaries. Owing to the disturbed state of the rest of the country, however, and the limited nature of the government's resources, they were painfully slow to assemble. Meanwhile, Russell would do nothing, and Exeter was under close siege. It was not until 12 July that Russell was authorized to raise 4,000 footmen, and Grey's force, as we have already seen, was delayed in Oxfordshire. Between 8 and 11 July no less than three proclamations were issued offering pardon to those who returned immediately to their homes, the last also threatening martial law against those who remained under arms. By 18 July the council considered that its commander in the South-west had adequate force to confront the rebels, and began to be exasperated by his inactivity. In fact Russell was elderly, and had never been a very skilful soldier, a fact of which Somerset was perfectly well aware. But he had been chosen for this mission because of his position and not because of his effectiveness. From 24 July onwards the council sought to drive him forward with a mixture of encouragement and rebuke. On 27 July he began to move towards Exeter, and on the following day fought an engagement with the rebels at Fenny Bridges. This was short, but sharp, and the insurgents were forced to retreat after suffering some 300 casualties. In spite of this Russell would probably have halted his advance if he had been left to his own devices, because of his concern over threats to his lines of communication. However by this time he had been joined by the tough and experienced Grey, whose positive counsel was strongly supported by the Carews. On 3 August he resumed his advance, encountering the main rebel host at Clyst St Mary on the following day. Twenty-four hours of fierce and confused fighting followed. Many were killed in the field, and prisoners taken by the royal army were executed out of hand. Because of the superior armament and discipline of their troops, Russell and Grey were completely victorious. Humphrey Arundell, the rebel captain, drew off the battered remains of his forces to the West, and the siege of Exeter was raised. Having achieved his main objective, the Lord Privy Seal then relapsed into querulous inactivity, and it was not until 18 August that Arundell was finally defeated, and his forces destroyed, appropriately enough at Sampford Courtenay.

It had been a messy and brutal campaign, and in London the relief was tempered with acute dissatisfaction. Mopping up operations resulted in minor massacres at Launceton in Cornwall and King's Weston in Somerset, and numerous executions under martial law. More seriously, once he felt himself to be secure, Russell began to conduct himself with a high hand. His provost marshall, Sir Anthony Kingston, went through Cornwall like an avenging angel; property was confiscated and redistributed without due process of law, and Russell ignored all instructions to disband the bulk of his forces. Perhaps as many as 4,000 died, directly or indirectly, for their part in the rebellion. For Somerset, this was a political disaster. He was equally discredited with those who had looked to him for redress, and with those who thought it his duty to uphold the law. He had failed to persuade the malcontents to trust him, and he had failed to control his agents in the area. It would be many years before the men of Devon and Cornwall would again venture to challenge the government in arms, but the 'wonderful hate against gentlemen' was not appeased. The city of Exeter benefited from its stout resistance, but the countryside was demoralized and resentful. The rebels had called upon God in their own way, and He had not responded. There was not much left but sullen acquiescence.

In Norfolk the disturbances took place at almost exactly the same time, but without any show of religious grievance. This was a county with many small freeholders, and the conversion of tillage to pasture was not the main problem. Much more serious was the enclosure of common land, which left the small freeholders without adequate grazing, and the engrossing of estates which were already pasture to produce very large sheep ranches. Unlike Devon, the local magistrates of Norfolk were mostly resident, and belonged to families with their roots in the county. The social friction, which had become evident as early as 1540, was consequently not the result of feeling exploited by strangers, but rather of constant abrasive competition. The gentleman had too many well-connected friends, he was literate and probably had a smattering of law. In fact he had too heavy a punch for the majority of yeomen farmers, even if they acted in concert, and it was this feeling that the odds were stacked in his favour which made the gentleman so unpopular. All too often, as a Justice of the Peace, he was prosecutor and judge in his own cause, and there was little confidence that either Somerset or the council would be able to clip his wings. As Norfolk was a prosperous county there were also a number of yeomen on the fringes of gentry status, some of whom endeavoured to ape the manners of their social superiors in order to become acceptable, and others were bitterly resentful at being excluded from functions to which their wealth alone might have entitled them. It was along this fringe that the trouble in Norfolk first developed, with a certain wry humour not seen anywhere in the South-west. Edward Flowerdew was a lawyer and minor gentleman, who had secured some of the lands of Wymondham Abbey from the crown and had carried out a number of enclosures. On 6 and 7 July there was a traditional summer gathering at Wymondham. This had originally been connected with the translation of Thomas Becket, but by 1549 seems to have become entirely secular and social. Inspired by the courage of numbers, and possibly fortified with ale, a number of the participants went over to Hethersett, about five miles away, and threw down some of Flowerdew's fences. He was too sensible to resist, and, understanding the mood of his assailants, persuaded them with small coins, and possibly more ale, to divert their attentions to the neighbouring enclosures of Robert Kett, with whom he was not on good terms.[19] Kett, however, turned the tables on him. Professing the greatest contrition for what he had done, he not only assisted the crowd to demolish his own enclosures, he then placed himself at their head, and returned to Flowerdew's land to finish the job.

Probably Kett allowed his hatred for Flowerdew – a neighbour who was just ahead in the competition for gentry status – to trap him in a situation from which he could not escape. The news of his leadership and dramatic change of heart flashed around the countryside and malcontents began to flock to Wymondham. Within a couple of days he had a force of several hundred men, armed with improvised weapons, and had little choice but to allow them a free hand against any enclosures within reach, including the charitable estates of the city of Norwich. By that time Kett could not turn back. He was already the leader of a riotous assembly, and his only chance of emerging unscathed lay in converting his unruly followers into a disciplined demonstration, which could then appeal to the Protector and council for the proper enforcement of the law. On 12 July the rebel camp was established on Mousehold Heath, and recruits came flocking in from all over Norfolk, together with many from the Beccles-Bungay area of Suffolk.[20] The speed and strength with which the movement gathered pace, and the large number of places throughout East Anglia in which it found echo and imitation, prove beyond doubt the strength of the feeling which existed. This fury seems to have taken everybody by surprise, including Kett. The sheriff, Sir Edward Windham, was almost captured when he endeavoured to persuade the demonstrators to disperse. The city of Norwich, totally unprepared for defence, warned the council of what was afoot, and maintained the best relations which it could with its dangerous new neighbour on Mousehold. As Kett's force grew, and his ability to control and administer so large a gathering became apparent, a curious atmosphere of unreality prevailed. There was virtually no local opposition. A few gentlemen were arrested, and others forced to contribute to the victualling of the camp, but there was no organized response from the justices of the county. Sympathizers within Norwich admitted the rebels, contrary to the intentions of the mayor, Thomas Codd and his brethren. These magistrates were ostensibly placed under arrest, but were soon deeply involved in advising Kett how to act. It seems that there was a serious intention to engage the council in peaceful dialogue, and the major efforts made by Kett and others to maintain good discipline should be seen in that context.

Within a few days of the establishment of the camp, about 17 or 18 of July a citizen of Norwich, one Leonard Sotherton, was sent to London bearing a petition to the Lord Protector which contained 27 hastily drafted articles. The tone of this petition was much more conciliatory than the 'demands' framed by the clergy of Devon, perhaps because of the influence of Codd. Half the articles were concerned with agrarian grievances, mostly common rights and copyhold rents, while others condemned the sale of wardships, clerical non-residence and the shortage of preachers. Insofar as they touched upon religion, they were sympathetic to the protector's policy, rather than the reverse, but this may have been a mere gesture to engage his sympathy. The principal target was the manorial lord who was endeavouring to exercise his rights in buying and selling land, exploiting fishing and keeping sheep and cattle. Nostalgia for a non-existent past, and a vaguely conceived desire for the king to intervene directly in social relationships, are the main characteristics of this document. Animus against the gentry is muted. Much stronger expressions of opinion were recorded both before and after the rising. In 1540 one John Walker of Griston had declared that there should be 'only as many gentlemen in Norfolk as there (be) white bulls . . .', while a decade later Robert Burnham expressed the view that there were 'too many gentlemen in England by five hundred'.[21] In contrast to Devon, no personal violence had been offered, and even attacks on property were limited to the destruction of hedges and fences. However, if this restraint was a strategy designed to draw a more favourable response from the council, it did not work. On 21 July the response came in the person of a herald who offered a general pardon in return for dispersal. As there was no attempt to address the petition, Kett refused. He could hardly have done otherwise if he had wished to retain any credibility; nevertheless, his action marked a turning point. As soon as it was known, the council decided to move from conciliation to intimidation. William Parr, Marquis of Northampton, was despatched with a hastily assembled force of about 1,800 men, including a contingent of Italian mercenaries. Parr's instructions were to cut off the rebels' supplies, and then to negotiate.

Parr did neither of those things. Arriving on 30 July, he promptly occupied Norwich, which had been virtually neutral territory. Kett, who by this time had some 10,000 men under his command, could not ignore such provocation. He counterattacked and, in two days of bitter house to house fighting, drove the royal forces out. There could now be no turning back. All the restraint and careful discipline; the attempts to maintain the facade of peaceful petitioning; all had been wasted. It had been Parr's incompetence rather than Somerset's aggression which had forced the issue, but probably such an outcome was inevitable. Whatever the citizens of Norwich might think, no Tudor government could have regarded the camp on Mousehold as anything other than a rebellion, and reacted accordingly. By 3 August the council was dealing with a crisis. Northampton was retreating towards London, having suffered heavy losses, and the whole of Norfolk was effectively in rebel hands. How much longer they would continue to exercise restraint over personal violence was unpredictable. A major military campaign was now imperative and urgent, while the operation in Devon still hung in the balance. Somerset should probably have commanded this army in person if he wished to recover the political ground which he had lost during the summer, but he did not do so, perhaps because he wished to distance himself from the bloodshed and the brutal punishments which would inevitably follow. The protector was not squeamish; he had demonstrated that in the Lowlands of Scotland, but he still believed that he could retain some credentials as a social reformer. In pursuing that will o' the wisp, he sacrificed his last chance to recover the confidence of his colleagues, and by appointing the Earl of Warwick to go in his place, handed his erstwhile friend a political ace. If Somerset hoped that Warwick might suffer the fate of Northampton, he was soon disappointed. The Earl moved with speed and efficiency. The border garrisons were depleted, and all the gentry of East Anglia were ordered by proclamation to join him in arms with their retainers. On 23 August he reached Intwood, just outside Norwich, with 6,000 foot and 1,500 horse. Warwick made an immediate, and perhaps somewhat formal, attempt to negotiate, but by this time Kett's men were in an ugly mood, and he had lost his control over them.

Not being a soldier, he did not know how to handle such a situation; while Warwick, having made his gesture, prepared for an all out attack.

On 24 August he moved into Norwich, but unlike Parr, he did so in adequate strength and with great effectiveness. The rebel troops were driven out in hand to hand fighting, and over 50 prisoners were hanged. The city was then garrisoned and supplies to the camp on Mousehold cut off. Perhaps for that reason, or perhaps from sheer inexperience, on 26 August Kett abandoned his fortified camp and descended to a nearby valley. Having his enemies now at his mercy, Warwick again offered pardon. Perhaps he was not trusted, or perhaps the rebels had fortified themselves with dreams and prophecies, but the offer was rejected, and on 27 August the Earl attacked, using mainly his German mercenaries and his cavalry. The result was not a battle but a slaughter. Over 3,000 men perished on this unknown field of 'Dussindale', and the last major revolt of a desperate summer had been crushed. Unlike Russell in the West, Warwick administered the inevitable punishments in Norfolk with moderation, and in strict conformity to the law. That did not mean that the toll was light; some 600 died on the gallows. But the propensity of the Norfolk gentlemen to take revenge upon those who they had failed to resist was effectively curbed. In the end Norfolk cost as much blood as Devon, although at first it had seemed as though the protests were framed in a very different spirit. In the end, there could be no such thing as peaceful protest, least of all for those outside, or on the fringes of, the political nation. The riots and risings of 1549 were not a cry of despair from a hopeless and exploited peasantry, but the anger of men who felt that what they held by law and custom was being eroded, and who thought that they had been given promises of adequate protection. As Jeremy Bentham was to observe, no pain is keener than the pain of disappointed expectation. The main responsibility for that lay not with an acquisitive and unprincipled aristocracy, who seem to have been no worse and no better than in most generations, but with those idealists who believed that they could transform human behaviour by appeals to conscience and to Christian principles. Somerset for his own reasons accepted many of their arguments at face value, and in so doing turned a harmless moral and literary fashion into a potentially explosive ideology. The blood of Dussindale, of

Sampford Courtenay and of Oxfordshire was the price – a price which the protector also eventually paid himself.

After 1549 the actual condition of rural society deteriorated rather than improving. The harvests, which had been consistently good for over a decade, were deficient in most of the next ten years, greatly exacerbating the dearth. And the Earl of Warwick, effectively in charge of the government from October 1549, made no attempt to sustain his predecessor's anti-enclosure initiative. Realistically if not very equitably, the council under his leadership concentrated on maintaining order by the traditional means of enlisting the support of the gentry. Sir Thomas Wyatt, arguing for a select militia under aristocratic control observed

'. . . touching the people alone, of themselves either they stir not, or if they do their fury faileth with a little delay of time . . . . Without order they rise and without order they are quieted, and all their blaze is soon up, soon down.'[22]

Warwick seems to have read Wyatt's proposal with sympathy, but he did not adopt it. Instead he reverted to the old procedure of licensing trusted noblemen and gentlemen to arm their retainers, experimenting with the idea of doing this at the king's expense, a scheme which had to be abandoned after about a year because of the cost. Mary also used licensed retaining, and the cause was the same in both reigns; fear of rebellion. Throughout the years from 1550 to 1558 the records of the Privy Council are littered with references to real or imagined 'tumults'. In the summer of 1550 there were disturbances in Essex and Sussex, and the Imperial ambassador reported that the whole realm suffered from a great malaise, which would erupt as soon as the harvest was in. He was mistaken, partly because he listened to too many rumours, and partly because he wished to believe that a heretical government of which he thoroughly disapproved was about to be overthrown. Under Mary both the French and Imperial ambassadors reported endless conspiracies, the first because he wanted them to happen, and the second because he feared them. Under Edward such sedition was believed to be the work of 'papists', and under Mary of heretics. The truth seems to have been that after the climactic years of 1548 and 1549 social and economic tensions returned to their high, but not explosive, level. Aristocratic authority had survived the crisis, because in truth there was no alternative, and the outbursts of those years were negative rather than positive. Revolution was not on the agenda. After 1550 the 'commonwealth' men lost their influence in high politics, reverting to their earlier role as a social conscience which could act as a form of harmless propitiation. By 1565 even the pulpits no longer echoed to the subversive rhetoric of Hugh Latimer. Faced with the choice between a 'just' society and an orderly one, neither Warwick, nor Mary, nor Elizabeth hesitated. Only Somerset had believed that he could have it both ways, and the events of 1549 proved him wrong.

In one sense, perhaps the protector was just unlucky, because although harvest failure may be a great stimulus to discontent, widespread famine and disease tend to have the opposite effect. Warwick faced the consequences of three bad harvests in a row, from 1549 to 1551, and by the latter year conditions in some areas were extremely difficult. However, one of the consequences of malnutrition is reduced resistance to infection, and a widespread epidemic of the sweating sickness effectively took the edge off popular agitation and riotous assembly. Six years later the same situation confronted Mary, in an aggravated form. The disastrous harvests of 1555 and 1556 brought on an influenza epidemic of major significance. Nationally the population may have dropped by as much as 5% between 1556 and 1561, and this not only had a most debilitating effect upon England's capacity to wage its war with France, it also pulled the plug on any possibility of domestic upheaval, whether for economic or any other reason. Had the harvests of 1547 and 1548 been equally bad, Somerset might have survived, for all his political ineptitude.

# III

## THE CHURCH

# 5

## POLICY AND DOCTRINE

Of the three major changes which were to affect the English Church during the sixteenth century, two had already taken place before 1540. The Royal Supremacy, which replaced the traditional jurisdiction of the pope with that of the king, had been created by legislation between 1532 and 1536. The smaller monasteries had been dissolved by the same means in 1536, and the larger houses had surrendered piecemeal over the following four years. The last, Waltham Abbey in Essex, had closed its doors on 23 March 1540, bringing to an end a thousand years of continuous religious practice. The result was a church both unique and isolated. During the last ten years of his reign Henry VIII was excommunicated and his realm in schism; but apart from a brief diplomatic flirtation represented by the Cleves marriage (1539–40), no bridges were built to the developing evangelical churches of Germany, let alone to the reformed communities of Zurich or Strasburg. Many such connections existed, but at a personal not at an official level. Henry had no time for Luther, and had probably never heard of Bullinger or Calvin; while they in turn had little sympathy with a king who, for all his anti-papalism, had ordered the executions of Thomas Bilney and Robert Barnes. The admirers of this first Anglican settlement, such as Stephen Gardiner, described it as catholic and reformed. Neither monasticism nor papal authority, they argued, were essential to the true faith. The former was an optional discipline, long since discredited by many abuses both moral and financial, and the latter was a confidence trick, played upon a gullible church in the early Middle Ages by a gang of unscrupulous Italian priests. A true church was one in which

131

jurisdiction belonged to a Godly prince, and in which the sacraments, particularly the central rite of the mass, were properly administered. Thomas Cromwell, who had engineered most of the changes of the 1530s, hotly denied that he was a sacramentarian[1] and was never accused of fully-fledged protestantism, but he was nevertheless far from orthodox by traditional standards, and his influence with the king was great. It was thanks to him that the attacks of reformers such as Hugh Latimer upon the doctrine of purgatory were translated into action. Starting in 1535 the great pilgrimage shrines were demolished and their cults denounced. Thanks to him also Archbishop Cranmer's vision of an authorized vernacular bible was brought to fruition in 1538. However, the ultimate arbiter of orthodoxy was Henry himself, who in 1545 informed his subjects that if they knew of any who taught false doctrine, they were to come and tell him or one of his council.

The king's doctrine, although he would certainly not have admitted it, was a mixture of tradition, learning and convenience. He remained totally committed to the mass in all its forms, and to the catholic positions on sacrifice and transubstantiation. On purgatory he was inconsistent, maintaining the efficacy of prayers for the dead, but abandoning his faith in pilgrimages and all that went with them. A humanist education inclined him towards the English Bible, more sermons and an emphasis upon education, whilst self-interest prompted him to accept the cases against monasticism and the papacy. The former gave him a great deal of land and money, while the latter enabled him to resolve his 'Great Matter', and gain a whole field of patronage and jurisdiction. However, because it was personal, the doctrine of the English Church also underwent several shifts of emphasis after the Royal Supremacy was established. In 1537, when the king was in an evangelical mood, he permitted a set of articles to be issued (although not in his name), which came close to a Lutheran position on the sacraments.[2] Two years later, alarmed by the radicalism of some of the preachers who were appearing in London, he encouraged parliament to reaffirm a strongly conservative position in the Act of Six Articles, and forced two of his more outspoken reforming bishops to resign. On at least two occasions after 1536 he contemplated re-opening negotiations with Rome, and failed to do so for practical diplomatic reasons, not as far as we can tell, on principle. For similarly practical reasons, in 1546 the French ambassador declared that Henry was trying to persuade his own master, Francis, to join him in replacing the mass with a communion service. If he had abandoned his life-long devotion to the mass, he failed to remove a large endowment for trentals from his will; and the likeliest explanation for this suggestion (if it was ever made) was simply to open a breach between France and the Curia. From 1539 to 1543 the king's stance was relatively conservative. Bible reading was discouraged, except among the aristocracy, and the 'King's Book' maintained all the seven traditional sacraments. However, during the last four years of his life he moved back towards the reforming sympathies of the 1530s, and this had major implications for the minority goverment which was to follow.

In 1544 the household of Prince Edward, who had been born in 1537, was reorganized, and formal arrangements made for his education. Richard Cox became his almoner, with the chief responsibility for supervising his studies, and John Cheke, the young Regius professor of Greek from Cambridge became his tutor. Various other specialist teachers were appointed slightly later, including a Frenchman, Jacques Belmain, to give the boy a native fluency in that language. It used to be thought that Henry's last queen, Catherine Parr, was largely responsible for these arrangements, and that they reflected her reforming sympathies. However, it is now clear that Catherine was both less educated and less influential than was supposed.[3] She only began to learn Latin after her marriage to the king, and although her evangelical piety was genuine enough, she had little or no influence over her imperious husband. Henry arranged his son's education himself, and it is therefore particularly interesting that the whole team which he chose consisted of reformers who subsequently became outspoken protestants. Belmain, later a stern Calvinist, was probably a protestant already. Since the king allowed the unfortunate Anne Askew to be tortured and executed for heresy as late as 1546, it seems unlikely that he was deliberately allowing Edward to be brought up as a protestant. The reforming party – the ideological heirs of Thomas Cromwell – enjoyed an increasing ascendency at court after 1543. Henry's favourite soldiers, Edward Seymour, Earl of Hertford, and John Dudley, Viscount Lisle, were of that party; so, too, was Sir Anthony Denny, the influential chief gentleman of the Privy Chamber, and Archbishop Thomas Cranmer. None of these men could be described as protestants before 1547. They seem to have paced their convictions by the king's tolerance, and Henry, who was a supreme egotist, probably believed that they would continue to do so after he was dead. In other words, he believed that he was establishing a humanist and evangelical church which would stabilize and perpetuate his own distinctive brand of reformed orthodoxy into the foreseeable future. Perhaps he also believed that that was the best way of securing the royal supremacy against popish subversion in the event of Edward succeeding as a minor.

If that was his intention, he miscalculated, but no more seriously than he did in making provision for the secular government. When Edward Seymour became protector and Duke of Somerset, the implications were as profound for the Church as they were for the state. Within a few weeks, Somerset and Cranmer began to move cautiously in a protestant direction. How far this had been planned in advance it is difficult to say. Cranmer had never been an orthodox archbishop. Secretly married before his elevation, he had immediately repudiated his oath to the pope, and had privately, in correspondence with the king, expressed the view that ordination was no more than an ecclesiastical custom. There was nothing heretical about vernacular scriptures until they were condemned by the Council of Trent, nor about the English litany which he had written in 1544. On the Eucharist, which was central to Henry's personal piety, Cranmer was a catholic until 1548, and if he had embraced justification by faith alone before 1547, he had kept very quiet about it. Nevertheless the promptness with which the first moves were made suggests that they must have been part of a prepared plan. In February, Cranmer petitioned for a new commission, as though his office had lapsed with the death of the late king. That was the case with all secular offices, but had never been applied to the episcopate. The conservative Gardiner was outraged, claiming that a bishop was an Ordinary, that is, one whose powers depended upon his consecration and not upon his appointment.[4] Cranmer took the opposite view, as being more consistent with the king's spiritual authority, and the commissions were granted. At about the same time, in his coronation sermon, the archbishop also made it clear that he saw the role of the Church as one of teaching and admonition, with no power to control the monarch however far he might stray from the path of righteousness.[5] Cranmer's very exalted view of the Royal Supremacy must have been calculated with the intention of using that authority to bring about for the first time an explicit and fundamental revision of the doctrine of the English Church. This began to happen with the issue of a book of homilies, or model sermons, in July 1547. Several of these were written by the archbishop himself, including that on justification, which was fully protestant in the Lutheran sense. Gardiner was once again swift to protest, pointing out (quite correctly) that the orthodox doctrine of the English Church was enshrined in the Act of Six Articles, and that justification by faith alone was an unlawful teaching. At the same time a royal visitation was held, and it was decreed that the *Paraphrases* of Erasmus should be placed in every church. Gardiner and Edmund Bonner, the Bishop of London, objected to the visitation and were imprisoned.

It soon transpired that the archbishop's conservative opponents were in a cleft stick, because what parliament had given, parliament could also take away. The session which lasted from 4 November to 24 December 1547 not only repealed the Act of Six Articles, it also swept away the Henrician treason laws and the statute *De Haeretico Comburendo*. Henceforth bishops were to be appointed by Letters Patent, confirming the initiative which Cranmer had taken earlier in the year, and an Act of Henry's last parliament for the dissolution of chantries was revived in a new form. Gardiner and his supporters were left baffled and apprehensive. They could hardly object to the Chantries Act, since it did no more than implement that of 1545, but the new preamble condemning all prayers for the dead as unprofitable superstition, would hardly have pleased Henry, and indicated a new ideological thrust to what was otherwise an act of old-fashioned acquisitiveness. Gardiner was released from prison under a general pardon of January 1548, and forced to rethink the basis of his opposition. He was rapidly becoming convinced that the Royal Supremacy, which he had helped to create, was being hijacked by a gang of heretics. No longer able to plead statute, he fell back on discretion. No change of importance should be made while the king was a minor, not because of any inadequacy in his authority, but simply to avoid confusion and embarrassment if the adult man turned out to have different opinions from the mentors of his youth. Moreover, it would present the papists with valuable propaganda if it began to appear that the Royal Supremacy would mean a change of religion with every change of monarch. These arguments were forcefully expressed, but they were based upon opinion and not law. In the first session of Edward's first parliament, Somerset had cleared the way for change, but in terms of positive action had not gone beyond the homilies of the summer. Perhaps he was testing the water. If so, the reaction must have been encouraging. An enormous surge of protestant writing flooded from the London presses, beginning even before the law was relaxed. Some of it was a good deal too radical for the protector's liking; but that was a small price to pay for the clear indication that protestant reforms would command a lot of articulate and committed support.[6] On the other side, Gardiner was not exactly a solitary voice – he was backed by a number of other conservative bishops – but there were few signs that the lay aristocracy would go out of its way to defend traditional doctrine.

Although it did not represent any new principle, the Chantries Act of 1547 was an important instrument of change. Unlike the dissolution of the monasteries, the confiscation of these small endowments got right inside the life of the ordinary parish church. Perpetual chantries had been in decline for some years – the peak of their popularity had been in the previous century – but smaller endowments for obits, lights and altar furnishings, were still being given in large numbers in the early 1540s. In 1535 there had been 36 foundations in Lincoln Cathedral, but the pre-dissolution survey of 1548 found only 11. Some may well have been concealed, or their funds redistributed to avoid the commissioners, but evidence from other areas also suggests that chantries were rapidly disappearing from the ecclesiastical scene before 1547. As many as 3,000 may have survived to be dissolved, along with some 90 colleges and 110 hospitals, but by far the largest number of confiscations would have come from minor parish pieties – the gifts of the poor.[7] Commissioners sat in every county, and were by no means arbitrary or unsympathetic in their dealings. Where chantry chapels had become necessary chapels of ease in large parishes, they were often allowed to continue; schools were refounded in the king's name when the foundations to which they had been attached disappeared; and where endowments had been redirected to parish purposes, these arrangements were often accepted. Nevertheless the disruption was considerable, and the message of impending religious change clear for all to read. The minor rites and cere-monies which had characterized the daily round of the parish church were now under threat, not just from royal com-missioners looking for money and objects of value, but from earnest reformers to whom they represented superstition. The endowments of the more substantial foundations were in lands, and for the most part these were kept in the hands of the crown. At first the universities feared that the endowments of their colleges were at risk, since they had also originally served a religious purpose, but it appears that no such attack was ever intended, and that the personal intercession of the Protector which was once thought to have saved them was a subsequent invention.[8] In fact the Chantries Act was more significant as a gesture of reform than it was as an act of plunder.

By the beginning of 1548 the council had realized that it would have to exert itself to control the pace as well as the direction of change. The signals which had already been sent out had proved more than sufficient for some ardent souls. Not only was the mass being violently attacked in print, but there had been a number of instances of iconoclasm in and around London. On 16 January 1548 a deliberate dampener was placed on this enthusiasm in a proclamation which carefully defended such traditional practices as the Lenten fast, and insisted upon its observance in the forthcoming season. The repeal of the Act of Six Articles had left the Church without any authoritative statement of doctrine, and although parliament had authorized communion in both kinds, the council was careful to point out that the doctrine of transubstantiation remained in place unless or until some official pronouncement was made to the contrary. According to his later testimony, it was at this time that Cran-mer was struggling with his own conscience over the question of the Eucharistic presence; and the rather futile finger wagging of several successive proclamations between January and March may reflect that fact. Having admitted that the matter was under consideration at the highest level, the council tried to suppress public debate, on the grounds that 'every man fantasy-ing and devising a sundry way by himself in the use of this most blessed sacrament' would lead to strife and disorder. Another equally contentious issue was the use of images. The reforms of the mid–1530s had removed those images which were being 'most notoriously abused', particularly those associated with shrines, but exactly what constituted superstitious use had never been defined, and there were many skirmishes between conservatives and reformers in the latter days of Henry's reign. The Edwardian council, as might be expected, took a strict view, and on 11 February 1548 instructed the archbishop to proceed with the removal of all images from churches and chapels throughout the kingdom. Given the centuries of custom which lay behind their use, the banishment or destruction of these familiar objects caused remarkably little stir. In most London parishes they had long since gone, mocked into oblivion by Bishop Barlow's famous iconoclastic sermon of 27 November 1547. Conservatives, like the Yorkshire priest Robert Parkyn, grumbled vigorously, but in general compliance was swift. If the defence of images played any significant part in the disturbances of the following summer, remarkably little was said about it on either side.[9]

By April the council was under attack from both sides. Cranmer was already heading a special committee instructed to produce a definitive new liturgy, and until that committee reported, there was little to be done except to dampen down the fires of controversy. On 24 April, in a proclamation denouncing unfounded and seditious rumours, the council inhibited all preaching until further notice, except for such clergy as might be licensed by the king, the protector or the Archbishop of Canterbury. However, the licensed clergy proved to be no more responsible or restrained than the others. Abuse of the Mass continued, and on 23 September all preaching without exception was forbidden until the archbishop's new liturgy should be unveiled. Meanwhile, Cranmer was seeking to broaden his approach. So far reform in England had proceeded on its own idiosyncratic way, owing more to the king, and to political leaders like Thomas Cromwell, than to the contemporary protestant movements of the Continent. As long as Henry VIII had been alive, that had been inevitable; but the developments which had taken place since his death had made closer relationships both possible and desirable. Cranmer had enough strategic sense to realize that division was the great enemy of the reformation, and that although the Schmalkaldic League could provide a political voice for German Lutheranism, no comparable organization embraced all protestants. By bringing England into the protestant camp, he hoped to provide both cohesion and leadership. In order to do this, and to strengthen his own position, he endeavoured to attract as many prominent theologians from the different reformed traditions as might be prepared to visit England. Up to a point, circumstances conspired to favour him. Martin Luther had died in February 1546, and thereafter no one enjoyed his unchallenged ascendancy. Moreover in April 1547 Charles V defeated the Schmalkaldic League at the battle of Muhlberg and destroyed its organization. As a direct result the Augsburg Interim was signed in May 1548, and several prominent reformers from the Rhineland became fugitives. On the other hand these misfortunes helped to tie down Luther's principal heir, Philip Melanchthon, in such a manner that he felt it impossible to leave Germany without abdicating his responsibilities. Consequently, in spite of repeated efforts on Cranmer's part, Melanchthon did not come to England; but Peter Martyr and Martin Bucer, men of equal stature in a different tradition, did come, and occupied the Regius chairs of Divinity at the Universities of Oxford and Cambridge respectively. For some five years England was also a place of refuge, and alien congregations were established, both in London, and at the dissolved Abbey of Glastonbury. All this fell far short of Cranmer's ecumenical vision, but it did mean that Continental influences were being brought to bear by direct personal contact at the most sensitive and formative phase of English protestantism.

Such influences did not, however, appear at once. When Cranmer unveiled his new liturgy before parliament in December 1548, it had a very moderate and conservative appearance. Basically a translation of the Sarum Use, its main novelty lay in its language, and in a few significant changes, such as the omission of the elevation of the host. The language of the central rite, the Eucharist, was ambiguous. Cranmer was a fine liturgical scholar, and had used a number of formulae, both ancient and modern, in the preparation of his text,[10] but at the time his work was more welcome to the politicians than it was to the theologians. It probably represented what he thought he could get away with rather than what he wanted to do. Parliament accepted it, and the first Act of Uniformity ordered its exclusive use from Whitsun 1549. When they looked at it closely, Cranmer's reforming friends were less happy than his conservative opponents. Stephen Gardiner declared that he could use it without violation to his conscience, while John Hooper, the chief protagonist of Zurich theology in England, pronounced it to be full of imperfections and dregs of popery. When it was introduced, the main objections were simply to its unfamiliarity; 'like a Christmas game' the Cornish rebels called it for no very substantial reason. Conservative priests hated it, and were full of ingenuity in their ways of disguising the communion as a Mass. They muttered, instead of speaking aloud as the rubrics enjoined them, so that the congregation could not tell what language was being used. They used all the traditional liturgical gestures, again contrary to the rubrics, and did not admit the laity to the communion. Throughout the autumn and winter of 1549 episcopal visitations endeavoured to root out these abuses, and in spite of the violent objections in Devon and Cornwall, or the loss of momentum which was occasioned by the fall of Somerset in October, a very high degree of acceptance was achieved. However much Swiss students like Conrad ab Ulmis might complain about the shortcomings of the Anglican Church, by the end of 1549 it was protestant in doctrine and usage. The parliament which met on 4 November removed all positive laws against clerical marriage, and decreed that all ecclesiastical courts should be held in the king's name.

Positive enthusiasm for the new order was limited. As early as March 1549 the judicious Dryander, writing to Heinrich Bullinger in Zurich, declared that religion was truly established, but that Cranmer was deliberately refraining from too specific a definition of doctrine, concentrating instead upon public worship, 'many puerilities are suffered to remain, lest the people should be offended by too great an innovation'.[11] The following May Martin Bucer was more pessimistic. Religion in England was 'very feeble' he declared, because it had been introduced by 'means of ordinances which the majority obey very grudgingly'. Good preachers were extremely scarce, and discipline was slack because the aristocracy who were the social leaders were more interested in subjugating the Church and taking its property than they were in promoting its work. Cranmer, however, was not discouraged. Having survived the crisis of October, and finding a somewhat unexpected ally in the Earl of Warwick, he rightly concluded that whatever men might think, or even say, there was no significant will to resist the new Church Order.

He was therefore free to proceed with the further reforms which were already in his mind. During the summer of 1549 he had been working on a new reformed ordinal, probably in consultation with Bucer, who was then his house guest and whose *De ordinatione legitima* was clearly one of his sources. When this work was presented to the council, early in 1550 it was greeted, like the prayer book, with abuse from both sides. Conservatives like Nicholas Heath rejected it because it no longer recognized the sacrificial nature of the priesthood; while John Hooper denounced it bitterly during a court sermon in February because the names of the saints were still invoked, and because the candidates were required to wear white vestments, which he declared to be unknown to scripture.

Over the next few months Hooper became a major embarrassment. He was a totally committed protestant, and a skilled and fearless preacher; just the kind of man whom the reformed Church needed in its struggles to dislodge conservative habits and convictions. However, he was also uncompromising in his refusal to accept any word or gesture which did not correspond with his own ideas of biblical purity. Offered the bishopric of Gloucester, he refused to be consecrated wearing the authorized garments. The case became a test of the king's ecclesiastical authority, and Hooper spent a period in prison before deciding that his defiance was doing more harm than good. Hooper has been described as the founder of English puritanism, and although he was not the first to have such scruples, this early 'vestiarian controversy' revealed that there was no natural and necessary link between protestantism and the Royal Supremacy.[12] Protestant commitment to biblical authority could be as inconvenient as catholic commitment to the papacy. The fact that the Royal Supremacy was used to introduce protestantism during Edward's reign led to a natural alliance between the reformed clergy and the council, but it soon became apparent that this was an alliance of convenience. Bucer's criticism of the aristocracy as 'carnal gospellers' and Hooper's quarrel with the bishops were two early signs of a mutual disenchantment which was to become steadily stronger over the last three years of the reign. The role of the episcopate was central to this conflict of priorities, and the reformers really only had themselves to blame. Cranmer's new commission, and persistent references to 'unlording' prelates by turning them back into working teachers and pastors naturally encouraged the view that bishops were royal officials who should work for modest stipends. Consequently when episcopal estates and revenues came under pressure, and began to be whittled down, it was hard for Cranmer and his colleagues to make a stand. There were strong arguments that a reformed Church should not have an episcopate at all. By retaining the whole traditional structure of bishops, ecclesiastical courts and canon law, the English Church was revealing itself to be only 'half reformed'. To the council, on the other hand, bishops were useful, even necessary, vehicles for the royal authority, which could hardly have worked through a powerful reformed consistory. So when Stephen Gardiner was at length deprived of his bishopric of Winchester, and John Ponet appointed in 1551, the crown retained the revenues of the see, worth some £3,000 a year, and paid him an annual stipend of 2,000 marks (£1,333). The following year, after the similar deprivation of Cuthbert Tunstall, the see of Durham was dissolved by statute, and a similar plan seems to have been contemplated for the new sees of Durham and Newcastle. It was never implemented, partly because the council seem to have had second thoughts, and partly because the king died before the Letters Patent could be approved.[13]

Meanwhile the steady progress of reform was maintained, for the time being without obvious disagreements. In November 1550 a campaign was launched, both by the bishops and the council with equal zeal, to secure the removal of all stone altars and their replacement with wooden communion tables. As with the removal of images, there was much grumbling but little resistance. A complete revision of the Prayer Book was also undertaken. Cranmer had probably begun this even before the first order came into use, and he had certainly consulted both Bucer and Peter Martyr by January 1551. Bucer wrote down his advice in the form of the *Censura*, and his influence may consequently have been over-estimated. Martyr may well have been more important, but English divines such as Cox and Cheke were also consulted, and there seems to have been a battle royal among the bishops over the extent of the revisions. What emerged, to be approved by parliament in the second Act of Uniformity of January 1552, was an unequivocally reformed liturgy. The Eucharistic wording was now clearly protestant, in the receptionist mode.[14] Prayers for the dead, and all reference to vestments, had alike disappeared. Not even the most ingenious conservative could fudge this liturgy to look like the Mass. However, in spite of the changes, Cranmer was by this time beginning to lose touch with the council, where the influence of Hooper and Knox was becoming increasingly strong. Against his wishes they insisted on inserting the so-called 'Black Rubric' which explained that kneeling to receive the communion was for the sake of good order, and not out of idolatry. The introduction of this book in November 1552 must have made a much greater impact in the average parish than that of 1549. Unlike the first book, it had almost nothing in common with the familiar and traditional rites. Nevertheless it was accepted with a minimum of fuss, and if anyone ventured to describe it as a Christmas game, their words were not recorded.

With the advent of the second Prayer Book, the worship of the English Church could be described as fully reformed. There were still enthusiasts for whom it did not go far enough, but Cranmer had achieved one of his objectives, and created a Church Order which was both distinctive and acceptable to the main Continental traditions.

'. . . we think it convenient that every country should use such ceremonies, as they think best to the setting forth of God's honour and glory, and to the reducing of the people to a most perfect and Godly living, without error or superstition.'

The Prayer Book did not, however, present a doctrinal system, and pressure for such a system had been growing since 1549. Cranmer complied reluctantly, partly because it was impossible to make any doctrinal statement which was not controversial, and partly because his own position was still evolving. John Hooper was using a set of his own articles to check on ordination candidates by 1552, and the possible proliferation of such unauthorized statements presented an obvious danger to which the council responded in 1551. Cranmer was then instructed to draw up a set of articles, and prepared a draft with the help of Nicholas Ridley, the Bishop of London, which was circulated to a number of other bishops in 1552. In May he was peremptorily ordered to submit them for examination. The council ordered certain revisions, and returned the draft to the archbishop in September 1552. By this time Cranmer was becoming thoroughly disillusioned by the dominant role which the council was assuming. In his eyes the bishops were the proper agents of the king's ecclesiastical authority, but their position was being steadily eroded, first by the reduction of their wealth and status, and now by the slighting of their function in the determination of doctrine. The final version of the Forty Two Articles was submitted on 24 November, with a covering letter from the archbishop expressing the hope that 'such a concord and quietness in religion' would be established as would last many years. The council however, preoccupied with other problems, did nothing with them until the following summer. They were not submitted to Edward's last parliament, nor to the convocation which accompanied it. Finally, on 9 June, less than a month before the king's death, they were promulgated, ostensibly on the authority of the 'bishops and other learned and godly men', but in reality without any proper consultation. Cranmer again protested, but received no satisfaction.

Because they were issued so late in the reign, and because Mary immediately abandoned her brother's religious policies, these articles had little impact at the time when they were issued. They have been described both as 'Calvinist' and as 'eclectic'. They were certainly protestant. Article 12 stated that good works done without the inspiration of faith 'have the nature of sin', and article 17 that 'predestination to life is the everlasting purpose of God . . .'. Several clauses were borrowed almost unchanged from the Augsburg Confession, while others seem to reflect the influence of Bucer or Martyr.[15] They were generally accepted by the other reformed churches, and were re-issued in a slightly modified form as the Thirty-Nine Articles of 1563, as a part of the Elizabethan settlement. In June 1553 they represented another example of the estrangement between the bishops and the council which was soon to undermine the Duke of Northumberland's attempt to engineer a protestant succession. A similar estrangement had also arisen over plans to issue a new canon law for the Anglican Church. Without the pope the traditional law was a thing of shreds and patches, but as the Church courts remained in place, they needed a body of law to administer, and reformed canons were obviously desirable. In February 1550 the king was empowered by statute to set up a special commission for the purpose of drawing up such a code, although several bishops (including Cranmer) objected because the proposed commission was to consist of clergy and laymen in equal numbers. In the event, it was to be two years before the work commenced, and although the commission worked with admirable despatch, no legislation resulted. Cranmer had a text ready to submit to the parliament of March 1553, but found his work strongly denounced, both by the common lawyers and by the Duke of Northumberland himself, on the grounds that the proposed canons would give the bishops too much power. With the dissolution of parliament the commission expired, and the project was abandoned amidst bitter recriminations. By the summer of 1553 even the more extreme evangelicals were concluding that the English Church had too little control over its own affairs. In approving the dissolution of the chantries, they had looked for the redistribution of the property for pious and charitable purposes. In the event only education benefited, and that not to the degree expected. The same was true over the confiscation of Church goods, frequently threatened, and finally made inevitable by the Prayer Book of 1552. By the time that a general expropriation was ordered early in 1553, such goods had long since been inventoried, and much had already been disposed of. Some had been sold to local laymen at knock-down prices, some simply embezzled. The evangelicals had no time for gaudy ornaments or lavish plate, but they were deeply (and somewhat naively) shocked by the way in which the carefully acquired assets of so many parish churches were stripped, with little benefit to the poor or the Godly, but only to local officials – and possibly the king, if there was anything left.

Consequently, when Edward VI died on 6 July 1553, the Church of England was thoroughly reformed, but scarcely in good heart, and certainly not at one with its political masters. Northumberland had undoutedly counted on protestant support in his bid to exclude Mary from the succession, because the princess made no secret of her devotion to the Mass. She had been a consistent and outspoken opponent of the religious policies of both her brother's regents, and it was generally assumed that she would return to her father's settlement when, and if, she ascended to the throne. In spite of this, even protestant London could find no welcome for Northumberland's puppet, Jane Grey, and of the bishops, only Nicholas Ridley preached publicly on her behalf. As a member of the council, Cranmer reluctantly acquiesced in the king's 'Device', but took no steps to implement it. Within a fortnight Mary had secured a bloodless victory, and seemed at first inclined to acknowledge the support she had received from such improbable sources as John Hooper and Sir Peter Carew. Her first proclamation, issued on 18 August, was studiously moderate, claiming that although her own conscience was fixed, she had no intention of coercing the faith of others;[16] not, at any rate, until due order had been taken by process of law. This was not intended to deceive, but the new queen, deeply insulated by the security of her own convictions, simply did not believe that anyone could honestly differ from her. In her eyes the Edwardian Church was merely a facade, a confidence trick perpetrated upon a gullible population by greedy and wicked men. Once the said greedy and wicked men had been deposed and dealt with, their dupes would gratefully return to the true faith which they had always secretly acknowledged in their hearts. Coercion would not be necessary, and therefore need not be threatened. At the same time Mary's notion of lawful proceedings was based upon a similar simplicity of outlook. Those conservative bishops, notably Gardiner, Tunstall and Bonner, who had been deprived for their resistance to the late king's ungodly proceedings were *ipso facto* unlawfully deprived. Their successors were consequently no true bishops, and their acts were invalid. So the deprived bishops were promptly restored, in advance of their legal rehabilitation, and the disputes over leases and other transactions carried out by the 'intruders' wrangled on for years.

In matters of religion Mary was guided first and foremost by her conscience, and only secondarily by considerations of law or political expediency. Consequently she encouraged, and allowed her officials to encourage, the restoration of the Mass and other traditional rites and ceremonies, while the statutes were still in place which made them illegal. At the same time her council arrested and imprisoned leading protestants such as Hooper and Latimer for upholding in public the doctrine which was still by law established. This was, of course, only a temporary situation, as everyone acknowledged. By the time that her first parliament was dissolved on 5 December, the whole of Edward's religious legislation had been repealed, and the Church stood roughly where it had stood in January 1547, except that the Act of Six Articles had not been resurrected.

The protestant reaction to this destruction of their hopes was chiefly one of resignation. In 1550, when he had been feeling particularly disgruntled with the 'carnal gospellers', Martin Bucer had prophesied that '. . . the dreadful wrath of God will very shortly blaze forth against this kingdom'; and now it had happened. 'Our king is taken from us by reason of our sins . . .'[17] declared Hooper. Resistance to the will of God was not to be contemplated, and although there were some demonstrations in and around London, none of the recognized leaders were involved. Had the queen left her settlement where it was in December 1553, the whole story of her reign might well have been different, but such half measures never formed part of her plan. At what point Mary reverted to being a convinced papalist is not clear. She had accepted her father's ecclesiastical supremacy under extreme duress in 1536, and had never given any public indication of having changed her mind. Throughout her quarrels with Edward's council, the office of the pope was never mentioned. Perhaps she had dissembled throughout, or perhaps the opportunities presented by her accession had suddenly jolted her back into familiar paths. By the time she discussed the matter with her council, and with her favourite mentor, the Imperial ambassador Simon Renard, early in August, her mind was made up. The schism must be ended and the papal authority restored. A secret emissary from Julius III, Gian Francesco Commendone, visited her during the same month, and received her earnest expressions of devotion to the Holy See.

The only person who was genuinely delighted by this news was her cousin, Cardinal Reginald Pole, a long time exile for his resistance to the Royal Supremacy. Renard, although he could not say so openly, was thoroughly alarmed. His brief was to arrange a marriage between the queen and his master's son, Philip of Spain, and he feared lest the queen's preoccupation with religion should distract her from this urgent priority. He also believed that English protestantism was deeply rooted, and that a full catholic reaction would provoke civil war. Of Mary's councillors some, particularly her household servants, were enthusiastic. The Chancellor, Stephen Gardiner, was also supportive; but the lay nobility, led by Lord Paget, were sceptical. They knew, and pointed out discreetly via Renard, that the biggest stumbling block would be the former monastic lands, now in the hands of innumerable laymen by lawful purchase. The queen was not to be deflected from her purpose, but she did agree to compromise, chiefly out of deference to the emperor's wishes as expressed by Renard. She would make a full restoration, but she would do it by due process of law, through parliament; and that would inevitably mean delays. Pole was horrified

> '. . . shall God grant his help to schismatics and heretics assembled in parliament to reform the affairs of the kingdom? . . . God has given the sceptre and the sword into her majesty's hands for no other reason than that ribaldry and disobedience to the holy laws may be punished . . . .'[18]

However, the Cardinal's simple world of first principles, attractive as it might be to Mary, was out of touch with reality. A law once made could only be unmade by repeal, and it soon became apparent that the repeal of Henry's anti-papal legislation would require long and hard negotiation. Meanwhile the English Church could only be restored to a semblance of the true faith by the authority which the queen most entirely deplored, that of the Royal Supremacy.

The spring of 1554 saw that authority being wielded vigorously. Royal injunctions were issued, ordering not only the restoration of the Mass, but also of all the old accustomed ceremonies, processions and patronal festivals. Images were to be restored to honour, and clerical celibacy re-imposed. This latter rule became something of an obsession with the Marian authorities, and many hundreds of clergy were deprived of their livings – a much more severe penalty than that imposed for mere incontinence. However, although ordinations soon began to recover from the low point reached in Edward's reign, there were not enough priests to replace such a large-scale drain, and many of the deprived clergy were subsequently re-inducted elsewhere. In theory they were supposed to have repudiated their wives, but in practice many did not do so, and the issue rumbled on throughout the reign. These were troubled months; a quick descent from the euphoria which had greeted Mary's accession in July. The religious riots which Renard feared did not materialize, but news of the queen's intention to marry Philip, which began to circulate in November, was 'heavily taken of many'. So heavily, in fact, that there was a major conspiracy, abortive risings in Leicestershire and Devon, and a sizeable revolt led by Sir Thomas Wyatt in Kent.[19] To what extent this movement was inspired by protestantism has always been controversial. Wyatt disclaimed a religious motive, making his rallying cry 'the avoidance of strangers', and the recognized protestant leaders denied any connection with him. Only a minority of his known followers can be shown to have had protestant connections, but on the other hand as soon as the rising was over the government insisted that it had been a heretical plot. Both sides had good reason to be dishonest. Wyatt may well have suspected that opposition to the marriage would be a more compelling reason to attract a following than the restoration of the Edwardian Prayer Book. At the same time the council wished to play down the marriage issue for obvious reasons, and Stephen Gardiner hoped that, by raising an heretical bogeyman, he could increase his own authority and recover the political ground which he had lost to Paget and his allies before Christmas. Unfortunately the Chancellor's propaganda was reasonably successful. As a result protestantism began to be associated with opposition to foreign rule, and thus to acquire patriotic overtones. To the uncommitted majority of the population of England protestantism, in spite of its established status during Edward's brief reign, had been German or Swiss in its associations. 'English religion' was that which King Henry had left. After February 1554 that began to change. There was nothing foreign about the Church under Mary's supremacy, but when Philip's arrival in the summer was followed by the restoration of the papal authority, the persecuting catholicism which then ensued was regarded by many as Spanish in inspiration and method.

Both Pole and Gardiner could see the danger of allowing Philip any say in the restoration of the papal authority. The 'old religion' was popular, but there was little enthusiasm for the pope, even amongst the most conservatively inclined. For this reason Gardiner made a final bid in the second parliament of April 1554 to secure at least a limited acknowledgement of the Roman jurisdiction before Philip arrived on the scene. The delicacy of the situation made him secretive, and his plan was derailed by Paget. So England was still in schism when the highly orthodox Prince of Spain celebrated his nuptials in Winchester Cathedral on 25 July. This fact was significant in a number of ways because the Spaniards were already fiercely proud of their orthodoxy and regarded the English with contempt as a nation of heretics. Consequently the hostility with which Philip and his followers were received was fully reciprocated, and even anticipated. The king himself exercised superhuman restraint. Confronted with an unsatisfactory treaty, an aging and inexperienced bride, and what he considered to be a barbarous and avaricious people, he managed to seem pleased with everything. But it was not long before skirmishes began to break out in and around the court, and Philip's entourage began to complain bitterly that the English had no fear of God or his saints. It was in this unpromising atmosphere that the king first began to interest himself in the reconciliation of his new realm. Two main considerations influenced him. Firstly, it was derogatory to his honour to rule over any realm which was not fully catholic; and secondly the successful reconciliation of England would be a major propaganda *coup* against the French. The Franco-Habsburg wars had been going on intermittently since 1521, and in the early 1550s the influence of the two parties in the papal curia was delicately poised. If he could bring England back into the fold, it would give his father a decisive advantage. However, he soon realized that this was easier said than done. Not only were the English aristocrats determined to hold on to their church lands, but Cardinal Pole, whose commission as Legate to England was now a year old, was equally intractable. No one, he argued, could claim absolution and expect to retain the fruits of their sin. If Pole was going to be allowed into England, he would have to modify his views, and the only person who could make him do that was the pope.

Early in October, therefore, Philip made two moves. First, he sent Renard across to Brussels in an attempt to persuade Pole to adopt a more flexibile attitude; and secondly he wrote to his father's ambassador in Rome, Manrique de Lara, to raise with Julius the possibility of giving Pole a new brief. Somewhat unexpectedly, both moves succeeded. Pole did not yield ground directly, but he agreed, in the event of his admission to England, not to take any action without the king and queen's consent. This effectively shut off the possibility of his summoning individual possessioners before the ecclesiastical courts, and made a general dispensation the only possible way forward. At the same time Julius reluctantly concluded that the former property of the English Church would have to be sacrificed if the present goodwill of the English government was to be exploited. He therefore issued a brief not merely permitting, but instructing the English legate to negotiate on a general basis. By the end of November Pole was back in England, to Mary's overwhelming joy, and the elements of an agreement were in place.[20] The queen believed herself to be pregnant, and was beginning to show signs of that condition; so the prospects for a long-term solution to the disturbed religious condition of the realm seemed to be brighter than at any time in the previous twenty years. On 30 November the members of both Houses of Parliament presented themselves at the Palace of Westminster, bearing a humble petition to be readmitted to the fellowship of the Universal Church, and amid scenes of great emotion, Pole pronounced a solemn absolution. Inevitably, the euphoria soon wore off. Parliament had still to repeal the laws enforcing the Henrician supremacy, and Pole had still to issue the full text of his dispensation. In spite of his apparent tractability, the legate had not changed his mind. His dispensation was *ob duritiam cordis illorum*, and conferred no legal title; consequently any subsequent pope could withdraw it. The common lawyers countered by including the full text of the dispensation in the statute of repeal thus making it, in their own eyes, part of the law of England. It was not a very satisfactory compromise, because no statute could be binding on the pope; but on the other hand, the Church could claim no jurisdiction over real estate. So the Act of Supremacy was repealed on 3 January 1555 and the twenty-year-old schism came to an end.

Philip did not obtrude himself upon the restored Church, indeed he maintained a low profile in England in many ways, but there was no doubt about the crucial part which he had played in the negotiations. Mary, increasingly preoccupied with her health and the crucial question of an heir, had allowed him to make most of the running. With Cranmer in prison and suspended from all ecclesiastical functions, and York vacant following the deprivation of Robert Holgate, the senior bishop of the English Church was Stephen Gardiner of Winchester. Pole's legatine jurisdiction superseded all lesser powers, but Pole was long out of touch with English affairs, and in practice the two men seem to have shaped ecclesiastical policy between them until Gardiner's death in November. The main problem confronting them was undoubtedly discipline. Church goods and revenues had been embezzled; spontaneous enthusiasm for the old rituals had fallen a long way short of total restoration; and there turned out to be far more genuine heretics than either of them had believed. Gardiner, like the queen, had seen heresy mainly as a matter of time-serving and opportunism, and he had had no chance to test his opinion because Mary would not allow any trials to take place until a lawful ecclesiastical jurisdiction was in place. However, by February 1555 that situation had changed, and Pole set up his first legatine courts. Responsibility for the persecution which then followed has been long debated. Formally, it lay with the legate, and Pole certainly had no objection to burning heretics; but to him it was at best a painful duty, and he was not averse to granting reprieves. To Gardiner, on the other hand, it was a calculated policy. He did not believe that any so-called protestants would stand the test of fire, and when a few leaders had recanted in abject terror, the rest would follow. Within a few months he knew that he had miscalculated, and in Foxe's words 'gave over the matter as utterly discouraged'; more realistically he started arguing for civil penalties, understanding that every burning was a propaganda defeat. But both Pole and the queen saw the persecution as duty rather than policy, and neither would listen. The most implacable persecutor was Mary herself. 'Touching the punishment of heretics . . .', she wrote '. . . it may be evident to all this Realm how I discharge my conscience therein and minister true justice in so doing.'[21] In other respects the queen could be a gentle and irresolute creature, but when her conscience was fully engaged she was ruthless and unswerving.

How far her resolution was stiffened by Philip is difficult to ascertain. Both he and his court theologians, such as Alonso à Castro, were committed persecutors in other circumstances. But in England they seem to have held back. This was not Spain, and there was no political advantage to be gained from championing the true faith. The reverse was more likely. Philip knew perfectly well that the English would blame him for any government action which they did not like, and the burnings were not popular. Starting with John Rogers on 4 February 1555, nearly 300 men and women were executed in this way in less than four years. Most of them were artisans and other people of humble status, and the vast majority suffered in the dioceses of London, Canterbury, Rochester and Norwich, where the protestants were most numerous, and the reaction consequently most hostile. If Philip was in any way responsible, it can only have been at the beginning, because he left England in August 1555, and apart from three months in 1557, which were preoccupied with the coming war against France, he did not return. By the summer of 1557 he had accepted the fact that Mary would have no child, and his interest in England was waning fast. Perhaps the Spanish theologians who remained in England, Pedro de Soto, Juan de Villa Garcia and Bartolomé Carranza, retained an influence at court in support of continued severity;[22] but it seems most unlikely that Philip himself either had, or wished to have, any say. To the protestants, on the other hand, a martyrology was a very welcome gift. Having been partly discredited, first by their association with the unpopular Northumberland, and then by his spectacular recantation in August 1553, their own non-resistance principles had seemed likely to destroy them. Presented by government propaganda with the credit for the Wyatt rebellion, their rehabilitation was completed by these burnings. 'Where there is martyrdom, there is the true faith', Latimer had once said, and by the summer of 1555 the reformed faith had become something that brave men would die for.

In the wake of the persecution therefore, protestant propaganda gained in both volume and confidence. Nearly a hundred polemical works were produced between 1554 and 1558. Devotional at first, they became increasingly political, culminating in John Ponet's *Short Treatise of Politic Power* in 1556, Robert Pownall's *Admonition to the Town of Calais* in 1557 and Christopher Goodman's *How Superior Powers Ought to be Obeyed* in 1558. The last of these was a strident call to Godly revolution, an appeal for the overthrow of Athalia as an unnatural as well as an ungodly ruler – a queen who was murdering her own natural subjects for the benefit of strangers and foreigners.[23] All this was a far cry from the resignation of Hooper or Cranmer, and signalled a potential transformation of the utmost importance in English protestantism. Had Mary not died in 1558, the next generation of English reformers might well have been revolutionaries of the same stamp as some of the French Huguenots. Elizabeth was to come to the throne just in time to rescue establishment Anglicanism from such a radical takeover. The actions of the Marian Church were only partly to blame for this dramatic development, however. Stephen Gardiner, who *pace* Foxe, was not a brutal man, decided in the early months of the reign that it would be better for all concerned if as many prot- estants as possible could be frightened into leaving the country. Nearly 800 went, and those who remained behind to suffer either did so deliberately, like Cranmer and Ridley, or because they were too poor to go. These exiles scattered widely through Germany and Switzerland, some of them picking up contacts which they had made during Edward's reign, when the boot had been on the other foot. Most of them settled down to penurious drudgery, waiting for better times. But some, and Ponet and Goodman were among them, took the opportunity to imbibe the pure waters of the reformation from the fountains of Zurich and Geneva. As they did so, they became increasingly dissatisfied, not only with Mary and her idolatrous regime, but also with the whole of their own tradition, Royal Supremacy, prayer book and all. It was these men who began to look for the establishment of a Godly commonwealth in England, by violence if necessary, and they were to be an intractable element in the Elizabethan Church. Their spiritual heirs were eventually to achieve their aim in 1649.

To Pole obstinate heretics were troublesome, but a relatively minor problem. The real mountain which he had to climb was the legacy of years of strife and even more of indifference. Bare, whitewashed churches, often falling down; misappropriated rev- enues; vacant cures; slovenly and ill-educated clergy. This situ- ation was only partly the result of deliberate action by the reformers; in many respects they found it as deplorable as he did, and had fought the same battle in their different way during their years in power. Considering that his mission lasted less than four years, the legate cannot be accused of either slackness or incompetence, but he can be accused of picking up the stick at the wrong end. Mary's health was never particularly good, and after the fiasco of her failed pregnancy in the summer of 1555 it would have required invincible optimism to foresee an heir to carry on her work. The catholic restoration therefore depended upon the queen's own life, and mortality was uncer- tain at the best of times. Nevertheless Pole went doggedly and systematically about his work of restoring order, discipline and financial stability. As a cardinal and a prince of the royal blood, he had an unmeasured contempt for the ordinary layman; the people were children who needed encouragement and rebuke. They should be punished if necessary, and protected from harmful influences. Good habits of devotion were more important than instruction in the faith, which most were incapable of comprehending.

'But this I dare say, whereunto scripture doth also agree, that the observation of ceremonies for obedience sake, will give more light than all the reading of scripture can do, if the reader have never so good a wit to understand what he readeth . . . .'[24]

Pole was a good humanist scholar, who had fought and lost a battle for scriptural translation at the Council of Trent. He could not bring himself to ban the English Bible, but he was deeply suspicious of its use by laymen. By the same token he was a great promoter of clerical education, and an energetic reformer of both universities, but had little enthusiasm for preaching. This was partly because his own spiritual crises had made him a reluctant theologian, and given him a deep suspicion of the counter reformation, then budding strongly in Italy and Spain. He ignored offers of help from Ignatius Loyola, and none of the new Continental orders established cells in England during this period. When he called a legatine synod in 1556 to co-ordinate the work of restoration, he modelled it on the Council of Constance, rather than Trent; and preaching came well down in its order of priorities, in spite of some pointed hints from the queen, who was anxious to counter 'the evil preaching in time past'.

Under this determined, but not particularly inspired leadership, the catholic restoration was patchy in its effect. Not all Mary's bishops shared Pole's indifference to the instruction of the laity, and several works of devotional guidance were published, such as *A plain and Godly treatise concerning the mass*, *An honest Godly instruction for the . . . bringing up of children*, and above all Bonner's *Profitable and necessary doctrine*, which went through many editions.[25] Nevertheless, little attempt was made to encounter protestant polemic head on, and such attempts as were made were by private enterprise rather than public authority, notably Miles Huggard's *Displaying of the Protestants*. The

155

council relied on censorship rather than counter-propaganda to support the Church in this connection. Great, and largely successful, efforts were made to restore the authority and revenues of the bishops, and good appointments were made; but the restoration of religious houses was slow, and small scale. The Bull *Praeclara* of 1555 had canonically extinguished the dissolved houses as a part of the bargain with the English parliament, but such new foundations as were made were made on the old sites. Only Westminster, with about 100 monks and an endowment of £1,460 a year, was on a significant scale. Altogether six houses were founded, and the total endowment of a little over £2,000 a year came entirely from the crown. Had the restoration lasted longer, of course, the story might have been different. Some laymen did resume the foundation of perpetual chantries, notably Sir William Petre and Sir Robert Rochester, and bequests for pious purposes in the traditional form were showing clear signs of revival by 1558. Nevertheless, in spite of their enthusiasm for images and ceremonies, neither Mary nor Pole made any attempt to restore those great centres of popular piety, the pilgrimage shrines. St Thomas Becket at Canterbury and Our Lady of Walsingham remained derelict, and the queen made no pilgrimage during her reign. When Mary wished to make thanksgiving offerings for her victories over Northumberland and Wyatt she gave additional endowments to the universities, in a manner more resembling her brother than her father in his early days. The only major shrine restored during the reign was that of Edward the Confessor, and that was rebuilt by the monks of Westminster. The piety of the restored Church, in fact, was not that of the Middle Ages, or that of the counter-reformation, but that of the humanist ascendency in the 1530s; the piety of Richard Whitford or Thomas More. Other legacies of the 1530s were also noticeable. Much of the devotional literature was based on such works as *A Necessary Doctrine and Erudition* of 1543, or even on Cranmer's *Homilies*, with suitable doctrinal adjustments. The lives of saints, very popular before 1529, are almost unrepresented, and neither Myrc's *Liber Festivalis* nor the *Legenda Aurea* was re-issued. Equally significant was the continuing role of the crown. Even after the restoration of the papal jurisdiction, catholic writers continued to refer to 'the Queen's Godly proceedings', with scant reference to Rome or the Church Universal; and the Privy Council continued to be the main agency of enforcement. It was the council which harried Bonner into doing his duty, and chivvied the Justices of the Peace into hunting down seditious preachers. It was the council also which reprimanded and punished local officers if executions were not carried out with sufficient despatch, or if there were accompanying disorders. Only a few of Mary's councillors were zealous persecutors as individuals, but as a body they were bound to implement their mistress's instructions. The shadow of the Royal Supremacy was heavy on the Marian Church, and the queen was not reluctant to take full advantage of it.

Even if she had been unwilling, Mary would not have had a great deal of option, because the papacy was a broken reed. Julius III died only two months after the reconciliation, and was succeeded, after a chapter of accidents, by the violently anti-Habsburg Paul IV. All Philip's careful politics were lost overnight, and tension immediately began to build up, culminating in open war in September 1556. Mary was not a party to the conflict, but she was caught between her husband and her Father in God, and Paul made it perfectly clear that he considered her behaviour reprehensible. Pole's task became increasingly difficult as he was bombarded with enquiries from the curia about the exact financial state of the English Church, enquiries which demanded laborious and time-consuming answers. Worse still the pope had long suspected his orthodoxy, a disagreement which went back almost twenty years, and on 9 April 1557 revoked his legatine commission. Shortly after he was summoned back to Rome to answer 'certain charges', and it was generally believed that he would join his friend, Cardinal Morone, in the papal prison. Mary refused to allow him to go, and informed the pope that she had full confidence in him to run the English Church. Since Pole had succeeded Cranmer at Canterbury after the latter's execution in March 1556, he had adequate canonical authority without a special commission, but he was deeply distressed. For years he had clung to the papal authority as the sheet anchor of orthodoxy, believing that salvation lay only in obedience, and now he was unable to obey. Furious at the queen's defiance, but fearful that England might again lapse into schism, Paul named another legate to England. But as his choice was the senile Franciscan William Peto, the breach was in no sense healed. Mary was insulted, and Peto very properly declined the mission. Pole struggled on, but he was a broken man during the last year of his life, described as 'lukewarm' and 'a dead man' by his Spanish critics. Had he outlived Paul and shared Morone's rehabilitation, he might have recovered his momentum, at least to the extent of being a major factor in the calculations of the new queen. But in the event he followed Mary to the grave within a few hours on 17 November 1558, leaving his task less than half accomplished; and the pope rejoiced that the heretical cardinal and his royal backer could no longer obstruct the true faith in England.

It is often said that Elizabeth faced an extremely difficult situation on her accession, but this is largely an optical illusion created by her own propaganda skills. The new queen was a protestant, although a somewhat idiosyncratic one, and perhaps not deeply committed. She knew that there was a small but vociferous party, both in England and among the exiles, willing her to return to the Edwardian settlement. She also knew that there were English protestants who no longer had the patience to 'tarry for the magistrate', and who regarded the Royal Supremacy with deep suspicion. She had conformed, with somewhat visible reluctance, to her sister's church, and this seems to have made her more suspect to the catholics than to the protestants. Elizabeth and Mary had hated each other very cordially, and that animosity played into the hands of the survivor. Mary's weakness had never lain in her adherence to the 'old religion', but in her dependence upon the Habsburgs and, ironically, upon the papacy. Elizabeth was determined to reverse both those policies, and re-establish the English priorities which had been her father's great strength. The shrewd Feria, Philip's envoy, commented almost at once that 'she has her way absolutely, as her father did . . .'. Had she been faced with a resolute papalist at Canterbury, and a Roman Catholic Church in full sail, such a process would have been truly difficult. As it was the shortness of Mary's reign, the continuing unpopularity of the papacy and the lack of strong ecclesiastical leadership made it comparatively straightforward. Although there was officially still war with France, peace negotiations had been under way for some time, and Henry II's need for peace made it unlikely that he would attempt to press the claims of his daughter-in-law, Mary Stuart, to the English throne. On the other hand that possibility, however remote, ensured Elizabeth of Philip's continued support, no matter what kind of a religious settlement she might make. So in choosing her course, the queen was not constrained by overwhelming pressures, and was largely free to choose her own way.

Some clear signals preceded positive action. Unlike Mary, Elizabeth was very scrupulous about insisting upon obedience to the existing law, so iconoclasm and attacks upon the Mass were suppressed. On the other hand the persecution abruptly ceased, protestant preachers again appeared at Paul's Cross, and the queen's carefully studied gestures during her coronation entry into London, left few doubts about her intentions. Perhaps she would have been satisfied, at least at first, with a return to her father's settlement; but too much had happened since 1547 for that to be feasible. No catholic bishops could be found to run such a church, and no protestants would accept office in it. If the queen wanted the Royal Supremacy, she would have to do a deal with the only important clerical group which was willing to accept it, the Edwardian protestants. The Elizabethan settlement, embodied in the Acts of Supremacy and Uniformity of 1559, represented that deal. It was fiercely resisted by Mary's surviving bishops, but apart from a handful of peers, there was no lay catholic party in parliament to back them up. The failure of the short-lived catholic restoration could not have been more clearly demonstrated than by the progress of these bills through the House of Commons. Convocation was solidly hostile, reflecting a sound policy of appointment to senior ecclesiastical offices, but was simply swept aside, and when the oath of supremacy was administered to the rank and file clergy, only about 300 refused it. Elizabeth made a few modifications to the Edwardian order, perhaps to mollify conservative opinion, or perhaps merely to please herself. The 1549 wording was added to the 1552 wording in the distribution of the communion; a vestments rubric was inserted; and she styled herself 'Supreme Governor' of the Church, rather than 'Supreme Head'. An ecclesiastical commission was established to exercise regular executive supervision, the new religious houses were dissolved and the clerical taxes (First Fruits and Tenths) which Mary had restored were again appropriated to the crown. To all intents and purposes, the Edwardian settlement was restored. With one exception the Marian bishops refused it, and were deprived, being replaced over the next eighteen months with an equally worthy bench of protestants, several of whom had been exiles and some of whom had been Edwardian bishops, but none of whom was tainted with radicalism. In the convocation of 1563 the Edwardian vestiarian controversy was revived, and the Forty Two Articles (reduced to Thirty Nine by the removal of the concern about anabaptism) were reaffirmed. In a sense the Marian restoration had been merely a hiccup in the continuous progress of the reformation.

However, such a view would be inadequate, if not mistaken. Elizabethan protestantism developed a patriotic drive which its Edwardian predecessor had not possessed, thanks to the Spanish overtones acquired by Marian catholicism. On the other hand Elizabeth's bishops benefited from the Marian restoration, and retained a measure of their recovered wealth and status. Above all, the Marian Church, with its persecution and its alien associations, created the Black Legend which was so skilfully exploited by John Foxe, whose *Acts and Monuments of the English Martyrs* was published in 1563. Religious conservatives, who continued to prefer the old ceremonies, and who deplored the 1559 Prayer Book, had no desire to be thought of as disloyal to the queen, or as agents of a foreign power. In effect they became detached from catholicism proper, with its papal allegiance and its increasingly Continental theology, and were gradually absorbed into a conforming Anglican Church. That was one reason why the queen tended to ignore them during the first ten years of her reign, to the bitter chagrin of her more zealous bishops, and concentrate instead upon enforcing the Royal Supremacy over those protestants who attempted to make their own conditions for acceptance. The danger presented by these Puritans was not that they wanted to remove such ceremonies as the queen chose to retain, but that, in the last analysis, their loyalty was to the bible rather than the crown. Elizabeth knew that it was part of her task to prevent that dichotomy from becoming explicit, and she succeeded very well, to everyone's annoyance and frustration, and to the great benefit of the Church. She was prevented from following a similar course with the catholics by the Bull *Regnans in Excelsis*, but that declaration of war came too late to derail a settlement which had taken deep, if unheroic, roots.

# 6

## THE FAITH OF THE PEOPLE

The medieval Church had been a collection of practices, habits and attitudes rather than an intellectually coherent body of doctrine. It had suffered no shortage of intellectual effort, even of the most distinguished kind, but the debates of the schools had not created certainty or coherence, even on some of the most important issues of christology or eschatology. In theory doctrinal disputes were resolved, either by the authority of the pope, or by General Councils. In practice over the centuries conflicting judgements had been handed down, and the scholarly enquirer could often choose that which suited him best. The confusion was made worse by the fact that this was not supposed to happen, and could not be openly admitted, because the Holy Spirit was supposed to dwell in the Church, protecting it (in its collective capacity) from all error in matters of the faith. Consequently intellectual curiosity came to be frowned upon as leading at best to uncertainty and at worst to heresy. The Church became for its lay members, and for the great majority of the clergy also, identified by what it did rather than by what it taught or believed. It was a visible and tangible world of devotion; a world of intercession, in which the supernatural was constantly invoked to cope with the spiritual and physical hazards of everyday life. Central to this world was the inaccessible mystery of the Mass, and the comfortable rites of confession and absolution. The crucifix held in the sight of the dying, or the holy water sprinkled for 'avoiding of evil spirits' contained a reassurance not easy to express in words.[1] There was consolation, too, in the corporate nature of such a faith. The processions on Corpus Christi Day or at Rogationtide; the pilgrimages and Church ales; the days of atonement and fasting; all were collective actions, which marked out the liturgical year and matched it to the agricultural seasons. The Church, often the only substantial stone building, was the centre of parish life, and often a symbol of the pride and identity of the community. When the Council of Trent assembled in 1545 to counter the onslaughts of the reformation, the fathers were well aware of the vulnerability of this unreflective piety. They were not averse to intellectual enquiry, but the evidence of its destabilizing consequences was all around them, and against the better judgement of many, they reaffirmed the infallibility of the Vulgate Bible, despite the fact that two generations of humanist scholarship had shown it to be full of errors of translation. Constrained to defend the historical authority of the Church, they could not afford to admit that the Holy Spirit had allowed it to function for nearly a thousand years with a defective text of its central revelation.

It was not only intellectual uncertainties, however, which had undermined the somewhat complacent security of the late medieval Church. Closely knit and mutually supportive groups are often deeply suspicious, not only of strangers but also of the non-conformists in their own midst. Not everyone found the external and somewhat mechanical nature of official piety satisfying. The doubts were often more a matter of temperament than of intellect, an instinctive groping for the inwardness of religion, but they set the doubters apart and might cause them to be ostracized or denounced to the authorities. Moreover, such views could be infectious, or could arise spontaneously, without having to be imported from ouside. The *Devotio Moderna*, widespread in the Rhineland and the Netherlands in the fifteenth century, was such a reaction against received wisdom. It was a quasi-mystical movement, not dependent upon higher education, and characterized by a withdrawal from the symbolic and ritual life of the community. In spite of its respectable links with reformed monasticism, the Church regarded it with suspicion. Although not heretical in any identifiable sense, it did not respond to conventional controls. To the mystic even the sacraments could be a matter of indifference, and absolution a question of private prayer rather than canonical penance. Eventually such indifference undermined the authority of the clergy, and consequently of the Church itself, replacing an accepted discipline with subjective judgement. The English equivalent of the *Devotio Moderna* was Lollardy, arising from the anti-sacramental and iconoclastic teaching of John Wycliffe, a late-fourteenth-century Oxford divine. Lollardy had always contained elements of explicit heresy, but in its early days it had been both intellectually respectable and politically significant. However Henry IV's need for papal support, followed by Sir John Oldcastle's rebellion in 1414, had driven it underground. By 1500 it had long been a grassroots movement, without either coherent teaching or recognized leadership. However that did not mean that it had become unimportant.[2] If Lollardy was a state of mind rather than a theology, it did not differ greatly from orthodox catholicism. It could be described as the reverse side of the same coin. If images were held in high regard, the Lollards wanted to burn them; if the sacramental host was venerated, they described it as nothing but mouldy bread; if pilgrimages were popular, they denounced them as superstitious folly.

Lollardy therefore represented a dissenting streak which had always existed in Western Christianity, and it is not surprising that the authorities lumped together all eccentric views, however they were derived, as 'Lollard'. Nevertheless, remnants of their founder's teaching lingered on, often in the form of apocryphal writings, so although there was no Lollard Confession there were some characteristic opinions. The most fundamental of these was the rejection of materialism, based upon the theological distinction between *Latria* and *Dulia*. *Latria* was the worship due only to the three persons of the Trinity, while *Dulia* was the reverence properly due to a creature, whether animate or inanimate. That distinction was easy to transgress, particularly in the climate of fifteenth-century orthodoxy. A genuine work of Wycliffe, *Tractatus de Mandatis Divinis*, returned to this theme in many places:

'Whoever sins in deed, as when he inordinately loves the creature, offends against the first commandment by committing idolatry . . .'.

'. . . so called Christians, like animals or beasts, having forsaken the faith of spiritual believers today exceedingly indulge the senses . . . senusous objects are provided by which all the senses are moved in irreligious ways'.[3]

This not only led to iconoclasm, but also to the rejection of transubstantiation, that central aspect of the late medieval Mass wherein the priest converted the Eucharistic elements into the 'real, carnal and corporeal' body and blood of Christ. The rejection of this miracle, so vital to contemporary piety, had wide-ranging implications. If the priest did not have miraculous powers, what claim had he to act as an intercessor? If he was not set apart by his office, what authority did he have to discipline his fellow Christians? The Lollard answer to these questions was instinctive rather than rational. The priest's power to celebrate any sacrament was not *ex officio*, but dependent upon his state of grace. In other words, his celebrations were valid if his congregation chose to regard him as a worthy man. By the same token it was often said that any good Christian could administer the sacraments, an opinion fundamentally subversive of the Church as it was then understood.

The other central tenet, shared by all Lollards, was that the scriptures should be available in the vernacular. Wycliffe himself had probably translated parts of the Bible, and a complete version appeared in about 1395, which was copied and circulated in manuscript for over a hundred years before it was superseded. The Lollards were great readers. This was a strength in so far as it kept them thinking and arguing about their beliefs, and in touch with their origins. But it was also a weakness in that books are hostages to fortune, and their discovery led to many arrests and punishments. By the early sixteenth century very few Lollards were educated men, and only a minority were literate, but the power of the written word was sustained by group readings. Moreover the illiterate frequently had excellent audio memories, and could repeat whole chapters of scripture by heart after a small number of hearings. Because their teachings had been condemned since the end of the fourteenth century, and because they were frequently regarded with disfavour by their neighbours, the Lollards had become secretive, and their numbers are hard to assess. They had no separate ministry, and did not withdraw themselves from the worship of their parish churches, but they did hold secret conventicles for reading and prayer, and evaded as many customary rituals as they could. They called themselves 'the known men', and groups in different places kept in touch through a network of messengers. They were numerous in the Chilterns, particularly around Amersham, in Essex, Kent and London. Most large towns had a cell; Coventry and Lichfield had several, and they were also fairly strong in the clothworking areas of Yorkshire and Nottinghamshire. On the other hand large areas of the rural West and North seem to have been entirely unaffected; only two possible cases were detected in the diocese of Exeter before 1530. Although many Lollard writings survive, and their opinions can be easily reconstructed, all that is known about the people themselves and the way in which they conducted their lives and worship, is derived from the charges brought against them. It is therefore not surprising that they often appear to have been ribald, and contemptuous of authority. One young man was hauled before the court of audience in York for describing the font as a 'stinking tarn', and for declaring that he would confess no sin to a priest who was a sinner like himself.[4]

There may have been an increase in Lollard activity between 1500 and 1520, or the authorities may have become more vigilant. There was certainly a large increase in the number of cases coming before the courts. Bishop Fitzjames of London tried 40 offenders in 1510, and a further 37 in 1517; Archbishop Warham investigated nearly 60 cases in Kent in 1511 and 1512; and 20 Berkshire Lollards did penance in 1499. In 1514 came the notorious case of Richard Hun, the London merchant arrested on a charge of heresy and murdered in the Bishop of London's prison. On the whole, however, Lollards were not made of the stuff of martyrs. Of the 77 tried by Fitzjames, 73 recanted and were penanced. The remaining four were burned as relapsed heretics, and of those three were reconciled to the Church before their deaths. Between 1527 and 1532 more than 200 abjured before the diocesan courts of London. By that time the problem of heresy was becoming much more complicated, as Lutheran ideas began to infiltrate from Germany. Wolsey carried out the first public burning of heretical books in 1521 – an honour which had never been accorded to Lollard manuscripts, although many were destroyed – and old-established Lollard groups were among the first customers for William Tyndale's English New Testament when it appeared in 1526. Nevertheless, popular heresy remained predominantly Lollard down to the end of

Henry VIII's reign, distinctively protestant ideas such as justification by faith alone being found mainly among the educated.
There were protestant divines, merchants, lawyers and gentlemen in England by 1545, although they had to conduct themselves with discretion. But the radical 'mechanic preachers', like
John Harrydance, the Whitechapel bricklayer, belonged to an
older tradition of dissent, emboldened and made more visible
by the general climate of reform.[5] The Lollards, we are told,
were 'much encouraged' by John Colet's famous sermon to
convocation in 1511, although it is unlikely that he would have
been pleased by the news. Some of the old dissent, although
branded as 'Lollard' went back a long way beyond Wycliffe,
and some of it had no doctrinal content at all. Resentment
against the canon law and the courts which administered it,
resentment against the Church as landlord, and resentment
against the paying of tithes; none of this had much to do with
spirituality, but was important in framing relationships between
clergy and laity.

It was once believed that anticlericalism was powerful in late
medieval England, and that it played an important part in
bringing about the reformation. Recently this received wisdom
has been challenged, and a great deal of evidence has been
presented to demonstrate that most clergy were well regarded
by their congregations, who called on them as mediators, coun-
sellors and advocates as well as priests, and who remembered
them gratefully in their wills.[6] The image of the corrupt and
ignorant vicar, dividing his time between the alehouse and the
favours of his female parishioners was, it has been argued, a
post-reformation fabrication; a *post hoc* rationalization of what
had been done. In truth, although often ill-educated, the average
parish priest of the late fifteenth or early sixteenth century was
an honest trier, a man doing his limited best, and making quite
a good job of it. The debate is likely to continue, but it is no
longer central to an understanding of the reformation, because
whatever else that may have been, it was not a spontaneous
religious movement. The English reformation was an act of state
(or more accurately a series of acts of state) which was facilitated
and retarded at different times by prevailing religious attitudes.
The Lollards were unquestionably anti-clerical, but they formed
only a small part of the population, even in the areas where
they were strong, and had no influence upon the formation of

policy. On the other hand the Church was a major property-owning corporation, and a huge vested interest, whose business interlocked with that of lay society at every level. It is not surprising that litigation between clergy and laity was frequent, or that bitter quarrels sometimes resulted. It was usually in the context of such quarrels that clergy were accused of abusing their spiritual authority. Excommunicating a tithe defaulter, or citing a parishioner before the archdeacon's court for the non-payment of a mortuary fee could lead to a lasting estrangement between a priest and his flock. Accusations of heresy, above all, were dangerously two-edged weapons because it was in such cases that the clergy were both accusers and judges. When Richard Hun was charged with heresy in the midst of a quarrel over money, the charge was probably justified, but his friends claimed that it was the pure malice of a defeated litigant who happened to be a priest. It is unlikely that many people embraced protestantism out of animosity towards the clergy; and both in 1536 and 1549 important groups of malcontents accepted clerical leadership in opposition to official policy, but when it was said in Mary's reign 'the priests are coming back to take their revenge', the speakers were not anticipating a reunion of old friends. Cardinal Pole did not mince his words when he confronted the Londoners in 1556 with what he perceived to be their most characteristic sin

'You have above all nations that I know, dishonoured the ministers of the church and priesthood itself; so you should now honour both the order instituted of God, and the persons for the order's sake, and him that they do represent, remembring ever what Christ sayeth, *Qui vos spernit, me spernit.* Above all obey their word speaking in God's name, whatsoever their lives be. . . .'.[7]

Pole's emphasis upon the duty of obedience made him extremely sensitive to the 'malicious mockers' who denied the clergy the reverence which he considered to be their due, but it was quite consistent with the role of the laity in the Church as he understood it.

It was perhaps a measure of the Cardinal's estrangement from the English situation that he should have laid so much emphasis upon clerical paternalism. The laity were 'little children', con-

167

stantly in need of protection against their own weakness and folly. Such views did not appeal to the followers of a more robust tradition, because it was not only the Lollards who had felt entitled to criticize clerical shortcomings. Nor was the role of the laity in the life of the Church a purely passive one. In the first place they were benefactors on a very large scale. One testator in five left money to the mendicant orders, and one in six to the monasteries and nunneries, even in the decade before their dissolution. Small benefactions to parish churches were almost universal, and a lot of expensive rebuilding was undertaken between 1500 and 1540. Above all, the lay fraternities catered for a variety of social needs under the guise of corporate piety, and played a major part in the religious life of many parishes, particularly in the towns. Basically a fraternity was a kind of funeral club, under the patronage of a particular saint, whereby the members undertook to give each departed brother the benefits of suitable burial and of regular prayers and Masses for the repose of his soul. They have been described as 'poor men's chantries', and testify to the continuing strength of belief in the doctrine of purgatory right down to 1547. Many fraternities, however, also developed more worldly functions. They subsidized young members trying to set up in business, and provided charitable relief for the old and sick. Some of the larger and wealthier guilds owned substantial amounts of property, including meeting halls for their own purposes, and ran schools, almshouses, and even hospitals.[8] Others looked after bridges and highways. At Wisbech the guilds maintained the sea-defences; at Ashburton in Dorset the guild of St Lawrence maintained the town's water supply, and many other specific instances could be quoted. Guilds provided feasts and entertainments, particularly on days associated with their patron saints, and through their regular religious observances a constant stream of intercession for the living and the dead. Yet in spite of their fundamental purpose, these fraternities were not directed by clergy. Their wardens, who exercised considerable disciplinary powers, were laymen and their chaplains were employees. At the end of Henry VIII's reign there were hundreds of such guilds in England. Some of them were shadowy organizations, perhaps short-lived, which have left little trace behind, but others were substantial and many of their records survive. There were about 120 in Lincolnshire; 7 in the town of Leicester; and another 7 in Yaxley in Suffolk, which was little more than a village. Collectively they provide a very good example of the bond which existed between the Church and lay society.

And yet these apparently robust organizations collapsed over-night in the face of statute law, and attempts to revive them when circumstances permitted after 1553 were surprisingly in-effective. This was partly due to the fact that some of the most powerful, like the London livery companies and the colleges of Oxford and Cambridge, managed to escape dissolution and continued under the guise of purely secular foundations. But it also partly reflects the paradoxical state of the pre-reformation Church. Ordinations were buoyant throughout the first 40 years of the sixteenth century, reflecting the general attractiveness of a clerical career, in spite of the fact that many of those who proceeded to priest's orders never secured a benefice. There was a great difference between the small minority of university educated clergy, who monopolized the best benefices, cathedral stalls and offices, and the large clerical proletariat. Many of the former were pluralists, in spite of frequent attempts to correct the abuse, while the latter worked as cantarists, chaplains and curates. In some cases curates served for 20, 30, or even 40 years in the same living, maintaining the substance of the parochial ministry, while rectors and vicars came and went. A good living could be worth £100 a year or more, but most were far less, and a curate's stipend was a mere pittance. When the colleges of Bishop Auckland, Chester-le-Street and Darlington were dis-solved in 1547, a vicar was provided for each; £20 per annum at Auckland, £16 at Chester and Darlington. Auckland was provided with three curates, and the others one each, at stipends ranging from £6.13s.4d to £8.[9] The minimum living wage at that time was considered to be about £5 a year. There were some 9,000 parishes in England at the time of the *Valor Ecclesiasticus* in 1535, and perhaps three times that number of clergy. The piety of the period must have guaranteed against unemploy-ment, and priests were entitled to charge fees for certain pro-fessional services – weddings and burials for instance – so the clergy were cushioned against the effects of economic malaise, and the rising population worked in their favour. There was little incentive to the average priest to improve his level of education, unless he could join the university elite. Otherwise appointments and promotions were controlled by patrons, often laymen, who commonly had little interest in the quality of the candidate, provided he satisfied the minimum conditions. Ordinations collapsed dramatically during the protestant ascendency from 1547 to 1553, as the bulk of the clerical proletariat faced redundancy, so that by the latter date there was not merely a shortage of acceptable clergy, but a shortage of any clergy at all. In 1554 the eleven parishes of Ipswich were served by just two priests. After Mary's accession the number of candidates recovered with equal speed, but the shortage was barely overcome by the end of the reign. The obvious conclusion is that the old piety was popular, and the new was not; but it must also be remembered that protestantism required a different kind of ministry, for which the bulk of potential ordinands were not prepared. Moreover the same considerations which made a clerical career attractive under the old regime, also made the laity resentful of their economically protected position. A high level of ordinations did not necessarily mean that all was well with the Church.

The religious orders, on the other hand, were having the opposite problem. Small bequests and gifts held up well, but major benefactions, let alone new foundations, were things of the past. The monasteries had never really recovered from the great plague visitations of the fourteenth century. Even the great houses, such as Westminster and St Albans, had far fewer monks than their spacious buildings were designed to house, and many small establishments, with fewer than ten brothers, had ceased to be viable. Unlike ordinations, vocations had been low throughout the fifteenth and early sixteenth century, and the great cloak of the monastic endowment hung loosely on its diminished body. The monks were partly the victims of changing fashions in piety. The *opus dei*, the constant fount of prayer and worship, was no longer valued, and less substantial foundations provided the intercession which was still very much in demand. The monasteries were no longer sources of intellectual or spiritual leadership. Many were orderly, decent and respectable establishments, but the only functions which they were clearly seen to discharge were those of hospitality and almsgiving. If Westminster and Durham are anything to go by, the monks were drawn predominantly from yeomen and merchant families, enjoyed a generous diet, spent a good deal of time out of their cloisters and were not seen to have any distinctive role in the spiritual life of the community. Some were priests, and served the abbey cures, but that did not require a monastic vocation. When the king moved against the lesser houses in 1536, there was a good case for his action. Wolsey had already closed some 30 small monasteries and nunneries, moving the inmates to larger houses, between 1524 and 1528.[10] Specific reactions varied greatly from place to place, often depending upon the local reputation of the house concerned. At Hexham in Northumberland the townsmen turned out in arms to defend their priory against the king's commissioners; while a few miles away at Tynemouth similar neighbours anticipated the commissioners by sacking the abbey before they arrived. Resentment against the dissolution played a part in the Pilgrimage of Grace, but that was a very complex movement, and probably less religious in its inspiration than some of its leaders wished it to appear. The monasteries were a familiar part of the English landscape, both physical and cultural, but with a few notable exceptions they were marginal, both to the spiritual and intellectual movements of the period, and to the religion of ordinary people.

The exceptions were two small and extremely austere orders of St Bridget and the Charterhouse. The Bridgettines had only one house in England, at Syon near Brentford, which consisted of about 50 nuns, many of them from aristocratic families, and some 25 male religious. These latter were drawn almost entirely from the educated clerical elite, and presented a unique combination of austerity and intellectual distinction. At Syon was based Richard Whitford, probably the most influential devotional writer of his generation, and the translator of the *Imitatio Christi* of Thomas à Kempis. Whitford was not a humanist, and not a reformer in the doctrinal sense, but his emphasis upon simple and practical piety in such books as *A work for householders* spoke to a popular need. Like Erasmus, he had little time for the outward trappings of religion, and had little to say about pilgrimages, images or processions. Although strongly opposed to heresy, his advocacy of prayer and penitence in preference to repeated ceremonial observances made him suspect to some conservatives. Whitford accepted the Royal Supremacy, more out of temperamental timidity than because he agreed with it, but his colleague Richard Reynolds stood with Fisher and More, and, like them, paid with his life. In the last days of its existence Syon was under constant scrutiny and pressure as a nest of potential papists. The Carthusians produced no writer of Whitford's skill or influence, but the very high quality of their regular life made them the only monastic order which was held in generally high regard on the eve of the Reformation. Both Thomas More and Reginald Pole spent extremely formative periods of their lives at the London Charterhouse, and it was the principled resistance of Prior Houghton and his monks to the oath of supremacy which goaded the king into ordering the most barbarous executions of his reign. Their heroism was to feed the hagiographical traditions of the future, but they did not inspire imitators and indeed the Carthusians were both too few and too austere to make much impact on the religion of the people.

A good monk scarcely appeared in public places, and his role was that of a surrogate rather than an example, but the same was not true of a friar. The mendicants were in many ways more relevant to the development of the Reformation, and although equally its victims, also provided a disproportionate number of the original protestant leaders. The reason for this lay in the distinctive nature of their ministry, which brought them directly into contact with the spiritual problems of daily life, but did not provide the institutional support of a parish church. There were about 3,000 friars in England and Wales in 1500. Unlike the monks, their recruitment had recovered well during the fifteenth century, and it is reasonable to conclude that the active life was more attractive than the contemplative on the eve of the Reformation. But active is a relative term, and with the exception of a small number of observant Franciscans the English friars of Henry VIII's reign were distinguished neither by intellect nor energy. Even Henry Standish, the belligerent Warden of the Greyfriars who defended the king's intervention in ecclesiastical affairs against Abbot Kidderminster, was an enemy of Erasmus and an extreme conservative in some aspects of his thinking. Nevertheless the academic tradition of the friars, and particularly of the Dominicans, was stronger than that of the monks, and it was at the University of Cambridge in the 1520s that the new generation of young men first encountered the theology of Luther. A friar's business was to preach and to argue, and energetic minds, such as Bilney, Coverdale and Bale, were quickly attracted by a technique of exposition which was both more compelling and more spiritually alive than their own somewhat arid dialectic. Nicholas del Burgo, a Florentine Franciscan, was one of Henry VIII's specialist advisers over the divorce; Robert Barnes, William Roy, an Observant of Greenwich, and Bartholomew Traheron all became prominent reformers, writers and polemicists. Such men were not necessarily characteristic of their orders. The Observant Franciscans at Greenwich as a house were deeply committed to the support of Catherine of Aragon, and several of them sealed their own fate by becoming involved with Elizabeth Barton 'the nun of Kent' in 1532.[11] The majority of the friars, like the majority of those they ministered to, remained loyal to the old faith, and after the dissolution of their houses became cantarists, chaplains and curates, sometimes remaining in the latter capacity well into the reign of Elizabeth.

As a body, the clergy responded only sluggishly to the dramatic changes of pace and direction which were imposed upon the Church between 1535 and 1560. Apart from the Carthusians only a handful refused the oath of supremacy, which was hardly surprising since an issue of high principle barely impinged upon their daily work. Many were unsettled and distressed by the changes of the 1530s; the attack on Purgatory, the reform of the calendar and the appearance of the Great Bible. Their constant grumblings were frequently picked up by Cromwell's alert agents; many were interrogated, and a few were imprisoned, but only those who refused the oath suffered. There was significant clerical participation in the Pilgrimage of Grace, but many of the monks from the dissolved houses who became involved seem to have acted reluctantly, because it was expected of them, and the man who was most insistent upon the religious nature of the rising was a layman, Robert Aske. By 1545 resistance to the king's 'proceedings' from the conservative side was minimal, and the principal dissidents were protestants. Some of these, like John Hooper and John Burcher, took refuge abroad, others no doubt dissembled and waited for better times. Henry continued to execute outspoken protestants, and clergy formed a high proportion of the victims. When the next dramatic change came, between 1547 and 1549, it was again the turn of the conservatives to be disgruntled. Complaint was very widespread, passive resistance common, and active resistance occasional. Lord Grey hanged several priests from the spires of their own churches in Oxfordshire, and a dozen clerical leaders were executed in Devon; but the vast majority conformed more or less willingly, and some began to show positive enthusiasm for the new ways. At the beginning of Mary's reign the real surprise is not the speed and spontaneity of the conservative reaction, but rather its patchy and hesitant nature. Robert Parkyn explained that, in spite of being required to say Mass by 'lords and knights catholic', many clergy hesitated 'although wholly inclined that way' because 'there was no act, statute nor proclamation set forth for the same'. In other words tarrying for the magistrate had already become a deeply ingrained habit. Mary was much more thorough in rooting out protestants and their fellow-travellers than either Edward or Elizabeth was with the catholics, but the largest number of deprivations was for marriage, and the majority of incumbents so deprived seem to have been rehabilitated. About 30 were burned during the persecution, and over 100 fled abroad, but the majority of those who had conformed to Edward's Church conformed to Mary's also, in spite of their incompatibility. At the beginning of Elizabeth's reign only some 300 refused to take the oath of supremacy, although many continued to celebrate the Mass in secret for years to come.

The most obvious explanation for this unheroic conduct is simply human nature. The clergy were men trying to protect their livelihoods, and in many cases no doubt feeling that conformity would protect their flocks as well as themselves. There was also a distinct shortage of episcopal leadership, not necessarily for unworthy reasons. With the notable exception of John Fisher the Henrician bishops accepted the supremacy out of loyalty to the king, and because they were willing to believe that he would do his duty in defence of the Church. The conservative bishops resisted Edward's changes, but *in camera*, in parliament and council, because, like their predecessors, they were loyal to the crown and unwilling to stir up sedition in the realm. The protestant bishops yielded to Mary on principle, adding an apocalyptic garnish to their political allegiance, and Mary's bishops did much the same to Elizabeth. As individuals they remained true to their confession, but they made no public attempt to encourage their clergy to resist. Such attempts were made, by polemical writers based abroad, just as they had been under Mary, but the outgoing hierarchy gave them no countenance. Nor was papal leadership particularly compelling, even when it was relevant. Paul III's excommunication of Henry VIII went off like a damp firecracker, and because it would have needed French or Imperial force to implement it, strengthened the king's hand rather than weakening it. And for the first ten years of Elizabeth's reign the papacy hung back for political reasons, leaving its followers in England in limbo.[12] By the time that it did act in 1570, there was only a residual Church left to protect. Either directly or indirectly the role of the crown explains the reaction of the clergy. Except for those with very assiduous consciences, the duty of Christian obedience was sufficient absolution in the sight of God, particularly if it also aligned with the course of safety and convenience. Moreover, the eyes of the council could not be everywhere, and there was plenty of scope for dissembling and evasion. Even Mary's vigilant bishops were still discovering congregations using the second Edwardian Prayer Book in 1556. Outward conformity was all that any government was able to demand, and all that the majority of the clergy were willing to offer. Ironically, the main casualty was the spiritual life of the English Church, the improvement of which was the declared aim of all parties.

'If gold rusts, what shall iron do?' If the shepherds were confused and irresolute, it is not surprising that their flocks followed the line of least resistance. Lollardy may have increased somewhat in the early decades of the sixteenth century, but there is no reason to suppose that, left to its own devices, it would have made any greater inroads into the traditional faith than it had done at the previous high point of its influence in the last decade of the fourteenth century. There were individual protestants in England from the 1520s onwards, but there were no Lutheran or Zwinglian congregations. Nevertheless there are clear indications that many traditional practices and attitudes had begun to lose their appeal before the official Church began to move in a protestant direction in 1547. The last edition of the once popular *legenda aurea* was published in 1529. In the fairly conservative diocese of Exeter 80% of the wills proved between 1520 and 1544 contained bequests for traditional pious purposes – Requiem Masses, obits, altar furnishings and so on – but only 20% of those proved between 1545 and 1569.[13] Church building and extension, still actively going on down to 1540, had virtually ceased a decade later. The explanation for this lies less in some spontaneous shift in religious priorities than in the actions of government. The destruction of the pilgrimage shrines particularly delivered a sharp rebuff to the whole practice of formal penance, and demonstrated that the Royal Supremacy spelled the end of ecclesiastical immunity. Neither thunderbolt nor plague struck the temerarious king or his agents to bear witness to the outraged dignity of St Thomas or St Cuthbert. No aura of sanctity had ever entirely protected churches from robbery or embezzlement, but the events of 1538 were unprecedented both in their scope and in their implications. The great Boxley Rood, venerated for generations, was burned at Paul's Cross on 22 February, its fraudulent nature having been exposed in an iconoclastic sermon. On 22 May the Welsh image of Derfel Gadarn was similarly destroyed at Smithfield. Not only were wagon loads of gold and jewels removed from Canterbury and Walsingham, but the whole devotion to which they had witnessed was called in question. The religious significance of this official iconoclasm was much greater than that of the dissolution of the lesser monasteries, important though that was.

'Religion is making favourable progress among us', wrote the protestant Nicholas Partridge to Heinrich Bullinger in September 1538, 'By order of the king, persons are sent to preach the truth in all parts of England. You have, I suppose, heard long since respecting the Lady of Walsingham, and the breaking in pieces of other idols.'[14]

When the royal commissioners visited the shrine of St Swithun at Winchester, they were careful to make the religious purpose of their action clear, lest it should be thought that 'we came more for the treasure than for the avoiding of the abomination of idolatry'.[15]

The psychological impact of this campaign was great because it was so widespread, and must have encouraged genuine religious doubt as well as a certain amount of cynical opportunism. A popular concept of holiness had been mocked and flouted, not by a few humble heretics but by the king and his council, with the bishops at least acquiescing, and sometimes preaching the sermons. The simplification of the calendar was another minor step in the same direction. First the relics of the saints, and then their festal days; if the company of heaven was so ineffectual in looking after its own interests, how effective would its members be in promoting the interests of their suppliants? At the same time the appearance of the Great Bible began to open up an altogether different style of piety. As with earlier Lollard works, the Bible began to be read publicly. Between 1538 and 1543, when its use was temporarily restricted by statute, Bible reading seems to have acquired a wide popularity. Such reading was not only favoured by protestants and Lollards, but also by many to whom the orthodox but simplified piety of Whitford also appealed. The decline of the old usages was not entirely a negative matter, but it would be a mistake to think that those who were no longer enthralled by the lives of the saints or the *Dialogue of Miracles* had necessarily abandoned the doctrines of the traditional Church. As we can see with particular clarity during the reign of Mary, a sensitive and practical spirituality was by no means confined to those who embraced justification by faith alone. The sermons of Thomas Watson were far removed from the crude materialism of Johan Tetzel. In linking faith to good works, he wrote 'The success of the work bringeth sweetness, and the increase of virtue new repaired bringeth gladness to our minds . . .'.[16] Unfortunately, as the enlightened on both sides acknowledged, the unsettling of popular faith resulted in the growth of ribaldry and indifference rather than the enhanced spirituality which both Cranmer and Gardiner were seeking.

This became increasingly obvious during the reign of Edward VI, when the already weakened fabric of traditional practice offered almost no resistance to the protestant onslaught. Between 1547 and 1549 the whole structure of intercession was dismantled. It is not surprising to find that, by 1552, only 6% of testators in Kent were still making bequests in the old fashion; what is slightly less expected is to discover that the percentage had already declined from 90 to 52 between 1530 and 1546.[17] By 1552 not only had images, processions and all the innumerable ritual actions of long-established custom been swept away, but the Mass itself had gone, and with it the altars and the elaborate furnishings which only twenty years earlier had been such a subject of pride and expenditure. As far as the evidence reveals, very few people positively wanted this to happen; more or less articulate regret was very widespread. As we have already seen, Martin Bucer commented upon the negative nature of the Edwardian changes, and ardent reformers such as Hooper and

Knox were profoundly disappointed by their own failure to inculcate any enthusiasm for sermons, congregational discipline or the reformed liturgy. Generally they blamed the shortage of preachers (which was real enough), but it was also true that protestantism was a highly literate and colourless form of Christianity, which seemed to have little to offer to the man or woman brought up with the comforts of a very visible and tangible piety. In due course the Prayer Book and the English Bible would develop a genuine popularity of their own, but that could not be created by decree, any more than inflation could be checked by proclamations. The protestantism of Edward VI's reign was not a natural growth, it was highly artificial and imposed by authority; nevertheless it was successfully imposed. Although vestments, images and liturgical books were often taken away and hidden, conformity was effectively enforced upon the parish churches. Not only were the ecclesiastical authorities surprisingly energetic in this respect, they were well backed up by the secular magistrates. This was partly because there were enough committed protestant clergy to carry out the visitations, and partly because the gentry had been too alarmed by the disturbances of 1548–9 to wish to encourage resistance to authority, even when it took a form with which they had much sympathy. Also, although Edward's reign was short, it was long enough to enable quite a lot of latent protestantism to crystallize. Old Lollards, humanist reformers and many individuals who had picked up a patchwork of evangelical ideas, were able to embrace the established faith, and to benefit from their willing conformity. It might be thought that Devon was a stronghold of conservative resistance, given the events at Sampford Courtenay in 1549 and their sequel; yet in 1536 Dr Tregonwell had been impressed by the 'conformity' of both Devon and Cornwall, a word which was again employed by the royal commissioners in 1553, and in a report from the justices in 1569. Churchwardens' accounts, where they survive, confirm the promptness with which the majority of parishes obeyed royal and episcopal orders.

Mary's policies provided the acid test for the Edwardian achievement, and it soon became apparent that the protestant preachers had accomplished rather more than their despair in the autumn of 1553 would suggest. The prevailing emotion was certainly one of contented willingness to return to the old ways.

But there were now congregations which were protestant in more than a conformist sense; in East Anglia and London particularly, but also in other large towns such as Exeter and Newcastle. Such congregations were nearly always the work of talented and respected individual ministers, such as Rowland Taylor at Hadleigh, and they did not form a large proportion of the whole; but they were significant out of all proportion to their numbers. When the persecution began in 1555, it was not only attacking individual heretics, as had been the case under Henry VIII, or a very amorphous association of the like-minded, such as Lollardy had been. It was dealing instead with congregations which supported and encouraged each other, which had a collective morale. This was one of the main reasons why the old Lollards recanted so easily, and the new protestants so often refused. They were, after all, much the same kind of people, artisans, apprentices, shepherds, small farmers, craftsmen, and their beliefs were not so very different. Perhaps justification by faith alone gave the new dissenters a sense of election which the old had lacked, but what principally strengthened the likes of Thomas Watts and Bartlet Green was the knowledge that the prayers of the faithful were being offered on their behalf, not in any notional or abstract sense, but the prayers of the families and friends with whom they had worshipped. It might seem that a protestant congregation lacked the collective identity provided by the corporate rituals of the old faith, but that would be to mistake the importance of fellowship in prayer. The Marian protestants, like the French Huguenots, derived their strength from their sense of belonging to the true Church, and that Church had a local habitation and a name. Several Prayer Book congregations continued to worship clandestinely throughout the persecution, and there may have been others which have left no traces. How long such entities could have survived, given their recent establishment, it is difficult to say, but by analogy with underground Calvinist congregations elsewhere in Europe, probably quite a long time. Unlike the radical groups, which tended to spring up and disappear within a few years, protestant Churches with an established and ordained ministry and a recognized membership, had considerable stamina.

The Marian Churches were also held together by an extensive polemical and devotional literature rather as the Lollard congregations had been. This was mostly printed abroad and the authorities tried in vain to suppress, or neutralize it. As the toll of deaths mounted towards its eventual total of about 280, an embryonic martyrology developed; and as we have already seen, traditional English xenophobia also contributed to the rising prestige of the victims in the eyes of the rest of society. By comparison, the restored catholic Church lacked edge. Pole's conviction that the faith would be restored by the natural momentum of conservative habits was understandable, but mistaken. Apart from persecution, the ardent convictions of the protestant minority were confronted with sound humanist devotion and a lot of traditional ritual, rather than with the tough-minded theology of the Jesuits or the Dominicans. 40% of the Kentishmen who made wills during Mary's reign reverted to the traditional formula. Had the reign lasted longer that proportion might well have increased, but there were few signs of large-scale generosity to the Church among the nobility and gentry. The tough battle which had been fought over secularized Church lands had not encouraged spontaneous gestures of repentance and piety. Under Mary the protestant settlement turned out to be much stronger at the grass roots than it was at the level of political action. The great majority of ordinary people followed the example of their betters and conformed, but the Marian Church was actually less effective in imposing conformity upon the reluctant than the Edwardian Church had been. This was partly, of course, because the catholic restoration cost money. Altars had to be rebuilt, images restored, new vestments purchased, and if the old 'massing gear' could not be brought out of its secret hiding place, then it had to be replaced. In many places all this was done with a good enough will, but it was not always heresy which made churchwardens and vestries drag their feet. There was often uncertainty, particularly after 1555, as to how long the Restoration was going to last. Margaret Sutton of Stafford, who left her best kerchief to be made into a corporas for the local friary 'if (it) go up again', was typical of this sort of doubt.[18] The restored religious communities were elderly, and attracted few new vocations. By 1558 traditional piety had not even recovered the level of 1546, let alone that of 1530; so it is not entirely accurate to attribute the relative failure of the old faith to recover its former allegiance to the shortness of time. Mary and Pole managed to halt, and to reverse, a process of inexorable decline that went back well before the advent of established protestantism. It would have required not only more time, but also a more positive policy, to have achieved more.

Just as Edwardian protestantism was tested by Mary, so Marian catholicism was tested by Elizabeth. Apart from the bishops, who were hamstrung (as Edward's had been) by their non-resistance principles, it was found wanting at both the political and clerical levels. However, among the nobility, gentry and commons alike, there was a tough survivalism, which fell well short of open defiance. The lack of open catholic resistance was due more to the tactics adopted by the queen than to the absence of robust conservative sympathies. Elizabeth did not really mind even if men and women who were close to her attended clandestine masses, provided that they took the oath of supremacy if required to do so, and abstained from intriguing with papal agents. The queen was not deceived (as her sister had been) into believing that a preference for conservative religious practices meant a conscientious allegiance to Rome. It was only when a pressing and unwelcome invitation to send representatives to the Council of Trent arrived in the spring of 1561 that Cecil and Bacon deemed it convenient to discover wide-ranging religious non-conformity, which appeared to threaten the 1559 settlement. Had Elizabeth allowed her bishops to be as thorough in rooting out the mass as Mary's had been in seeking heresy, the first decade of her reign would have looked very different. But to their bewilderment and chagrin they were checked, and their zeal discouraged. Survivalism was common, but we should beware of making it appear more common than it was by the selective use of evidence. In the Kentish wills already cited, traditional formulae had dropped to 9% by 1560, only slightly higher than in 1552, and the conclusion should be that, once again, the overwhelming majority of the population conformed. Before 1570 Elizabeth was willing, up to a point, to indulge the conservative sympathies of her subjects. Thereafter, thanks to belated papal action, she was forced to adopt a tougher stance, and catholic recusancy came into existence. There were, of course, those, particularly among the clerical elite, to whom a heretical Church was unendurable. There was consequently a clerical exodus, modest in scale but formidable in quality, from the universities to France and the Low Countries between 1559 and 1565. From their retreats in Paris and Louvain men like

Thomas Harding kept up a formidable polemical barrage against the Elizabethan settlement. But they lacked the popular appeal of their protestant predecessors, and there was little incentive to run the risk of defying a lawful government for the sake of an ecclesiastical principle which had little grasp on the public mind.

Those who point out that England was not a protestant country in 1560 are perfectly correct in the sense that only a minority of the population believed in justification by faith alone, or could honestly say that they preferred the Prayer Book to the Mass. On the other hand it was not a catholic country either, if by that is meant not only a preference for traditional ritual but also a refusal to accept the Royal Supremacy. We should beware of attributing too much importance to minorities. Just as Lollard activity before 1520 does not mean a general dissatisfaction with the late medieval Church, so conservative survivalism after 1560 does not mean a general rejection of the Elizabethan settlement. There were also tiny radical minorities, which run like a scarlet thread throughout the whole period. Often called 'anabaptists' by their contemporaries, they cannot really be classified under any general heading, because their views were so diverse.

> 'The anabaptists flock to this place (London), and give me much trouble with their opinions respecting the incarnation of the Lord . . .'

John Hooper had written to Bullinger in 1549. Nine years later, the story was much the same, as Chedsey complained to Bonner,

> 'Would to God the honourable council saw the face of Essex as we do see it. We have such obstinate heretics, anabaptists and other unruly persons here as was never heard of . . . .'.[19]

Some of these radicals were individual eccentrics, some were Lollards, and some, like Joan Bocher and George Van Parris, the only heretics to be burned in Edward's reign, probably derived their views from the Low Countries either directly or indirectly. The Free-Willers under Edward, the followers of 'Father Brown' at Islington in Mary's reign, or the Family of Love under Elizabeth, were all radical groups. None of them could properly be described as a sect, let alone a Church, and their protestantism is debatable. They form an interesting element in the English Reformation, but the brief upsurge of political sectarianism in the seventeenth century has exaggerated their importance. They represented a genuine element in the religion of the people, but being neither intellectually nor politically acceptable to any government, they catered only for the temperamental or congenital non-conformist. The safest generalization is that the religion of the people was conformity, and that the eventual triumph of Anglicanism by the end of the sixteenth century owed more to Elizabeth's longevity and the consistency of her policy than it did to any inherent appeal of protestantism to the people of England.

# EPILOGUE: THE LEGACY OF THE MID-TUDOR PERIOD

An Englishman born in about 1520 would have found the land of his middle age different in a number of respects from that of his youth; but it is unlikely that he would have been much distressed or excited by the changes. A woman sat on the throne which for centuries had known only kings, but she was a Tudor who had acquired the crown by lawful inheritance, and she had already demonstrated the political competence of her family. The constitutional changes which had taken place during his adolescence, and which had so upset some men of his father's and grandfather's generations, had become accepted and familiar. The structure of government as it affected him had changed but little. If he was a countryman, the Justices of the Peace had a few more duties, and were perhaps a little more intrusive than they had been. If he was a townsman, there was a greater chance that his town would have been recently incorporated, and that he would be enjoying the privileges of corporate citizenship. But such privileges were cast in the traditional mould of rule by mayor, aldermen and elected councillors; no radical adjustment would have been necessary in his perception of authority. The system of law under which he lived was the same, the courts were the same, and so were the familiar punishments. Statutes had created some new offences, and modified his duties if he should chance to sit on a jury, but the roots of the law were still in immemorial custom. There would have been a 10% chance that our notional man would have been affected by some change of land use or farming method, which might, or might not, have worked to his advantage. But economic vicissitudes of that kind happened in every generation, and his father's bitter grumbling

184

about enclosure seemed less relevant by the end of the first decade of Elizabeth's reign. He could hardly have failed to notice the great influenza epidemic of 1557–9, which would certainly have cost the life of at least one member of his close family, and laid others low for months at a time. By 1565 the effects might have faded, but the memory would not. The military duties of a citizen had been redefined in 1557, and a husbandman or craftsman was less likely to be conscripted for overseas service in 1565 than twenty years earlier; a return to the proprieties which Henry VIII had often ignored. In spite of the brief and heady convulsions of 1548–9, of which he might well have been keenly aware, nothing very much had changed in the social order. There were rather fewer noble retainers around, but the gentlemen were as powerful as ever, and whether you liked it or not, it was as well to keep a deferential tongue in your head, and to doff your bonnet when addressing your betters.

The most noticeable changes related to the Church. There was no longer an abbey in the next valley, or a friary in the nearest town. The familiar buildings had been converted into large houses, but their owners had probably been the monastic stewards, and only the absence of doles at the abbey gate would have made much practical difference. The parish church, on the other hand, was transformed in everything except its basic structure. Gone were the colourful rituals, and most of the comforting rites of passage. If you feared supernatural terrors, there was little 'church magic' left for consolation. The small benefactions which his father and his aunt had left to the high altar had been taken by the king's commissioners, and he could no longer have a Requiem Mass celebrated for the child which had died prematurely. On the other hand, there was something to be said for being able to follow the services, and a lot to be said for hearing the word of God read out Sunday by Sunday. It might even be worth learning to read, since the Bible was open for all to come at. The parson had survived all the changes, and was no more of a preacher now than he had been twenty years before, but at least he read the homilies and visited the sick. Corpus Christi had gone, and so had creeping to the cross, but the meaning of Christmas and Easter had not changed. There were fewer feasts than there had been, but they were kept with as good a will. Visually the Church was drab; no candles,

185

no gaily painted images; nothing really to fôcus a sense of identity. But praying and singing together maintained as much unity as the constant feuding of a closely knit community had ever allowed. And one thing had not changed; a word or a gesture out of place, or the rumour of a scandalous relationship, and the churchwardens would still present you at the archdeacon's visitation, as their forebears had done for generations. Like the Justices of the Peace, the churchwardens were becoming more noticeable, as they collected the contributions for poor relief, and decided who was to receive it. The other most noticeable change was the price of everything. A penny did not go nearly as far as it used to, and the government seemed to be more interested in controlling wages than prices. If you took more than the justices had decided was your due, you could be in serious trouble. There seemed to be rules and regulations about everything. Surely there was more government than there had been a generation before.

It is very unlikely that the ordinary man would have had any sense of having passed through a great crisis. His better educated and more alert contemporary, however, might have seen it rather differently. Having a queen instead of a king upon the throne had not made much difference to the effectiveness of government, but it had raised all sorts of questions about the relationship between the monarch and the state, some of which had not been resolved. There had been a serious attempt to prevent Mary from claiming the throne when her brother died, not because she was a woman, but because she was an unmarried woman, and the country feared an unknown and possibly foreign king. The attempt had failed for a variety of reasons, but most particularly because Mary's claim had been solidly rooted in the law and sanctioned by statute. Men might fear a foreign king, but they feared even more a king who could set the law aside by his own whim, especially when he was not even a grown man. So there had been a crisis in the state in July 1553, and the fact that it had been overcome did not make it any less real. And then the dreaded foreign king had come, in the person of Philip of Spain. Philip had allowed himself to be restrained by an elaborate treaty, and his time had been mercifully brief; but there could be no guarantee that if the new queen chose similarly, the country would escape so lightly. No marriage meant no direct heir, but marriage was hazardous for the realm, in whatever direction Elizabeth's fancy might move. No one wanted another foreign adventure, but then no one wanted Lord Robert Dudley either. An unmarried queen was a crisis in herself. Elizabeth was using an imagery of marriage between herself and the realm, and that would be very acceptable, provided that she meant it.[1] Fortunately the machinery of government – the council, parliament and commissions of the peace – was stable and functioning well. The nobility appeared to have accepted their greater dependence upon the crown; and after the fright that they had received in 1548–9, nobles and gentlemen seemed to be collaborating effectively to maintain order. The commonwealth intellectuals had frightened themselves into virtual silence after that debacle, and although social tensions remained, nobody was now trying to exploit them for ideological reasons. After the bad harvests and epidemics at the end of Mary's reign a period of recovery was urgently needed, and the fact that the early harvests of Elizabeth's reign were good, and that the recoinage temporarily checked inflation, had a calming effect upon the situation.

Looking further afield, there was change in the air, although it would have required a far-sighted man to appreciate how important that was going to be. Relations with France were improving, and with Spain deteriorating, so that the possibility of a diplomatic revolution could not be ignored. The loss of Calais had finally been accepted at the Treaty of Troyes,[2] and the King of Spain's ambassador was complaining almost monthly of the depredations of English pirates upon his master's shipping. Moreover, the queen was definitely encouraging the same pirates, especially when they posed as merchants and crossed the Atlantic. The horizons of the Merchant Adventurers, confined for so long to Antwerp and Middleburg, were widening rapidly, and English navigators no longer had to go to school to the Iberians. England had not turned her back upon the Continent – she could not afford to do that – but the queen was no longer interested in European adventures to the extent to which both Henry VIII and Mary had been. Thoughtful men like John Dee were already beginning to say that England's future greatness should be sought upon the seas. The English had always been a proud and xenophobic people. Even during the Hundred Years War they had claimed a special relationship with the Almighty, and that sense of a distinctive providence was powerfully reinforced by the advent of protestantism. Henry VIII's subjects had supported his eccentric course, partly out of loyalty to him, and partly out of contempt for the foreign powers which had tried to recall him to the path of orthodoxy. But they had not particularly warmed to the new theology coming in from Germany and Switzerland. Hugh Latimer had greeted the birth of Prince Edward in 1537 with the announcement that God was English, but that was an endorsement of the king's proceedings rather than reformed doctrine. However, the official adoption of protestantism under Edward VI began to change that perception. Whether they liked it or not, the young king's subjects were driven at last to accept that the reformed faith represented the personal conviction of the Supreme Head, and not just the fancy of his regents. Determined conservatives such as Gardiner and the Princess Mary took refuge in the fact that he was not technically of age, but no one who knew Edward was in any doubt as to where he stood. Gardiner attempted to claim that being 'a good Englishman' meant the defence of Henry VIII's settlement, but such an argument became less and less convincing as the reign advanced, and by 1552 anything less than protestantism savoured of disloyalty to the crown.

Such, at least, was the official position. In fact only a minority saw their patriotism in religious terms. Luther, Zwingli and Calvin were just as foreign as the pope; and the perception of a distinctly English protestantism, based on Cranmer's liturgy and tracing its origins back to Wycliffe, was only just beginning. Mary unintentionally furthered that process. In spite of never having been outside England, the experiences of her adolescence had alienated her from her father's people, and caused her to look towards her Habsburg relatives for identity and support. Not understanding the strength of English prejudices, she blamed the obvious and sometimes physical hostility to Philip and his followers upon the heretics, thus presenting them with the credit for defending England's interests. Worse still, she allowed Philip a very high profile role in the reconciliation, which he was anxious to embrace for his own purposes. A foreign pope was thus brought back by a foreign king, and the ironic fact that they were soon bitter enemies did nothing to mitigate the effect of the association. When Mary's pregnancy failed in 1555, and then the harvest failed, and then there was lethal influenza, and then Calais was lost, the persecuted protestants did the obvious thing. They cried judgement at the tops of their voices. Mary became

'Another Athalia, that is an utter destroyer of her own kindred, kingdom and country, a hater of her own subjects, a lover of strangers . . .'.[3]

and martyrs for the faith could also be represented as martyrs for the freedom of England. In 1558 there was nothing irresistible about this tide. An upturn in the queen's fortunes, peace with France and a few good harvests, and it would have remained the view of a dissident minority. But Mary died before any recovery could be sighted, at the nadir of her fortunes, and her successor exploited the situation for all it was worth.

'Englishness' was as important to Elizabeth as it had been unimportant to Mary, and at the very beginning of her reign she was given a unique opportunity to blend protestantism and patriotism into a compelling ideology. 'Come, give me your hand my dear lover England', says the character 'Bessy' in William Birch's ballad *A song between the Queens Majesty and England* of 1559,

'My sweet realm be obedient to God's holy commandment, and my proceedings embrace, For that is abused shall be better used, and that within short space . . . .'

By 1565, reinforced by the patriotic eschatology of Foxe's *Acts and Monuments*, such ideas were rapidly gaining ground. John Wycliffe had become the 'morning star' of the Reformation, which had thus taken its true beginning not in Germany, but in Oxford. Elizabeth's survival, and the stability of her regime, gave them time to take root, and to become an established orthodoxy. By 1580 William Charke could write, in his *Answer to a seditious pamphlet*, 'Religion and policy are, through God's singular blessing, preserved together in life as with one spirit; he that doth take away the life of the one doth procure the death of the other'.[4] Of all the seeds sown during the middle years of the sixteenth century, this was the most dynamic, and ultimately the most fruitful. But without the solid continuities of law, administration and effective royal government, it would have accomplished nothing. The years from 1545 to 1565 saw no revolutions either in society or in politics. What they did see was a system of government tested in various ways, and found adequate for its task. More by accident than design they also saw a new national myth forged out of the achievements of Henry VIII and the misfortunes of Mary by the good luck and dexterity of Elizabeth and Sir William Cecil. But more good luck was needed, because the queen was unmarried, and her heir was the Franco-Scottish catholic Mary Stuart. Anyone looking at the situation of England in 1565 could have been forgiven for thinking that the crisis was still to come.

# NOTES

## Introduction

1. W. R. D. Jones, *The Mid-Tudor Crisis, 1539–1563* (London, 1973), pp. 1–6.
2. D. M. Loades, *Mary Tudor; A Life* (Oxford, 1989), p. 327.
3. R. B. Outhwaite, *Inflation in Tudor and Stuart England* (London, 1969), p. 10; P. Ramsey (ed.), *The Price Revolution in sixteenth century England* (London, 1971), pp. 38ff; J. Thirsk (ed.), *The Agrarian History of England and Wales* (Cambridge, 1967), p. 865.
4. C. Haigh (ed.), *The English Reformation Revised* (London, 1987); J. J. Scarisbrick, *The Reformation and the English People* (Oxford, 1984); Patrick Collinson, *The Birthpangs of Protestant England* (London, 1988).

## Chapter 1

1. R. A. Griffiths, *The Reign of King Henry VI* (London, 1981), pp. 867–8.
2. Mortimer Levine, *Tudor Dynastic Problems, 1467–1571* (London, 1973), p. 120.
3. Sir Thomas Smith, *De Republica Anglorum*, ed. Mary Dewar (Cambridge, 1982), pp. 78–9.
4. *Calendar of State Papers, Spanish*, eds Royall Tyler et al. (London, 1862–1954), Vol. IX, p. 38.
5. J. G. Nichols, *Narratives of the Reformation* (Camden Society, Vol. LXXVII), pp. 225–6.
6. W. K. Jordan, *Edward VI; the threshold of power* (London, 1970),

p. 527; *Vita Mariae Reginae of Robert Wingfield of Brantham*, ed. D. MacCulloch (Camden Miscellany, Vol. XXVIII), p. 255.

7.   Loades, *Mary Tudor*, pp. 288–9.
8.   Philip was descended via his mother, Isabella, from the marriage between King John of Portugal and Philippa, daughter of John of Gaunt.
9.   Christophe d'Assonleville to Philip, 7 November 1558; *Calendar of State Papers Spanish*, Vol. XIII, pp. 437–8.
10.  J. A. Muller, *The Letters of Stephen Gardiner* (Cambridge, 1933), p. 299.
11.  J. Strype, *Ecclesiastical Memorials* (London, 1721), Vol. III, p. 55.
12.  D. M. Loades, 'Philip II and the government of England', in *Law and Government under the Tudors*, eds C. Cross, D. Loades and J. Scarisbrick (Cambridge, 1988), pp. 177–94.
13.  Derek Wilson, *Sweet Robin; A biography of Robert Dudley, Earl of Leicester, 1533–1588* (London, 1981), pp. 134–43.
14.  J. A. Guy, *The Cardinal's Court; the impact of Thomas Wolsey on Star Chamber* (Hassocks, 1977).
15.  J. A. Guy, *Tudor England* (Oxford, 1988), pp. 198–9; H. Miller, 'Henry VIII's unwritten will; grants of land and honours in 1547' in *Wealth and Power in Tudor England*, eds E. W. Ives, J. J. Knecht and J. J. Scarisbrick (London, 1978), pp. 87–105.
16.  The Groom of the Stool was in origin the king's most intimate body servant, with constant access to the person. By this time he was head of the Privy Chamber. D. E. Hoak, 'The King's Privy Chamber, 1547–1553' in *Tudor Rule and Revolution*, eds D. J. Guth and J. W. McKenna (Cambridge, 1982), pp. 87–108.
17.  D. E. Hoak, *The King's Council in the Reign of Edward VI* (Cambridge, 1976), pp. 55–71.
18.  That is, the ability to command personal service.
19.  PRO MS State Papers Domestic, Edward VI (SP10), Vol. XV, no. 66.
20.  D. M. Loades, *The Reign of Mary Tudor* (London, 1991), pp. 57–95.
21.  Ibid., pp. 200–201.
22.  *Acts of the Privy Council*, eds J. Dasent et al. (London, 1890–1907), Vol. IV, p. 398.

# Chapter 2

1. G. R. Elton, *The Tudor Constitution* (2nd edn, Cambridge, 1982), pp. 233–9.
2. A. G. R. Smith, *The Emergence of a Nation State; the commonwealth of England 1529–1660* (London, 1984), Appendix D2.
3. There had been a precedent for this level of activity in the early fifteenth century, but it had not been consolidated.
4. *Acts of the Privy Council*, Vol. II, p. 193; W. K. Jordan, *Edward VI; the threshold of power*, p. 184.
5. *Acts of the Privy Council*, Vol. II, pp. 248–56; J. Loach, *Parliament under the Tudors* (Oxford, 1991), p. 90.
6. J. Loach, *Parliament and the Crown in the reign of Mary Tudor* (Oxford, 1986).
7. R. A. de Vertot, *Ambassades de Messieurs de Noailles en Angleterre* (Leiden, 1763), Vol. V, p. 171.
8. Loach, *Parliament and the Crown*, pp. 148–50.
9. D. M. Loades, *Two Tudor Conspiracies* (Cambridge, 1965), p. 226.
10. Loades, *Reign of Mary Tudor*, p. 219.
11. R. S. Schofield, 'Parliamentary Lay Taxation, 1485–1547' (Cambridge Ph.D, 1963), pp. 198–215; J. A. Guy, 'Wolsey and the parliament of 1523', in *Law and Government under the Tudors*, pp. 1–18.
12. G. W. Bernard, *War, Taxation and Rebellion in Early Tudor England; Henry VIII, Wolsey and the Amicable Grant of 1525* (Brighton, 1986). The Amicable Grant was a Benevolence, and repayment was never promised, which intensified resistance.
13. J. A. Guy, *Tudor England*, pp. 143–5. The figures for income from monastic lands recently been raised by Dr. P. A. Cunich in an unpublished Ph.D thesis (Cambridge, 1991).
14. C. E. Challis, *The Tudor Coinage* (Manchester, 1978), pp. 81–111.
15. These figures are based on contemporary summaries and their precision may be doubted.
16. PRO MS State Papers Domestic, Mary (SP11), Vol. I, no. 14.
17. *Calendar of the Patent Rolls, Mary* (London, 1936–9), Vol. I, p. 72.
18. PRO MS State Papers, Domestic, Mary (SP11), Vol. IV, no. 6.
19. PRO MS Exchequer (E405), no. 484, ff. 1–3.
20. British Library, Cotton MS Titus C VI, ff. 198–9.
21. R. S. Schofield, 'Taxation and the political limits of the Tudor state' in *Law and Government under the Tudors*, eds C. Cross, D. Loades and J. Scarisbrick (Cambridge, 1988), pp. 227–56.
22. Loades, *Reign of Mary*, pp. 360–61.

# Chapter 3

1. *London 1500–1700; the making of the metropolis*, eds A. L. Beier and R. Finlay (London, 1986); S. Rappaport, *Worlds within worlds; the structures of life in sixteenth century London* (Cambridge, 1989).

2. D. M. Loades, 'The dissolution of the Diocese of Durham, 1553–4' in *Politics, Censorship and the English Reformation* (London, 1991), pp. 167–80.

3. Robert Tittler, 'The emergence of Urban Policy, 1536–1558' in *The Mid-Tudor Polity, c. 1540–1560*, eds J. Loach and R. Tittler, (London, 1980), pp. 74–93.

4. A. D. Dyer, *Decline and Growth in English Towns, 1400–1640* (London, 1991), Appendix 5.

5. Tittler, 'The emergence of an Urban Polity', pp. 76–7.

6. Thomas Starkey, *A Dialogue between Pole and Lupset*, ed. T. F. Mayer (Camden Society, Fourth Series, Vol. XXXVII), p. 118.

7. *A Discourse of the Common Weal of this Realm of England*, ed. E. Lamond (Cambridge, 1954), p. 130.

8. 'An act for avoiding of divers foreign wares made by handicraftsmen beyond the seas' (5 Elizabeth, c.7); *Tudor Economic Documents*, eds R. H. Tawney and Eileen Power (London, 1924), Vol. I, p. 126.

9. Loades, *Two Tudor Conspiracies*, p. 61.

10. C. S. L. Davies, 'Slavery and Protector Somerset; the vagrancy Act of 1547', *Economic History Review*, 2nd series, Vol. XIX, no. 3, 1966; John Pound, *Poverty and Vagrancy in Tudor England* (London, 1971); A. L. Beier, *Masterless Men; the Vagrancy Problem in England, 1560–1640* (London, 1985).

11. 'An act for the punishment of vagabonds, and for the relief of the poor and impotent' (14 Elizabeth, c.5); *Tudor Economic Documents*, Vol. II, pp. 328–30.

12. Jordan, *Edward VI; the threshold of power*, pp. 489–93; *Tudor Economic Documents*, Vol. II, pp. 37–47; Sir William Foster, *England's Quest of Eastern Trade*, (London, 1933).

13. G. Connell-Smith, *Forerunners of Drake; a study of English trade with Spain in the early Tudor period* (London, 1954), pp. 100–26.

14. *The Chronicle and Political Papers of King Edward VI*, ed. W. K. Jordan (London, 1966), p. 70.

15. J. A. Chartres, *Internal Trade in England, 1500–1700* (London, 1977), pp. 9–12.

16. PRO State Papers Domestic, Elizabeth (SP12), Vol. CV11, ff. 39–40.

17. R. H. Tawney and Eileen Power (eds), *Tudor Economic Documents*, Vol. I (3 vols., London, 1924) pp. 247–9.
18. Chartres, *Internal Trade*, p. 32.
19. *Tudor Economic Documents*, Vol. I, p. 126.

# Chapter 4

1. *Tudor Economic Documents*, Vol. III, pp. 51–6.
2. Robert Crowley on the causes of Kett's rebellion, *Tudor Economic Documents*, Vol. III, pp. 57–60.
3. R. H. Tawney, *The Agrarian Problem in the Sixteenth Century* (London, 1912).
4. Lawrence Stone, *The Crisis of the Aristocracy, 1558–1640* (Oxford, 1965).
5. E. Kerridge, *Agrarian Problems in the Sixteenth Century and After* (London, 1969), pp. 17–31.
6. That is, land which he was farming himself.
7. Philip Massinger, *A New Way to Pay Old Debts*, Act II, scene 1.
8. *Discourse*, p. 17.
9. R. B. Outhwaite, *Inflation in Tudor and Stuart England*, p. 10.
10. *Tudor Economic Documents*, Vol. III, p. 63.
11. J. E. Jackson, 'Wulfhall and the Seymours', *Wiltshire Archaeological Magazine*, 1875, Vol. XV, pp. 179–80.
12. C. S. L. Davies, 'The Pilgrimage of Grace Reconsidered', *Past and Present*, 1968, Vol. XLI, pp. 54–76; Davies, 'Popular religion and the Pilgrimage of Grace', in *Order and Disorder in Early Modern England*, eds A. Fletcher and J. Stevenson (Cambridge, 1985), pp. 58–91. M. L. Bush, ' "Up for the commonweal"; the significance of tax grievances in the English rebellion of 1536', *English Historical Review*, Vol. CVI, 1991, pp. 299–319; also Bush, 'Tax reform and rebellion in Early Tudor England', *History*, Vol. LXXVI, 1991, pp. 379–400.
13. *Tudor Royal Proclamations*, eds P. L. Hughes and J. F. Larkin (New Haven, Conn., 1964–9), Vol. I, pp. 427–9.
14. Loades, *Mary Tudor; a life*, pp. 137–9.
15. Julian Cornwall, *Revolt of the Peasantry, 1549* (London, 1977). The fact that many citizens of Exeter sympathized with the religious grievances of the rebels, but fought against the revolt, serves to emphasize this point. R. Whiting, *The Blind Devotion of the People*, p. 146.
16. *Tudor Royal Proclamations*, Vol. I, p. 461.

17. Jordan, *Edward VI; the young king*, p. 448. Religious conservatives were also behind disturbances in Yorkshire, but no clergy were among the known leaders.
18. Robert Whiting, *The Blind Devotion of the People; popular religion and the English Reformation* (Cambridge, 1989) pp. 125–44.
19. S. K. Land, *Kett's Rebellion* (Ipswich, 1977), p. 42.
20. Jordan, *Edward VI; the young king*, pp. 481–2; J. Strype, *Ecclesiastical Memorials*, Vol. II (i), pp. 271–2; D. MacCulloch, *Suffolk and the Tudors* (Oxford, 1986) pp. 301–4. MacCulloch presents a picture of widespread disaffection in Suffolk, pointing out that other 'camps' were set up in East Anglia, and that the extreme violence of the Norfolk confrontation arose through accident and ineptitude. Several of the other camps were pacified by negotiation, and preserved the same good discipline. The violence in Norfolk seems to have resulted from a degree of ineptitude on both sides, rather than from uncontrollable fury.
21. *Tudor Economic Documents*, Vol. I, p. 47.
22. *The Papers of George Wyatt*, ed. D. Loades (Camden Society, 4th series, Vol. V), p. 56.

# Chapter 5

1. That is, one who denied any spiritual presence in the Eucharistic elements, a position held at this stage by the reformers of Zurich.
2. A. G. Dickens, *The English Reformation*, 2nd edn (London, 1989), p. 200. The text of *The Institution of a Christian Man*, commonly called *The Bishops' Book* is printed in *Formularies of Faith*, ed. C. Lloyd (London, 1825), pp. 21–212.
3. Maria Dowling, *Humanism in the Age of Henry VIII* (London, 1986), pp. 66–8.
4. Gardiner to Lord Paget, 1 March 1547; Gardiner, *Letters*, p. 268.
5. J. Strype, *Memorials of . . . Thomas Cranmer*, Vol. I (London, 1694; Oxford, 1840), p. 206.
6. D. Loades, 'Books and the English Reformation to 1558', in *Politics, Censorship and the English Reformation*, pp. 127–50.
7. Dickens, *The English Reformation*, p. 231.
8. G. J. R. Parry, 'Inventing the "Good Duke" of Somerset', *Journal of Ecclesiastical History*, Vol. XL (1989), pp. 370–80.
9. Margaret Aston, *England's Iconoclasts; Laws against Images* (Oxford, 1988), pp. 252–4.
10. Dickens, *The English Reformation*, pp. 242–4.

11. *Original Letters relating to the English Reformation*, ed. H. Robinson (Parker Society, 1846), Vol. I, p. 351.
12. J. H. Primus, *The Vestments Controversy; an historical study of the earliest tensions within the Church of England in the reigns of Edward VI and Elizabeth* (Kampen, 1960).
13. Loades, 'The dissolution of the diocese of Durham, 1553–4'.
14. A receptionist was one who believed that the Divine presence in the Eucharist was induced by the faith of the recipient.
15. A good text of the articles is printed in Gilbert Burnet, *The History of the Reformation of the Church of England*, ed. N. Pocock (Oxford, 1865), Vol. V, pp. 314–29.
16. Hughes and Larkin, *Tudor Royal Proclamations*, Vol. II, p. 5.
17. Bucer to Calvin, 16 May 1550; *Original Letters*, Vol. II, p. 546; Hooper to Bullinger, 3 September 1553, ibid, Vol. 1, p. 100.
18. *Calendar of State Papers, Spanish*, Vol. XI, p. 419.
19. Loades, *Two Tudor Conspiracies*, passim.
20. Loades, *The Reign of Mary Tudor*, pp. 262–8.
21. British Library, MS Harleian 444, f. 27.
22. Carranza later claimed that, but the Spanish historian J. I. Tellechea Idigoras believed that if he exercised any influence, it was in the opposite direction. Loades, *The Reign of Mary Tudor*, p. 175.
23. Robert Pownall, *An Admonition in the town of Calais* (Unknown, 1557).
24. Strype, *Ecclesiastical Memorials*, Vol. III (ii), p. 503.
25. Loades, 'Books and the English Reformation prior to 1558'.

## Chapter 6

1. S. E. Brigden, *The Reformation in London* (Oxford, 1989), pp. 5–15.
2. J. A. F. Thomson, *The Later Lollards, 1414–1520* (Oxford, 1965).
3. J. Wycliffe, *Tractatus de Mandatis Divinis*, eds J. Loserth and F. D. Matthew (London, 1922), p. 158.
4. Aston, *England's Iconoclasts*, pp. 110–1.
5. Brigden, *The Reformation in London*, pp. 273–4.
6. J. J. Scarisbrick, *The Reformation and the English People*, pp. 1–18.
7. Strype, *Ecclesiastical Memorials*, Vol. III (ii), pp. 484–5.
8. Scarisbrick, *The Reformation and the English People*, pp. 19–39.
9. D. Loades, 'The collegiate churches of County Durham at the time of the dissolution', in *Politics, Censorship and the English Reformation*, pp. 159–65.

10. David Knowles, *The Religious Orders in England; the Tudor Age* (Cambridge, 1961), p. 470.
11. Knowles, *Religious Orders*, pp. 206–12.
12. C. G. Bayne, *Anglo-Roman Relations, 1558–1565* (Oxford, 1913).
13. Whiting, *The Blind Devotion of the People*, pp. 262–3.
14. *Original Letters*, Vol. II, p. 612.
15. M. Aston, *England's Iconoclasts* (Oxford, 1988), p. 236.
16. Watson, *Wholesome and Catholic Doctrine* (London, 1558), Sermon XV, f. 86.
17. Whiting, *The Blind Devotion of the People*, pp. 262–3.
18. A. F. Bartholomew, 'Lay piety in the reign of Mary Tudor' (Manchester M.A., 1979), p. 158.
19. British Library, MS Harleian 416, f. 77.

# Epilogue

1. Marie Axton, *The Queen's Two Bodies* (London, Royal Historical Society, 1977), pp. 38–60.
2. 11 April 1564, following the unsuccessful English occupation of Le Havre.
3. R. Pownall, *An Admonition to the town of Calais*, see above, p. 153.
4. W. Charke, *Answer*, Sig. C 1, r & v.

# SELECT AND ANNOTATED BIBLIOGRAPHY

## Bibliographies

Conyers Read (ed.) *Bibliography of British History, Tudor Period, 1485–1603* 2nd edn (Oxford, 1959, rep. 1978).
The standard bibliography for all works published before 1958.

M. Levine (ed.), *Tudor England, 1485–1603* (Cambridge 1968).
Produced for the conference on British Studies; useful but not comprehensive.

H. J. Creaton (ed.), *Writings on British History, 1967–1974* (London, Institute of Historical Research, 1982–6).
The last part of a series started in 1937 by A. T. Milne. The whole series is useful, but these last volumes bridge the gap between Levine and the RHS bibliography.

G. R. Elton (to 1984) and D. M. Palliser (eds), *Annual Bibliography of British and Irish History* (Brighton, 1976 – ongoing for the Royal Historical Society).
Comprehensive for all work published since 1975.

## General

G. R. Elton, *Reform and Reformation; England 1509–1558* (London, 1977).
A partial rethink of his classic *Tudor Revolution in Government* (1953); mainly about Henry VIII.

J. A. Guy, *Tudor England* (Oxford, 1988).
The standard textbook covering the whole period; based on the latest research, including the author's own. Excellent bibliography.

W. R. D. Jones, *The Mid-Tudor Crisis, 1539–1563* (London, 1973).
A specific, but dated, examination of the period; the proponent of the 'general crisis' view.

W. K. Jordan, *Edward VI; the Young King* (London, 1968).
A detailed narrative; a mine of information on the years 1547–9. Interpretation controversial, particularly on Protector Somerset. Should be read in conjunction with Bush (see below).

W. K. Jordan, *Edward VI; the Threshold of Power* (London, 1970).
Similar narrative of the years 1549–53; very useful. Argues that Edward was really in control by 1552.

J. Loach and R. Tittler (eds), *The Mid-Tudor Polity c. 1540–1560* (London, 1980).
A valuable collection of essays by the editors and others on specific aspects; no overall theme.

D. M. Loades, *Politics and the Nation, 1450–1660* (London, 1986).
An overview, placing the period in a long interpretative context.

D. M. Loades, *Mary Tudor; A Life* (Oxford, 1989).
Argues the influence of Mary's personal background on the policies of her reign.

D. M. Loades, *The Reign of Mary Tudor* (London, 1979; 1991).
The fullest history of the reign.

D. MacCulloch, *Suffolk and the Tudors* (Oxford, 1986).
The best study of any county during the period; contains excellent material on the disturbances of 1548 and 1549.

A. G. R. Smith, *The Emergence of a Nation State; the commonwealth of England, 1529–1660* (London, 1984).
Very well presented textbook interpretation; excellent appendices of information; readable and easy to use.

R. Tittler, *The Reign of Mary I* (London, 1983).
A 'seminar study', brief but useful; a good introduction to the reign.

## State

B. L. Beer, *Northumberland; the political career of John Dudley Earl of Warwick and Duke of Northumberland* (Kent, Ohio, 1973).
So far the only study of this important and controversial politican.

M. L. Bush, 'Tax reform and rebellion in Early Tudor England', *History*, Vol. LXXVI (1991), pp. 379–400.
The most recent re-examination of the role of tax demands in the creation of popular discontent. Emphasizes their importance.

M. L. Bush, *The Government Policy of Protector Somerset* (London, 1975).
The most intelligent treatment of the subject; a supplement and corrective to Jordan.

G. R. Elton, *The Tudor Constitution* (Cambridge, 1982).
An invaluable work of reference for consultation on the workings of the institutions of government.

S. R. Gammon, *Statesman and Schemer* (Newton Abbot, 1973).
The only full-length study of William, Lord Paget; useful, but not entirely satisfactory.

D. E. Hoak, *The King's Council in the Reign of Edward VI* (Cambridge, 1976).
A first class monograph, which is standing up very well to subsequent research.

D. E. Hoak, 'Rehabilitating the Duke of Nothumberland; Politics and Political Control, 1549–1553; in *The Mid-Tudor Polity* (see above).
Defending the Duke's record of financial and political management; useful.

D. E. Hoak, 'The King's Privy Chamber, 1547–1553' in D. J. Guth and J. W. McKenna (eds), *Tudor Rule and Revolution* (Cambridge, 1982).
A very useful supplement to his study of the council; contains fresh research.

J. Loach, *Parliament and the Crown in the Reign of Mary Tudor* (Oxford, 1986).
A detailed examination of the events of each parliament, with interpretation. A valuable study.

D. M. Loades, 'Philip II and the government of England' in C. Cross, D. Loades and J. Scarisbrick, *Law and Government under the Tudors* (Cambridge, 1988).
Argues that Philip's role was minimal, except over the reconciliation with Rome.

D. M. Loades, *Two Tudor Conspiracies* (Cambridge, 1965).
The Wyatt rebellion of 1554 and the Dudley conspiracy of 1556. Somewhat dated, but the only detailed study of these events.

W. T. MacCaffrey, *The Shaping of the Elizabethan Regime; Elizabethan politics, 1558–1572* (London, 1969).
The most complete and satisfactory overview of the complex politics of the first decade of Elizabeth's reign. Argues that she was very much in control.

Conyers Read, *Mister Secretary Cecil and Queen Elizabeth* (London, 1955).
Extremely detailed and scholarly, but has never been replaced as an account of Cecil's career and influence.

Elizabeth Russell, 'Mary Tudor and Mr. Jorkins', *Historical Journal*, Vol. LXIII (1990), pp. 263–76.
In spite of its slightly eccentric title, a serious attempt to argue that Mary was a highly-skilled politician. A viewpoint which must be taken into account.

Derek Wilson, *Sweet Robin; a biography of Robert Dudley, Earl of Leicester, 1533–1588* (London, 1981).
A well-written and sensible life of Leicester, soundly based upon the sources.

## Society

B. L. Beer, *Rebellion and Riot; Popular disorder in England during the reign of Edward VI* (Kent, Ohio, 1982).
A sensible modern survey; should be read in conjunction with MacCulloch (see above).

A. L. Beier, *Masterless Men; the Vagrancy Problem in England, 1560–1640* (London, 1985).
The best survey of the problem within a moderate compass.

C. E. Challis, *The Tudor Coinage* (Manchester, 1978).
Authoritative, and by far the best account of the fiscal basis of the sixteenth-century inflation.

J. A. Chartres, *Internal Trade in England 1500–1700* (London, 1977).
A brief summary, with useful figures and bibliography. The only study of its kind in this field.

P. Clark and P. Slack (eds), *Crisis and Order in English Towns 1500–1700* (London, 1972).
The most relevant of several collections on urban history put together by these editors, who are the acknowledged experts.

Richard Holt and Gervase Rosser, *The Medieval Town; a reader in English urban History, 1200–1540* (London, 1990).
Valuable insights into the background of the sixteenth-century situation.

J. Cornwall, *Revolt of the Peasantry, 1549* (London, 1977).
A different view from those of MacCulloch and Beer (see above).

C. S. L. Davies, 'Slavery and Protector Somerset; the Vagrancy Act of 1547' *Economic History Review*, 2nd series, Vol. XIX (1966), pp. 533–49.
Explains the motivation behind this piece of legislation, and why it did not work.

Ralph Davis, *English Overseas Trade 1500–1700* (London, 1973).
A brief and useful treatment of a complex subject; gives adequate context for the period.

A. D. Dyer, *Decline and Growth in English Towns 1400–1640* (London, 1991).
Brief, but contains useful information; a valuable update on a complex and popular subject.

G. R. Elton, 'Mid-Tudor Finance', *Historical Journal*, Vol. XX (1977), pp. 737–40.
A review article surveying several contributions to the debate on just how bad the financial situation really was. Incisive.

Eric Kerridge, *The Agrarian Problems in the sixteenth century and after* (London, 1969).
Documents, with an introduction. Excellent on the questions of law and tenure involved in the enclosures controversy.

S. K. Land, *Kett's Rebellion* (Ipswich, 1977).
Useful information, but should be read with MacCulloch, Beer and Cornwall; somewhat slight.

John Pound, *Poverty and Vagrancy in Tudor England* (London, 1971).
A seminar study. Useful introduction, with illustrative documents.

Peter Ramsey, *The Price Revolution in Sixteenth Century England* (London, 1971).
A collection of essays approaching the problems from several different angles; good statistical information.

R. H. Tawney and Eileen Power (eds), *Tudor Economic Documents* (3 vols, London, 1924).
An immensely valuable and varied collection of source material, to be used in connection with any of the standard analytical accounts.

Joyce Youings, *Sixteenth-Century England* (London, 1984).
A volume in the Pelican Social History of Britain; rich in anecdote and illustration.

# The Church

Margaret Aston, *England's Iconoclasts; Laws against Images* (Oxford, 1988).
Very useful on both the Lollard background and the Edwardian campaign; very thorough and learned.

Susan Brigden, *The Reformation in London* (Oxford, 1989).
A very full and detailed study, full of information about both popular and official religion. Shows the extent of protestant advance by 1547.

Patrick Collinson, *The Birthpangs of Protestant England* (London, 1988).
Argues that it took a long time for England to become protestant, in spite of a precocious start in some areas.

J. F. Davis, *Heresy and Reformation in the South East of England, 1520–1559* (London, 1983).
Usefully targeted study of protestantism in its strongest area; tends to the opposite conclusion from Collinson.

A. G. Dickens, *The English Reformation* (2nd edn, London 1989).
The most comprehensive study of the Reformation down to the early Elizabethan period, recently updated. Essential reading, but its conclusions have been challenged by Haigh and Scarisbrick (see below).

A. G. Dickens, *Lollards and Protestants in the Diocese of York, 1509–1558* (Oxford, 1959).
A convincing case study of the early development of dissent in a supposedly conservative area.

# Bibliography

W. P. Haugaard, *Elizabeth and the English Reformation; the struggle for a stable settlement of religion* (Cambridge, 1970).
A useful account, but now somewhat dated in its interpretation.

C. A. Haigh, *The English Reformation Revised* (Cambridge, 1987).
An attack on the interpretation of Dickens (see above). Argues that the English Reformation remained primarily political until well into Elizabeth's reign.

C. A. Haigh, 'Anticlericalism in the English Reformation', *History*, Vol. LXVIII, (1983), pp. 391–403.
Argues that there wasn't any – or at least that it has been greatly overestimated.

P. Hughes, *The Reformation in England* (3 vols, London, 1950–54).
The standard Roman Catholic account; learned and detailed. The interpretation originally challenged by Dickens.

N. L. Jones, *Faith by Statute; parliament and the settlement of religion, 1559* (London, 1982).
Effectively challenging the interpretation of the settlement advanced by Sir John Neale in 1950. The best account, but now challenged in its turn.

J. N. King, *Enlgish Reformation Literature* (Princeton U.P., 1982).
A scholarly and informative study of the whole range of learned and popular writing connected with religious and moral issues. The most complete examination.

David Knowles, *The Religious Orders in England; the Tudor Age* (Cambridge, 1959).
The fullest and best account of the Dissolution and Marian Restoration written from a sympathetic point of view.

D. M. Loades, *Politics, Censorship and the English Reformation* (London, 1991).
A collection of essays, many of them about the role of printing.

D. M. Loades, *The Oxford Martyrs* (London, 1970).
A study of the Royal Supremacy in action.

D. MacCulloch, *The Later Reformation in England, 1547–1603* (London, 1990).
A brief summary of the history of the Church during these years; a useful introduction.

J. W. Martin, *Religious Radicals in Tudor England* (London, 1989).
A collection of essays dealing mostly with the Marian dissenters; useful.

T. F. Mayer, *Thomas Starkey and the commonweal; Humanist politics and religion in the reign of Henry VIII* (Cambridge, 1989).
A study of the intellectual thrust towards non-protestant reform, and socially responsible government.

Andrew Pettegree, *Foreign Protestant Communities in Sixteenth Century London* (Oxford, 1986).
A thorough examination of these settlements and their influence, mainly between 1540 and 1570; the most complete treatment of the subject.

J. J. Scarisbrick, *The Reformation and the English People* (Oxford, 1984).
Ford lectures; argues that nobody really wanted a reformation, which leaves the problem of why it happened.

Robert Whiting, *The Blind Devotion of the People; popular religion and the English Reformation* (Cambridge, 1989).
A study of the diocese of Exeter; demonstrates that the vast majority of people simply did what they were told; valuable.

# INDEX